MICHIGAN ON FIRE

by Betty Sodders

Edited and designed by Don Weeks

DEDICATION

This book is dedicated to our son Bruce, who planted the seed in my mind, where it daily germinated to reality. Both he and I were amazed at the wealth of subject matter that resulted from researching this subject. At this point in time, we both realized we had birthed a "winner."

Kudos also go out to:

Bill Sodders, my husband, for suffering through the writing of yet another book (the fifth, to be exact). We share so much togetherness that in order not to lose this special part of our lives, I research quietly at 5:30 a.m. and type mainly in the evenings.

Special thanks go out to Gerry Prich of Bad Axe who did my Thumb Area leg-work regarding the 1871 and 1881 forest fires that so completely ravaged this section of Michigan—not once, but twice.

Thanks also to Robert Haltiner, Chief of Resources at the Jesse Besser Museum in Alpena, for searching files to obtain historical data and photographs that greatly added to the chapters on the Metz tragedy.

Robert Zeil and Gregory Lusk, along with their superior Don Johnson—all DNR forest fire specialists—contributed text, information, records and photographs toward this book and have again pledged the use of their files should a sequel result, bringing the forest fire story up to modern times.

All the people from the U.S. Forestry Service and U.S. Park Service who contributed freely with both material and advice warrant thanks as well.

Huzzahs go forth to the scores of historical societies that became involved in my project and literally scoured their specific areas for little-known, never-before-published facts and family accountings.

But I will never forget the man on the street—he is the backbone of all my writing. Archives are great, but everyone has access to them. I like fresh material. By placing "open letters" with newspapers in targeted former fire areas I received a wealth of material from interested citizens. These added the "human interest" touch to *Michigan on Fire*. Thanks, people.

Everyone who helped in some large or small way will see their contributions throughout this publication. Indeed, this was a combined undertaking of many, many individuals, societies, museums, libraries and government institutions.

And last but not least, special thanks are afforded to my friend David Hacker, who so many, many times through his encouragement kept me from simply giving up.

Published by Thunder Bay Press
Publisher: Sam Speigel, Thunder Bay Press
Edited and designed by Don Weeks
Cover photo courtesy Michigan Department of Natural Resources, Greg Lusk Collection

ISBN: 1-882376-52-8

Printed in the United States of America

97 98 99 2000 1 2 3 4

Contents

Michigan On Fire

Introduction

October 8, 1871 was forever known as "the day Michigan burned." But it was not the first nor the last of the great Michigan forest fires. Fires had burned through Michigan's Thumb area as early as 1853, 1861, 1862, 1864 and again in 1881.

Michigan's first recorded catastrophic forest fire occurred in the fall of 1871 at the time of the great Chicago fire and the Peshtigo, Wisconsin fire. These fires, together with the numerous concurrent Michigan blazes, took a devastating toll of some 1,500 lives. The 1871 forest fires ate their way through parts of Menominee County, most of the territory from the shores of Lake Michigan to Lake Huron, downward into the Thumb. In its course, Holland, Manistee and Glen Haven were destroyed, as were at least 40 smaller villages and hamlets.

In my estimation, the Thumb Fire of 1881 proved to be the worst of these disastrous conflagrations. You will read of 70 townships burned, 1,521 homes destroyed, over 220 people dead and some 13,000 victims left in need of assistance. A chapter is dedicated to the relief work performed by the American Red Cross, for this forest fire proved to be the organization's first actual disaster test.

The Upper Peninsula fires are covered in great detail, from the burning of the town of Ontonagon, which pitted corporate greed against the general population, to a rescue by sea of two lighthouse keepers threatened by high seas on one side, and an approaching wildfire on the other.

In 1908 the tragedy of Metz took place. Here, a rescue train left this small village with men, women and children loaded into a steel gondola car, only to run directly into an advancing wall of flames. The men escaped; the women and children did not. Simply stated, all were cremated!

Twin towns of Au Sable and Oscoda faced the wrath of twin fires—one a forest fire started by land clearing, the other caused, perhaps, from a spark of a passing railroad engine. Nevertheless, this 1911 holocaust proved to be traumatic. A vital part of our Michigan heritage.

The fire story is taken from 1871 to 1946. Later chapters include the "History of Forest Fighting and Equipment in Michigan." The final chapter is supplied by the Michigan Department of Natural Resources as a conclusion—and as a reminder that our state once again is "ripe" for a similar happening.

Section One

The Great Fires of 1871

Extent and Causes
The Great Fires of 1871

During the period known as The Great Fires of 1871, old-time lumberjacks coined a phrase that aptly applied to this far reaching holocaust. These related and unrelated fires swept through Illinois, Wisconsin and Michigan on wings of flame. Woodsworkers claimed that 1,000 moose birds were born from the ashes that remained. A "moose bird" is lumberjack jargon for the obnoxious Canada jay, also known as a "camp robber." An uncounted number of lumberjacks died during these various conflagrations that were swept by tornado-like winds. Many deaths were never tabulated, but the "jacks" believed that thousands were reincarnated as moose birds on that fateful day of October 9th, 1871.

Perhaps they really were!

Extent and Causes
The Great Fires of 1871

Only charred stumps remain on the Kingston plains after a devastating fire passed through.
Photo courtesy Michigan Department of Natural Resources, Greg Lusk Collection

Rev. E.J. Goodspeed's *History of the Great Fires in Chicago and the West*, written in 1871, states: "In our foolish American haste we have wastefully cut down the trees, dried up the springs, raised the temperature so that precipitation of moisture is reduced, and have driven the rain away in useless clouds of invisible vapor over the Atlantic. We have prayed for rain one day of the week and driven it away with an axe on six. Now, whose fault was it? We are not inclined to shift blame to heaven. It is **we** who have created these dry summers. Men, not providers, brought this calamity upon us."

It appears that the Rev. Goodspeed was a conservationist of the first order. All throughout the pages of *Michigan on Fire*, you will read of people blaming God for these disasters by fire.

Wildfire has been an enemy of man since the beginning of time. Even then, early man deemed their "manitous" responsible for the fire monster as it swept through their forests, jumped streams and hungrily destroyed all in its path. But

Extent and Causes—The Great Fires of 1871

Photo courtesy Michigan Department of Natural Resources, Greg Lusk Collection

A drawing of an early forest fire.

while this is surely true, modern man's trial by flame was, in essence, man-made.

Michigan's first recorded catastrophic fire occurred in the fall of 1871, at the time of the great Chicago Fire and the Peshtigo Fire in Wisconsin which took over 1,500 lives. These two famous fires overshadowed those that swept our state of Michigan, literally from shore to shore, rendering some 15,000 citizens homeless. To date, the death toll remains incomplete, with most research sources declaring a ballpark figure in the range of some 200—plus or minus—deaths. Similar to other great conflagrations, these fires of 1871 were actually a series rather than just one large inferno. But often, these smaller fires joined together and created walls of flame and their own breed of "hell" on earth.

A 1950 booklet—a cooperative effort between the Michigan Department of Conservation and the U.S. Department of Agriculture—offers a true perspective as to the course these fires followed:

> The summer of 1871 was one of the driest on record. From early August no rain fell, pastures and gardens dried up, wells went dry, streams shrank to a mere trickle, and crops failed. Set carelessly or by settlers in clearing land, fires burned everywhere, and ran uncontrolled into the woods and swamps where they continued to smoulder. September was equally dry. On October 5, forest fires were reported raging in northeastern Wisconsin. On the 6th, according to the Detroit *Free Press*:
>
> "The lurid sun and warm winds which have prevailed here for several days past continues (and) fires in the woods keep up the smoky atmosphere which renders everything obscure..."
>
> On October 7 it was reported that "the great woods and prairie fires in Wisconsin still continue and almost incalculable damage has already been done with no immediate prospect of extinguishing the flames," and that "navigation at Detroit has been suspended owing to the dense smoke and fog unparalleled within the memory of the oldest navigators."
>
> Word of the Chicago fire reached Detroit at 12:30 a.m. Sunday, October 8, the day that Peshtigo was destroyed. On the eighth also, the following news item appeared:
>
> "Owing to the uncommon drought, dryness of timber and fallen leaves, numerous fires are raging in the southern portion of the State."
>
> On the 10th, details of disastrous Michigan fires began to arrive. Holland, it seems, had been "reduced to ashes;" Manistee "nearly consumed;" Glen Haven "destroyed;" and fires had swept across the state to Lake Huron. The Saginaw Valley and territory northwest (as far as the Au

Sable River) was reported fire swept, and fires were said to be raging in Genesee County and the Thumb. On the 12th, word was received that Huron City, Sand Beach, White Rock and Forestville had been completely destroyed, that a number of persons had been burned to death, and that "two-thirds of the population of Huron and Sanilac counties were homeless."

On the 14th, fires were reported to be increasing in Newaygo, Isabella, Gratiot and Tuscola counties, and getting worse along Lake Huron. Sixty people were said to have been rescued from the lake where they had fled to escape the flames. On the 18th, "a large section of the State" was reported to have been "utterly desolated" and the U.S. Revenue Cutter *Fesenden* cruised along the shore to aid and transport victims of the fire to safety.[1]

The following contemporary account of conditions appears in E.J. Goodspeed's *History of the Great Fires in Chicago and the West*:

Extreme drought had prevailed throughout the west for many weeks and there had not been a rainy day since the beginning of June. During this time fires were raging in the woods in many localities. The same gale which blew upon Chicago Sunday night, October 8th, swept over the burning woods of Michigan and Wisconsin, and in places increased to tornadoes, fanning the scattered fires into a general conflagration.

The disaster was most complete between Saginaw Bay and Lake Huron, Here "an area 40 miles square was completely devastated, and over 50 people were found burned to death." While the worst was over by the 18th, the fire was not completely out for nearly a month. As late as October 24, smoke was reported "troublesome" and "lake navigation difficult," while on November 13, "contributions of money and clothing" for homeless refugees were "still being received." No accurate record of the area burned or the loss sustained was ever made, but it has been estimated that more than two million acres burned over, that hundreds of families were rendered homeless, and that at least 200 lives were lost. The only reason that the loss of life and improvements was not greater is that the country at the time was sparsely settled.[2]

The United States Commissioner of Agriculture in his "Report on Forestry" that was submitted to the Congress in 1872 stated:

> ...these fires, spreading far into the interior, not always continuously, but everywhere with most destructive energy, had destroyed a multitude of hamlets, mills, dwellings, buildings and bridges, which were never counted up, and had consumed farm fences, fields and forests to an extent that never could be estimated.[3]

The information just presented failed to mention that the holocaust that literally wiped out Peshtigo, Wisconsin jumped state lines into Michigan's Upper Peninsula. Flaming boards of lumber actually were borne by the tornado-like winds some 14 miles where they literally flew over the great Menominee River and set numerous fires along the Michigan-Wisconsin border. A painted sign that had become airborne during the Peshtigo conflagration was discovered near the burned village of Birch Creek.

Other evidence indicates that the fires all along the west shore of Michigan's lower peninsula during this period were also fanned by tornado-like winds. This fire storm, as one could easily describe it, left nothing in its wake. Historians speculated that an abnormal event sparked those great fires of 1871 from Chicago to Michigan.

Section 1, Chapter 1
Extent and Causes—The Great Fires of 1871

Many claimed severe lightning storms were the culprit. Others said no, meteor showers were to blame. Author Mel Waskin, who wrote *Mrs. O'Leary's Comet*, stated that a comet collided with the earth, and that Chicago, Wisconsin and Michigan were all showered with fiery particles at exactly the same time. He made a strong case by declaring that the multiple blazes were just too "hot" to be a normal fire. Some facts support his theory, others simply do not.

True, the air itself seemed almost electrified—buildings exploded before the fire actually invaded them; walls of flame jumped thousands of feet through the air as they advanced.

But on the other side of this ledger, it appears that many—if not most—of these fires started out as a single runaway blaze, totally out of control due to high wind gusts, finally joining with other such fires until the fire became an enormous beast that simply could not be stopped for miles—for days—until it ran out of fuel and the winds to fan it.

October 8, 1871 was forever known as "The Day Michigan Burned." But it was not the first nor the last of Michigan forest fires.

The 1871 fire was known as a treetop inferno which left a tanglement of downed deadwood and debris littering the forest floor. The 1881 blaze covered literally the same avenue of entry but actually was deemed far worse in its intensity, for the ravaging flames consumed the downed forest litter that had been drying for a decade. Other great fires followed. The question always remains: Were they spontaneous, erupting simultaneously? Or did each and every segment maintain a birth, a life and finally a death?

An extreme dry spell was evident before these fires spelled out their disastrous consequences. Here's how the U.S. Forest Service summarized conditions, in a 1969 booklet titled *Climatic Conditions Preceding Historically Great Fires in the North Central Region*:

> The data indicate that abnormally hot weather for the season is not a prerequisite to large fires in the north-central region. Although records show above-normal temperatures at some time during the fire year in all instances, most of the departures occurred early in the year. If we restrict temperature analysis to just the prolonged season of dry weather, then the 1871 fires can not be truly classed as hot and dry.
>
> Short-term temperature fluctuations, however, do appear to be highly significant. Some weather stations recorded normal or even below-normal temperatures on a seasonal basis, but well-above-normal temperatures during the 10 days before the fire.
>
> [Author's note: The Chicago weather station was completely consumed in the great Chicago fire of that year. Nevertheless, within a short period of just seven days, the weather station was relocated a few miles from town, so actually there was but a week of weather data missing from the big picture]
>
> When we combine temperature and precipitation and use them to analyze agricultural drought, we find that vegetation was below wilt stage for from 1½ to 2½ months preceding the conflagrations. These conditions contributed to the serious fire problem by increasing the amount of available fuel.
>
> Solar radiation, as revealed in the percentage of possible sunshine records, was generally above normal during spring and summer of the fire years. This, of course, substantiates our contention that drought was severe.
>
> Lowered relative humidity in most cases also appears to have contributed to the drought conditions. The Michigan data of both the 1871 and 1881 fires show near or above-normal humidity during the prefire seasons.

Over the past 50 years many of the once-burned forests have been regenerated and protected from fire. Moreover, residue from logging, thinning, and pruning in many of these forests provides an ample source of fuel for conflagrations. Arnold (1968), for example, believes that the Michigan forests today "provide a ready source of large amounts of fuel," and therefore Michigan has the basic ingredient needed for mass fires.

...There is no reason why the unusual climatic conditions could not recur in the future; i.e., 1) below-normal precipitation for 3 to 8 months, 2) low vegetation in drought or wilting stage for 1½ to 2½ months, 3) long-term below-normal humidity, 4) above-average sunshine duration. In addition, the daily weather patterns that preceded these fires were not unique.

Present ignition potential is much more difficult to assess. All the fires studied burned extremely large areas in short periods of time. Today's large fires that commonly originate from one ignition point never approach the size of these historic fires. However, public awareness of the

Photo courtesy Michigan DNR, Greg Lusk Collection

Debris slashings left behind after logging operations often provided fuel for rampaging forest fires.

> importance of fire prevention and constant fire control efforts by State and Federal agencies have dampened the threat of major conflagrations. But until man learns how to fireproof the forest or modify the weather, he must remain constantly alert to the threat of new fire disasters, and continue to intensify forest fire prevention and control activities.[4]

One of the most ironic instances of The Great Fires of 1871 that seemed to be yet another freak of nature was the fact that the day after the fires—with much of the entire northwest lying in ruin and total devastation—torrential rains fell, just some 24 hours too late.

Under The Lilacs

The fires that ravaged Wisconsin leaped state boundaries and invaded Michigan's Upper Peninsula near the Mich-Wis county of Menominee. A small village of some one hundred residents lost one-fourth of its population to this fire fiend. Birch Creek was helpless before the terrible onslaught of flames.

When the holocaust was completed many of the dead could not be identified. Strangers had been in this area, employed by the railroad to extend their rails toward Escanaba. Furthermore, traveling salesmen often visited the town and it was believed several had been there during the blaze.

Many of the area's citizens were poor farmers. Cemetery plots and tombstones cost money—more than was readily available, especially following just such a disaster. So in essence, many of the victims were simply laid to rest in the warm bosom of Mother Earth with naught more than a lilac bush to serve as grave marker.

Under the Lilacs

On Sunday, October 8, 1871 the city of Chicago burned. Ninety thousand persons were left homeless, 300 died and $200,000,000 worth of property was destroyed. As horrifying as this holocaust proved to be, a far worse scenario was played out simultaneously in Wisconsin and Michigan.

It is estimated that more than 1,200 people died in these fires that swept through Wisconsin from Peshtigo to Marinette, then jumped the Menominee River to Menominee, Michigan as flames roared up an alley of forest and farm-land to consume the small hamlet of Birch Creek.

The actual Michigan/Wisconsin death toll was listed at 1,152 on the assumption that 600 had perished in Peshtigo, 255 in the nearby forest settlements, 75 in Kewaunee and Door County communities, 22 residents of the small Michigan settlement of Birch Creek and perhaps another 200 or more lost their lives throughout lower Michigan before the multitude of flames had finished its across-the-border rampage.

The Wisconsin town of Peshtigo had little warning of the impending danger. The summer of 1871 was very dry—no rain fell after June until in October. Streams were mostly dry, as were many of the shallow wells. Swamps were peat-filled. Forests were littered with tinder dry leaves. Many fires had broken out but the populace felt little apprehension. Only the domesticated animals and the resident wildlife provided clues to the possibility of a serious calamity. Dogs howled. Cats ran in packs like wolves. Deer ran into town seeking safety. Totally exhausted flocks of birds took refuge in the village, but as the wall of flame swept into Peshtigo, these birds seemed to commit suicide by flying directly into the flames.

As the flames drew closer, deer and wolves were seen running side-by-side, driven relentlessly on by the scorching heat of the forest fire. Bears, dogs, pigs, cows, small wild animals, deer—all sought safety in the Peshtigo River alongside humans. Their world was topsy-turvy; their flight for survival made for strange bedfellows.

Within the hour Peshtigo was totally destroyed and the fire demon headed toward Marinette and Menominee.

These twin towns each boasted a population of 2,500 citizens, but neither village owned a fire engine. Their city fathers viewed fire equipment as a waste of good public money.

The moraines—ridges of sand, earth and rock—spared Marinette, but the flames leaped across the Menominee River near the rapids and invaded Menominee County.

The Menominee County Historical Society has granted permission for all the following reprints:

A Boy's Memory of the Big Fire

By Kirk Shepard

My father had the first drug store in Menominee and I recall that the store was quite a hang-out for captains of the sailing vessels from Chicago and Milwaukee that loaded lumber.

...The summer of 1871 was unusually dry. I don't think a drop of rain fell during August and September, and on quiet days when no wind was blowing, a pall of smoke hung over the bay, so dense at times that the vessels coming into and leaving Menominee had difficulty in navigating.

Sunday, October 6, was warm and sultry, with no wind to speak of, and the people went to church as usual. Father was visiting at his old home in Hartford, Connecticut. A neighbor was running the store, and the clerk was spending Sunday at his home in Green Bay.

About 9 p.m. the wind started to blow quite hard from the west. Mr. Farrier had charge of the store during Dad's absence and had closed up rather early. Our family lived over the store. Between nine and ten o'clock Joe LeRoy, who ran the Menominee House, came down to the store for a gallon of kerosene. He got Farrier out—he lived next door to us—and I heard LeRoy say, "There's a big fire coming up in the southeast." The next thing I remember was mother waking us up and telling us to get dressed as quickly as we could.

When I got downstairs and looked out the window, the sky was a red glare from horizon to horizon, and the wind had increased to a gale. Pieces of tree limbs and siding from houses all ablaze were flying overhead and dropping in the bay. Mother said that orders had come that all the women and children were to take to the boats at once. We didn't stop to pack, but I grabbed a small tin box belonging to dad, containing papers and rushing into the store, I took all the money in the till and put it in the box. I still have the box.

The Kirby Carpenter docks, where the boats were, jutted out into the bay a short distance north of the mouth of the river at the foot of PenGilly street. On one side of the dock was the *Favorite*, commanded by Capt. Hutchinson, and on the other side the large towing tug *Dunbar* was tied up. I think the *Dunbar* was towing barges for a couple of Wisconsin mills, though I'm not sure. Mother and her brood of three went aboard the *Dunbar*. The barge *Golden Harvest* was tied up at the other dock. The Kirby Carpenter Company had two docks with a slip about 100 feet wide between.

By this time the wind was blowing hot, like the breath from a furnace. The *Dunbar* had a long overhanging stern, and when we went aboard I noticed a dozen women sitting in a circle, all praying. Such sights were common that night. The boat crew stood by, ready to cast off, but the fire never reached the docks. Some say that the wind shifted a trifle to the north and carried the fire to the south and east where it cleaned the point at the river mouth. Gilmore's mill, boarding house and other buildings, also Menekaune across the river, caught fire.

As I wouldn't stay put in one place very long, I sneaked off the boat and went out on the dock. It was light as day, and from the end of the dock I could plainly see the point at the mouth of the river, also Menekaune. Buildings would suddenly burst into flames with apparently no fire near them.

...From the dock I could see the side wheel steamer *Union* tied up at Philbrook's ship dock in Menekaune. The *Union* ran from Green Bay to Menominee and other bay ports. The *Union* was commanded by Capt. Hawley, whose son became chief of police in Green Bay. Some have said that when the fire got close, the *Union* left the dock and started for the bay, but on account of the heavy load of women and children she carried and the gale that was blowing, she turned back at the mouth of the river and returned to the dock.

...Sometime on Monday the news came—I don't remember how—that Peshtigo was entirely destroyed and a lot of people burned to death. It seemed that everyone was in a kind of daze, not knowing what to expect.

Monday afternoon a man came around and told the women to take the children and go aboard the boats again as the danger wasn't over yet. So right after supper we went aboard the barge *Golden Harvest* lying at the Kirby Carpenter Company south dock. We brought along blankets and pillows and were herded down into the hold as no lumber had been loaded, all the men were fighting the fires.

During the night a number of Peshtigo survivors came aboard. Some of them were quite badly burned.

Sometime during the night, the mate from the *Favorite* came down into the hold where we huddled. “Say,” he said in a very loud voice, “there’s a woman on the *Favorite* going to have a baby and I’ve got to have help.” Mother volunteered.

Just as it was getting daylight we heard rain pattering on the deck overhead. Then the tenseness broke. Someone started a hymn and all joined in. At daylight we all went home. Menominee had been saved, probably by some freak of the wind. Those who saw that fire will never forget that awful glare covering the whole sky. I was ten years old at the time, and I’ll never forget it. Monday noon the propeller *Truesdal* of the Goodrich Line came into the dock and I heard the captain say, “Chicago is burning up and the whole country is doomed!” [5]

☒☒☒☒☒

Birch Creek, First Farming Settlement

The farming settlement at Birch Creek was begun about 1855. Among those who made their homes in this community were Henry Bade, Sr., William Hackeman and the Sieman brothers and their families. One of the early land transactions shows that Frederick Sieman secured a deed for his land June 10, 1856, from the government of the United States.

A brief account of the life of Wm. Sieman tells of the experience of his family at the time of the Peshtigo fire October 8, 1871 when Birch Creek was swept by flames.

“At the time of the great Peshtigo fire on the 8th of October, 1871 Mr. Sieman and his family were living on a farm at Birch Creek. When they saw the fire approaching like a beast of destruction and sweeping the whole country, there was no time to save property and not even time to flee. With his wife, Mr. Sieman seized their four children, whose ages ranged from 2½ months to 10 years, and rushed out in a vacant field about an acre in extent.

"The crops had been gathered and the field burned over, leaving a bare spot that offered a chance of safety. On a little knoll in the field, the children were huddled and wet blankets placed over them. Here the harassed father and mother stood, dashing water upon them while the holocaust swept by and listening to the crash of their burning buildings, the maddened cries of their dying cattle and horses, while not 40 rods away their neighbors were burned to death."

Probably not all those who lost their lives in this fire were ever placed on the death records, but these names appear of persons burned to death at Birch Creek, October 8, 1871: Mr. and Mrs. Peter Bockling and five children, James Hill and three children, Carl Koeniger, Mrs. Eames and child, two strangers.

Birch Creek was settled largely by thrifty and industrious families, and in spite of the setback of the 1871 fire, the community continued to develop into one of the most progressive sections of Menominee County. The farms have good buildings and are well-stocked and equipped. The community is scattered so that it can hardly be called a village, but it retains its distinctive name and substantial character. It has a two-room school, a Catholic church, a cemetery and a few scattered business buildings.[6]

Mrs. Elizabeth Brown of the Menominee Historical Society also forwarded a copy of the May 12, 1990 edition of the Menominee *Herald-Leader* which contained an article by Penny Mullins titled, "Lilacs Mark the Graves of Fire Victims." This article presents an unusual twist to the Birch Creek disaster:

MENOMINEE COUNTY—In the next few weeks, the lilacs, lilies, trilliums and lady slippers will line the road in glorious color.

But in Menominee Township, near the township hall, the lilacs on the west side of the road are said to mean more than just signaling the start of spring. Legend has it that the lilacs mark the burial site of several victims of a fire which destroyed portions of Menominee and Marinette counties more than 100 years ago.

Many stories have been told and written about the Peshtigo fire, which, at the time, was overshadowed by the famous Chicago fire. In one evening, which was preceded by months of drought, more than five times the victims of the Chicago fire died in Peshtigo.

Stories of the flaming devastation of Peshtigo and the surrounding areas, the unbelievable loss of human life and the awesome display of nature gone awry the night of Oct. 8, 1871 have been passed down through the years.

But few remember that the same night, traveling flames from the Peshtigo inferno found their way to Birch Creek where it is estimated that between 27 and 40 people died.

...On Bay de Noc Road, just across from the Pullman House Supper Club and over the railroad tracks to the left, is a large clump of purple lilacs. Those lilacs, it is said, are planted over the graves of eight people who died the night of Oct. 8, 1871.

Alice Knuth, a lifelong county resident, said she is not sure who is buried under the lilacs, or who actually buried them, but she guesses they were some of the German immigrants who had come to homestead in the area.

She says some caring soul must have planted the lilacs there to mark the spot, where no stone could be placed without the names.

Photo by Betty Sodders

Unknown fire victims were buried together; instead of a tombstone or marker, lilac bushes were planted over the graves. Just off M-41, north of Menominee at Birch Creek, aged lilac bushes mark the spot.

...Martha Rice LaMack taught at the Birch Creek School between 1947 and 1952. She said the two-room school building, still standing across from the cemetery, is on the same site as the log school which burned in 1871.

While a teacher there, she heard many accounts of the 20-odd people who had reportedly died that night, but only of one location where the lilacs stand to honor the unknown victims.

She said the families who survived the fire in 1871 told her of other victims, which hadn't been counted in the official death toll. She heard that a number of men, working in Birch Creek to build the railroad bed for the line which went only as far as Oconto, were caught by the indiscriminate flames and fireballs which roared through wooden homes and buildings. Of the 100 residents of Birch Creek, more than a quarter were officially listed as dead. Those not listed, and buried by the compassionate people who came afterward to give their assistance, were not known, but still given a decent, dignified burial.

Little remains but the legends and the lilacs![7]

The next piece is an eyewitness accounting of the Peshtigo Fire, which first appeared in 1960 in the Marquette *Daily Mining Journal*:

Delta Woman, Survivor of Peshtigo Fire, Recalls Blaze on Anniversary

This day 89 years ago was a Sunday (Oct. 12, 1871). It was a Sunday that will never be forgotten by persons who lived it out in the Peshtigo, Wis. area.

That Sunday evening a forest fire swept over the little lumbering town south of Marinette and a wide area about it and took more lives than any other forest fire on the North American Continent. An estimated 1,200 persons burned to death in the holocaust.

Since the death of Mrs. Helen Smith of Escanaba on Oct. 1, the only survivor in the Escanaba area is Mrs. Elizabeth Wilke of Ford River. Mrs. Wilke is 94 and in pretty fair health. She has scars on the hands and legs as a reminder of that dreadful experience of 89 years ago. She reads, plays cards, enjoys baseball on television and likes to reminisce about the great fire.

She says that the story of the fire has been much exaggerated with retelling, but that it was "just terrible." She was aroused by her mother, Mrs. Henry Merkatoris, about 9 o'clock the night of the fire. Church bells were ringing an alarm and the wind roared and the air was full of flames. The five-year-old girl accompanied her mother and two sisters and two brothers to the Peshtigo River, which flows through the village.

They were burned as they crossed the flaming bridge and once across they entered the river and climbed onto a saw log and endured the fiery night there.

"All you could see was flames," said Mrs. Wilke. The river was filled with domestic animals and wildlife as well as people, and the general terror lasted until 3 a.m. when the fire burned out, but the pain of the burned continued. There were hundreds of dead along the stream.

...There were many side strikes of the fire, which burned an estimated 1,280,000 acres of timber land. There was a large loss of life in Birch Creek north of Menominee in Menominee County, Michigan and a larger one on the Door County Peninsula in Wisconsin across the wide expanse of Green Bay.

The fire threatened the cities of Menominee and Marinette and their populations were up through the night ready to be moved out into the bay on barges if the fire entered the cities. It burned a sawmill in Menekaune on Marinette's bay front, but did not sweep into the city.

North of Menominee it burned across the Menominee River and to the shore of Green Bay, destroying Birch Creek in this sweep.

All survivors told of the roar of the fire and said that the air was full of fireballs which spread it widely and wildly so that it over-ran fleeing hundreds and cremated others who stayed in its path and tried to find refuge in cellars, wells and trees.

In Peshtigo historical interest in the fire grows and many visitors stop to inspect the mass graves in the old cemetery there in which victims of the fire were buried.[8]

Perhaps the most graphic of the eyewitness stories regarding the Birch Run fire was written by Josephine Ingalls Sawyer. Her father was a well-respected judge of that time. During his later years he became a Menominee County historian (The Hon. E.S. Ingalls, Menominee, Michigan). Ms. Sawyer's accounting of the Great Fire of 1871 comes from a collection of stories contained in a book—*Menominee Revisited*, published in 1982:

The Big Fire of 1871 (The Peshtigo Fire)

The summer of 1871 was hot and dry. There were frequent forest fires in various parts of the northern states and for weeks before the big fire of October 7th and 8th the smoke hung so heavy that the sun looked like a ball of fire. Just when and where the fires started, no one can say, but the woods and swamps between Oconto and Peshtigo had burned at intervals, controlled only by occasional rains. These fires were supposed to have caught from the camp fires of the laborers who were building the Chicago and Northwestern railroad track through to Escanaba. The culmination began the evening of October 7th. In describing this, I will have to give it from a personal standpoint, as that is the way I remember it.

I think everyone had a feeling of uneasiness and premonition for weeks; to my people, our first alarm came in this way. At that time my father, E.S. Ingalls, had a water mill on Little River, about five miles from Menominee. October 7, being Sunday, most of the crew had come downtown leaving the boarding house keeper, his wife and two children, and about ten men there. The bookkeeper, Mr. Merrill, had spent the day at our home. About 6:30 p.m. my brother Fred put the team on a light wagon and, accompanied by my younger brother, sister and myself, started to take him back.

After passing Frenchtown, we noticed an occasional log burning beside the road. Mr. Merrill told us to go back; he would walk the remaining mile and a half. There was already a roaring in the air and the sky was lighted up over towards Peshtigo. The smell of smoke was strong before we were half way back; the roaring became loud and the wind came in fierce hot gusts, which fanned the smouldering logs into flames. Often a standing tree took fire. Our horses needed no urging home. Afterward, Mr. Merrill told us his experience.

All Buildings Afire

It took him some time to make his way over the logging road to the mill, for the whirling wind had carried the fire to one side and over Marinette, and struck the mill and surrounding forest. All the buildings were on fire when he got there. He hastily got the books from the office, and taking the cook's baby, ran with the rest to the river. He buried the books in the earth on the river bank. The cattle and the horses had been turned loose, though one ox fell and was burned on the river bank. Each person had grabbed a pail or something to hold water, and carried it with him. Mr. Merrill said the heat was so intense that the instant they rose out of the water their clothes caught fire and when they inverted wooden buckets of water over their heads, the bottoms of the buckets would catch fire.

Rescue

...Late the next day, my brother-in-law got a team as far as Frenchtown. From there he had to walk the rest of the way to the mill, over fallen timber and hot ashes. He found them all alive but blind from smoke and heat and badly blistered, especially the 18 months old baby, which could only be held under water a few minutes at a time. He roped them together, so he could guide them, and so carrying the children, and sometimes the women, they stumbled along, helping each other as best they could, often falling over burnt logs, or burning their feet in hot ashes till they reached Frenchtown. We kept them at our house for two weeks, feeding them like children, until their eyes recovered. The woman and baby died two or three months later.

Marinette Escapes

As I have said, the whirling wind carried the fire, now high, now low. Marinette, directly in its path, escaped. Only the brush and low growth around the town caught fire, though it kept men busy to control it. Menekaune was caught in one of the whirls of fire. My remembrance is that everything burned, even fences, walks and the sawdust-covered streets. The fierce hot wind carried burning shingles a mile and more out into the bay and set fire to sails of ships. Where the fire struck it was so sudden and fierce that everything caught at once. In one house a woman was in confinement, with the upper part of the house burning, the doctor and neighbor woman attending her. As soon as the child was born she was lifted, mattress and all, and put into a sawdust cart, not a minute too soon, and carried to safety. Menominee, like Marinette, was rimmed with fire, and Birch Creek was entirely burned. The loss of life in this farming village was appalling...the survivors found safety in root cellars, holes in the ground and in Birch Creek.

Two girl survivors came to Menominee in 1878. I took my horse and buckboard and we went to visit near their old home farm and spent the day wandering through the growth of poplar and fireweed that always follow a woods fire. The tree trunks were still lying all in one direction like mown hay. These girls told me there were nine in their family. When the fire struck, the father and mother each took a small child and all ran to reach the creek if possible. These little girls, ten and eleven years old, soon began to stumble and fall. The father suddenly threw them both into the water and mud under roots of an overturned tree, telling them to crouch down and stay there, until he came for them. They alone survived in that family.

Frenchtown Refugees

Soon people began to drift down from Frenchtown. They said the jack pines back of the village are burning. We had lived there when we first came to Menominee (1862) and knew many of them. They camped in our back yard near the bay. I do not know how many there were. I heard my mother say she counted eight babies in her bed at one time, and children were asleep all over the house. I know we gave bread and coffee to 40 or more the next morning. Their homes did not burn and they went back. There were constant alarms.

Water Lowered in the Bay

My brother, Charles Ingalls, had personal proof of the lowering of the water in the bay. He was getting out cedar posts on my father's Hay Creek farm which ran from the Magnus Nelson farm clear through to the bay, joining John Quimby's land at Poplar Point. Charlie had a lumber ship anchored off the point and a crew of twelve or fifteen men. Sunday morning (October 7) most of them had come up town. Seven people were left, including the farm keeper's daughter, who had remained to get meals for the men. When the fire struck the forest and outbuildings, the cattle and horses were turned loose, except one team Charlie had kept, hoping to get to town or to shore. Charlie begged the men to get into the wagon, but four of them hastily threw some planks over a hole in the ground and crawled in. Someone spoke of the girl. Charlie looked for her and found her in bed, with the clothes drawn over her head. He grabbed her, quilt and all, and chucked her into the hole as he started for the shore, for the road was already cut off by flame. One of the men in the hole begged him to write their names on a piece of paper and fasten it on a stump near the hole. Charlie headed for water with one man with him; the team need no urging.

Loss of Animal Life

When a hot gust would come, the cattle and horses, running ahead, would throw themselves down and bury their noses in the sand for a minute or two. The loss of animal life was terrible that night. Several deer, wolves and bear were on the edge of the farm yard in the morning; live rabbits ran into the hole with the men and the girl. By some freak of wind, the house did not burn, though barns, fences, and surrounding woods all did. Charlie said the horses ran into the water until it reached the wagon box. He and the man lay down and went to sleep in the wagon and were awakened when the returning water covered them in the morning.

...Of course, people in nearby towns were not idle. Men from Marinette and Menominee forced their way through burning logs and hot ashes and brought sufferers from Peshtigo to Marinette. Women of the towns were volunteer nurses. We in Menominee helped. We had the Birch Creek refugees and outlying farmers to look after also. From far and near, food and clothing poured in; it continued coming for months.

After the fire destroyed Birch Creek, it leaped over about ten miles of green forest and burned the beautiful forest near what we call Greenwoods. Several days after the fire, I went with some friends to try and locate some of their relatives who lived there. I had spent some weeks with them before the fire. We could not get beyond Birch Creek. It was strange to see these great forest trees lying row after row, as though cut with a scythe, their tops pointing toward the north. The trunks of some of these great trees still lie in the birch grove beyond Birch Creek.

The fire burned so deeply into the peat bogs near Cedar River that it was still burning a year later. At times, during the first winter after, smoke came up through the snow. The fire got a good start early in the evening of the 7th of October 1871, but the height of its fury and destruction came in the morning of the 8th between one and five a.m. approximately. [9]

Michigan's West Coast In Danger

On the lOth day of October, details of disastrous western Michigan fires began to arrive at Detroit. Holland had been reduced to ashes; Manistee was nearly consumed by flames; Glen Haven destroyed. It appeared as though this monstrous fire demon could not be stopped. Had Judgment Day arrived?

Mrs. R.H. (Ginny) Steele, Secretary of the Newaygo County Society of History and Genealogy, White Cloud, had the following comments:

"When the fire of 1871 struck the surrounding areas of Michigan, the Village of Newaygo proved to be no exception. But for a sudden wind shift, the town was saved, for the forests were tinder dry and fires had simply popped up all over the county. One of these blazes crept within 30 yards of Kritzer's Grist Mill at the west end of town and Jarse's home at the east end. Fires were reported near Hess Lake and also threatened the community of Hessville."

Yes, Newaygo was one of the lucky ones; others were not so fortunate.

Michigan's West Coast In Danger

PROCLAMATION!

Sister City of Holland is nearly destroyed by fire. More than 2,000 people are left homeless and exposed to the pitiless storm. Food and clothing is the immediate want .

I, HENRY GRIFFIN, Mayor of the City of Grand Haven, do hereby call upon all good citizens to contribute to the relief of these sufferers.

For this purpose I have caused Subscription Papers to be opened at my office.

Any provisions, cooked or otherwise, and clothing, will be of comfort, and such donations taken to the Office of E.P. Ferry, will be there received and record kept of donors.

HENRY GRIFFIN, Mayor
Grand Haven
October 10, 1871

(Courtesy: Michigan Historical Collection)

Fires ran like the wind! On October 8th, the City of Manistee was consumed. Glen Haven proved next on the fiery fiend's hit-list. At Holland, a forest fire went out of control at three o'clock in the afternoon of October 9th. By the setting of the sun, flames were eating away at homes located on the city's outskirts. Long before daylight of the following day, Holland lay in ashes—75 business establishments were completely destroyed, 243 homes were burned to the ground.

The woods located along the railway of the Michigan Lake Shore Railroad that ran between Holland and Pigeon River were in flames. Miles and miles of marsh were on fire. Trains traveled with extreme difficulty. Heat inside rail cars was intense. Finally, trains were forced to hold back schedules until the rains came, subduing the flames along the line's rights-of-way.

Manistee

In an article which appeared in The Manistee *News Advocate Broadside* October 8, 1983—112 years after the fires—Manistee County Historical Museum director Steve Harold said that, while much has been said about the Fire, very little was actually recorded at the time. Harold reports that the office, print shop, and mailing list of the Manistee *Standard* were destroyed and it was many months before the paper reappeared on the streets of Manistee.

Harold's article contained the following account of the Great Fire, written by *Standard* editor Orlando H. Godwin for the first issue published after the Fire—April 6, 1872:

On the seventh day of last October we issued our *Standard* as usual, little thinking that would be our last for so long a time, that in the short space of 36 hours the greater part of our young city would be in ashes. The event of the fire being of so much importance and forming such an interesting part of Manistee's history, and the *Standard* not then being able to give a full and accurate accounting of it, we must now make some record of it, or else our files would be incomplete.

We doubt not our people were as devotional that Sunday as ordinary, went to church with the same reverence and sincerity they were wont to do, partook of their food with the usual relish and thankfulness to their Maker, set by their fire and enjoyed its comforts, read their Bibles with the attentiveness and interest that was their custom, without an uncommon thought of the future of fear of its bringings.

We had had a long droughth, making everything thoroughly dry and ready to burn at the first touch of fire. There had been fire in the adjoining woods for some time which, fanned by the wind throughout the day, reached great proportions by night, and then, with the aid of a heavy gale from the southwest, the flames increased in unabated fury until beyond our control. In the day time our firemen found a duty to perform near Gifford & Ruddock's mill, and succeeded in subduing the fire; but before they had fully recovered from the fatigue of these labors, the fire alarm sounded (about eight o'clock p.m.) calling them at the mouth of the river, where the fire was burning furiously among the dry driftwood along the shore of the lake. There was quickly gathered a large concourse of people at work, determined to get rid of the fire with as little loss as possible; but during the fury of the conflagration, when men were laboring in Hope, the engine gave out, and all were forced to abandon everything to the caprice of the destroyer, and naught was saved west of Canfield's mill save the steamers and Tyson & Robinson's barges lying in the river.

The fire in the woods on the south boundary of the city was now rapidly nearing the city and threatening it with total destruction, and every man was looking out for his own house and household. The fire again started at the house of J.G. Ramsdell, on Maple Street, and was driven by the wind with astonishing rapidity toward the river, widening in its course until it reached that point, when it extended from Oak Street to Sorenson's boarding house on the south side of the street, and on the opposite side nearly to Tyson E. Robinson's boarding house, and the *Standard* office in connection with everything within its fiery track, was shortly but a mass of ruins. The fire did not stop here, but leapt over the bridge as if in search for further prey, and on reaching the other side, continued its destruction until there was hardly a thing left to tell that it was once inhabited.

This was but the work of a few hours, and thousands of our people were without a home who before were comfortable and happy; but those of our citizens who had not lost their residences invited the less fortunate neighbors to take meat and drink with them, and shelter from the storm, and there were few who suffered from hunger, thirst or cold.

This, we thought, was hard indeed; but when news was received that Chicago and many smaller towns were also burned, and that many insurance companies could pay but an insignificant portion of their loss, then came the most unkindest cut of all.

Our appeal for aid was nobly responded to. Papers asking relief for sufferers from the fire were circulated in every village and city from Maine to California, and even in the old world charity was at work. Every one had a contribution to make—the laborer his day's wages, the millionaire his thousands of dollars—for there was no heart so hard but was moved in sympathy, no man so mean but would give something.[10]

Holland

The following personal accounting of the fire at Holland, printed in the Oct. 9, 1980 Holland *Sentinel*, was written in 1948 by Mrs. Ben Wolters (Anna Speet) at the age of 87. Speet was born in 1861 and died in 1960. The Speet farm was located on the northeast corner of 62nd Street and 146 Avenue, west of Graafschap. The Speet Family built a new home on the property after the fire, and much of the structure remains standing today.

Sunday October 9, 1871
A day of anxiety and distress

It seems like only yesterday, although it is 77 years ago. In the forenoon the people were all in church. By midday they were all fighting the fire. There was great excitement in the area. The fire was raging on all sides, through the forest and brush. Instead of going to church again in the afternoon they all had to fight the fire. Friends and neighbors came to see if they could help, and everyone was talking about the threat to their property. It was a day of anxiety and fear.

The fire continued to spread and became more fierce. People were running back and forth with sweat pouring down their faces. The fire came flying like a hurricane through the forests and countryside, over hills and valleys—it was everywhere. The atmosphere was luminous with it, people were gasping for air. The flames were crackling through the trees, raging like a hurricane. The people could withstand it no longer and fled, leaving all their possessions behind.

The fire was coming closer and flaming brands were flying through the air. We and the neighbor children were all crying and didn't know where to go, so we all went back to our homes. We were all alone. Our father and brother were fighting the fire with the other men, each one trying to save his house and barn. But my father thought, "I must take care of the children and bring them to safety." He came and took us by the hand and led us to a plowed field which was the safest place under the circumstances. Then he himself went back to the fire. There was nothing he could do but he could not give up the battle.

The fire crackled all around us and our eyes became irritated. Our barn was ignited and soon collapsed. The house was also encircled with flames and before long it was no more. Everything in and around our home lay in ashes. My father saw all his hopes disappear.

He left the ruins and came to look after us children and arrived just in time, for my little sister, seven years old, was lying on a feather bed. A fragment of burning wood, blown by the wind, fell on the feather bed and it began to burn. My father rescued her.

But we were still not out of danger. We had to get out of the area. My father led us to the home of our aunt, but there also everything was in an uproar. No one knew what to do or where to go. They ran here and there but found no refuge. It was a night of terror and suffering. They prayed, and God answered. He sent rain and the fires subdued.

The morning dawned, now what to do? My aunt proposed breakfast and she prepared food for all of us. We all knelt down and thanked God that He had brought us thus far in safety.

But the old home was gone. The grain that had been stored in the barn lay in ashes. Shocks of corn in the field were burned. There was much damage and loss. The first task was to build another house and they started at once. I think it was ready to move into in about 10 weeks. Now we could go home again under one roof, but it was no life of ease. Each one carried his own cross. Each one had to make a new beginning. They had to work with all their might but each one did rebuild his house. We all had to scrimp and save.

Father had a difficult time during those years, although he was at the peak of his strength. He had to do it all alone, for my mother had three years previously gone to be at home with her Lord.

I was ten years old at the time but I remember it all very clearly. I will never forget it![11]

The next two accounts of the burning of Holland were found in the Joint Archives of Holland. The first was published in a joint issue of Dutch publications *De Grondwet, De Wachter*, and *De Hollander* on October 12, 1871:

Holland Was, But Is No More
CATASTROPHE
Days of Terror, Distress and Suffering

We now face one of the saddest and most difficult tasks, one which we never faced before. Our minds are unable to grasp and our hands are unwilling to write about the details of the terrible series of catastrophes that befell us. We are unable to describe everything. We must limit ourselves. Because of the goodwill of the publishers of *De Hope*, we are able to publish this paper and we thank them very much.

1876 Atlas of Ottawa and Kent Counties, courtesy Donald vanRekin

Hope College's Van Vleck Hall, right, survived the Holland Fire of 1871.

The Almighty has spoken and the effect of that Voice is fearful. It may be said that our beloved city is no more. The entire business section is in ruin. Whole streets have disappeared. Every businessman has lost all he had and between 200 and 300 houses were burned down.

The most beautiful part of our city was turned into smoking and smouldering heaps of ruin. Fierce forest fires were burning during the past week, especially around the Graafschap area. There was then already a danger for some parts of the city and during the night on Wednesday of this past week. Efforts to save the Hope printery, Dr. Crispell's home, and the College building was successful.

Since the fire kept smouldering here and there destroying barns and houses. But there seemed to be no danger for us. Then Sunday afternoon a heavy storm from the south moved in and before the end of the afternoon church services, alarms were sounded.

Still there seemed to be more danger for the surrounding areas than for the city itself. If only the wind had remained from that direction, then Holland would be here today. But between 11 o'clock and 1 o'clock the wind moved westward and increased in strength almost to hurricane force.

The so-called creek, a low area which contained felled and half rotten trees, etc. soon became a sea of fire. The wind blew sparks toward Sprietsma's and Elferdink's tannery and next to the large steam tannery of Capon and Bertsch which immediately was engulfed in flames as well as 3,000 cords of bark alongside and from there the fire jumped to 8th Street and then crept through the entire length of River and a couple of side streets, sweeping away and destroying everything in its way...The flames spread with unbelievable speed and in less than one hour the largest and most beautiful part of Holland lay in ashes. The entire business district is completely burned down and that 7/8ths of the city is destroyed... About 150 to 200 families lost their homes, clothing, furniture, practically everything and now must depend upon handouts...We can say, Holland is no more...the city has perished. Only a few rows of houses on the outskirts of town are left.

The circumstances are shattering and people do not yet comprehend the terrible series of tragedies. Twenty-five years of labor has been wiped out. Adding to an already terrible situation of the fire is the well grounded fear that because of the fire which almost destroyed Chicago, the fire insurance companies are bankrupt. Many of our citizens who had some insurance on their property may even lack that help and being totally poor and helpless, will have to start again from nothing.[12]

Tells How and Where The 'Big Fire' Started

At about 2:30 on the afternoon of Sunday, October 8, 1871, while services were being conducted in the six churches of this city, reports were brought in to the respective pastors that a threatening forest fire was raging in the swamp back of the Third Reformed Church.

Immediately the congregations were dismissed and a large number of people flocked to that part of the city to do what they could to bring the fire under subjection. After cutting down a number of trees, killing the fires in the brush tops, killing the fires in the brush along the ground and plowing up a large territory to prevent spreading of the flames, the people returned home convinced that all was safe. And it was safe at that time as far as any human being was able to foresee.

Shortly after midnight, however, on October 9th, it began to blow out of the southwest, and in a very short time a genuine storm developed. Add to this that we had no rain to speak of for several weeks previous to this, and we were surrounded by a number of large forest fires, and we need not state that the outlook was at once truly alarming

...We had a fire department at that time, known as Eagle Fire Company No. 1, but, considering that they had only a hand fire engine to work with and had to pump the water from open wells, which generally gave out after from 20 to 30 minutes pumping, one can readily see the handicap in that way. The fire department with the best will in the world could accomplish very little, and especially on an occasion like this when they were all surrounded by fire. They made their last stand at Cappon's Tannery. After this establishment caught fire, they gave up, and the firemen scattered to their respective homes to save as much as they could of their own goods as was yet possible, as everybody could plainly see that a large part of the city was doomed.

At about one o'clock that night, we—and everybody else living in the direction the fire was spreading—began packing our beds and other clothes, getting ready to vacate the houses. After this was done, my mother and three children, the youngest of which was only one month old, and the other two, 6 and 16 years, left the house and departed for the home of a relative living on the southwest corner of Ninth Street and Lincoln Avenue.

When they had left, my father, my grandfather and myself—I was a kid of only 14 years of age—began lugging the goods out of the house located one door east from the northeast corner of Seventh Street and Central Avenue, placing them temporarily on the street.

Sketch depicting the burning of Holland, 1871. Courtesy Donald vanRekin.

We had just begun with this work when an old gentlemen, living on West Eighth Street, driven out of his home by the fire, approached our house carrying a large feather bed on his back. He asked my father if he could leave this bed in our care. My father told him he had no objection to this, but considered it useless since we were vacating ourselves and the fire would also reach us in a very short time.

Thinking a moment, he said, "You are right," grabbed up his bed again and walked with it to the house on Lincoln Avenue, where my mother and the children were staying, threw it down on the floor and said, "There it lies; I cannot carry it any further."

In order to be sure that we could get our goods—the furniture we simply threw out on the street—away from the street in front of the house before the fire would overtake us, we began lugging the bundles from there to the southwest corner of 7th St. and College Avenue, and threw them temporarily on a heap there alongside of a lot of goods brought there by other people. There was a large collection of goods on this corner, including even four showcases taken out of a hardware store on Eighth Street, which were filled with all sorts of stuff.

After we had made a couple of trips to this corner, we noticed that the buildings on the west side of Central Avenue, between Eighth and Seventh Streets, had started to burn. A neighbor across from our place, living on the lot in the rear of what is now the Warm Friend Tavern and used at present as a parking place for automobiles of the hotel guests, was working with might and main to save his house by carrying pail after pail of water up a ladder, and in this way was trying to keep the roof wet. He kept this going for only a short time, when the heat from Central Avenue's burning buildings drove him off the roof. Coming down, he ran into the house, grabbed a feather bed, shouldered this, and, emerging with this on Central Avenue, he tried to come around the corner of Seventh Street. Before he could succeed in this, however, his bed caught fire and he was forced to throw it from him, and in a few moments it went up in smoke on account of the rain of sparks.

A neighbor to the west of us, living on the lot now occupied by the Yellow Cab Company's garage, had two fat, three hundred pound hogs which he let out of the pen and tried to drive out on the Central Avenue side of the street. Just as soon as these hogs caught sight of the raging flames opposite them, they ran right back in the yard. He tried repeatedly to drive them out but always with the same result, and at last had to give it up. I saw these hogs the next morning lying dead and half roasted near the ruins of their pens.

Another neighbor, after bringing his wife and children to a place of safety, came back to see what he could still save of his household goods. As he had no time any more to lug his goods to safety, he did the next best thing, and this consisted in tearing the covering off the well—we all had open wells at that time—and dumping his goods in there. In his excitement, he forgot all about throwing a lot of chairs in first in order to keep the stuff out of the water, and the result was that what he saved was largely spoiled by becoming watersoaked. He saw and admitted his mistake right there and then, but it was too late, as what was done could not be undone.

Before we could succeed in bringing all of our goods from the house to the before mentioned corner, all of Eighth Street till about the middle of the block between Central and College avenues was burning as was also the whole of the west side of Central Avenue, from Eighth Street to Sixth Street. Also Seventh Street from Central to River avenues and beyond, was a roaring furnace of fire. Never mind where one looked from our house—everywhere was a raging sea of flames.

About the middle of the east side of Central Avenue, between Seventh and Sixth Street, stood a barn in which a sewing machine agent kept his horses. When the man drove away with his horses, he left the barn open, with the natural result that a few seconds after this the barn took fire. From here the fire spread rapidly to Sixth Street, back to our houses—our house and the adjoining buildings being still untouched—and swept in a northeasterly direction over what is now the city dumping grounds, but this was a big swamp at that time, in which a number of trees were still standing. After Sixth Street and the dump territory was overswept, and everything was destroyed that would burn, the fire reached the river and destroyed a large stave factory located at the foot of Columbia Avenue.

When we got our last bundles of goods from our house—Sixth Street back of our block being entirely swept away at this time—we noticed that our house, the one west and the one east of us had also begun to burn as well as some buildings on the opposite side of the street from us, showing us conclusively that it was high time to get out of this block.

Our block on Seventh Street at that time was only a sand road on which the owners of the above mentioned stave factory—who used this part of Seventh Street quite frequently—had strewn a thick layer of 4 x 4 inch pieces of oak, cut off from the ends of the staves, to improve this sand road a little. These small pieces of oak, being cork-dry, burnt like tinder, and the result was that not only the buildings on both sides of this block began to burn and were burning, but the very street was burning.

Flames from a foot to a foot and a half high could be seen all over the street, and all the furniture, which was largely left behind on the street as we were escaping, was consumed to the last piece.[13]

Perhaps the most complete and factual accounting of the Holland fire came from Donald L. vanReken of Holland. Mr. vanReken had written a book titled *The Holland Fire of October 8, 1871,* which includes the following newspaper clippings:

Grand Rapids Daily Eagle

It is reported that Grandville, on Grand River, in the township of Wyoming about seven miles south and west of the city, is threatened with destruction. ...Holland City was completely destroyed...the railroad bridge across the river was burned and the whole surrounding country was in flames. It is said that the woods have burned throughout the whole extent of the county from Holland to Grand River, a distance of at least 20 miles

...About the only goods that could be saved in the burning district were clothing and such articles as could be hastily buried. Many trunks and valuable articles were thus buried, but even of these many were found so heated and charred when dug up and opened as to burst into flames, and were thus destroyed. This was the case with some of the goods of Rev. C. Van der Veen and others.

☒☒☒☒☒

***Holland City News*, July 24, 1897**

[From the obituary of Henry D. Post]

The fire of 1871 destroyed one of the finest private libraries and geological collections in this section of the state owned by the deceased.

Section 1, Chapter 3
Michigan's West Coast in Danger

☒☒☒☒☒

[Author's note: A few of the multitude of newspaper articles held some fallacies. In his book, Mr. vanReken points out that the next article, by the editor of the *Hartford Day-Spring* was an eyewitness account that contains, as vanReken put it, "obvious errors."]

Holland City News, February 21, 1907

About 2 o'clock on the morning of the 9th of October, the terrible conflagration commenced that destroyed the pleasant city of Holland. Most of the bells of the city which had sounded the cry for help of the doomed city shrieked for succor and protection as the flames from the burning church and dwellings in the south part of the city lit up the heavens above and the forests for miles away. Soon the second church and the Methodist Episcopal were on fire, now the City Hotel and the finest stores on Main Street. Here the fire became terrific and women, men and children fled the city in panic stricken horror...At 2 o'clock a young woman died and her husband took her slim body in his arms, and by the humanity of Mrs. Bostwick, it was watched and cared for in the open air in the outskirts of the city until daylight came, when it was buried. One old lady, delirious with despair, rushed into the swamp and was mired up to her body, but was rescued by her children before the flames had reached her. A poor woman, whose infant lay a corpse in her parlour, grasped the stark body and ran frantically to the woods. The next day she visited the blackened site where stood her home, still carrying her dead baby which she refused to have buried, saying it was all she had left. One woman, who was under the doctor's care, arose from her bed for the first time in 24 hours, and saved herself by flight and, strange to say, has been well ever since. An old lady, who lived alone, was burned in her cabin, she probably not having awakened until the flames reached her body. Mrs. Vervena, a widow lady who buried her husband in May, grasped her two small children and involuntarily found refuge in the cemetery a mile away, and was found about noon wailing over her husband's grave, wailing his name piteously in that hour of her great disaster.

...For miles around, the heavens were aglare with the light of the burning city and vessels tossed on Lake Michigan on that eventful night were lighted towards the port of Holland full fifty watery miles away.

☒☒☒☒☒

***Holland City News*,** March 9, 1872

We learn that the State central committee has made final shipment to the sufferers at Fillmore, as follows: 50 bbls. flour, 10 bbls. pork, 400 bu. seed oats, 400 bu. potatoes, 20 plows, 100 kegs nails, 6 doz. hoes, 2 cook stoves, and furniture, and $3,000 in cash to be drawn to pay for saw bills, lumber, hay, etc.

☒☒☒☒☒

***Holland City News*,** May 30, 1874

Many a relic of the fire, in the shape of old iron, were shipped last week by Messers. Van Landegend & Melis. Amongst the rubbish we noticed the hammer and fire alarm of the Third Church bell, also a part of the old *Hollander* press to this place in September 1850 from Allegan by Messrs. Hawks & Bassett. This press was a Peter Smith's No. 83, and rumor here has it that the Chicago *Tribune* was once printed on that press.

☒☒☒☒☒

Holland City News, July 22, 1876

While digging a cellar under the store of D. De Vries, on River St. & Ninth St., they found some relics of our great fire such as burned coffee, lumps of grease, etc. This is the spot where Koffers & Gringhuis used to do business.

☒☒☒☒☒

Holland City News, October 10, 1874

Three years ago this week, while Chicago was being partially burnt, Holland was almost totally obliterated...

...Holland was settled by a colony of Hollanders in 1847. Two or three Americans had preceded them, but the town was, from the start, Holland to the heart and is the same today. Three-fourths of the signs on business houses are hard to spell. A graduate from any of the best American colleges could spend a day profitably here in learning to spell and pronounce people's names.

☒☒☒☒☒

The Burning of Holland

by Gerrit J. VanSchelven

[Excerpts taken from this long essay by Holland's eminent historian of the late 19th century]

...The grounds of Hope College, somewhat isolated as they were, seemed to be the only spot where one could escape with his life. Many took to the waters of Black Lake, escaping in small boats.

The fierceness of the wind and the rapidity with which the fire spread may be inferred from the fact that over 250 dead horses, cattle and swine were found in the burned district, and a canceled bank check, partly burned, drawn by the firm of DeJong, VanSchelven & Oggel, upon Nathan

Kenyon, banker, was picked up the next day on one of the farms in Tallmadge Township, in this county, a distance of 25 miles.

...The loss of human life was limited to one aged widow woman, Mrs. J. Tolk. She lived in a small house on Ninth Street, west of the present residence of E. Van Der Veen. Over 300 families were left without shelter.

The number of buildings destroyed is about as follows: dwellings, 210; stores, shops and offices, 75; "manufactories," 15; churches, 5; hotels, 3; misc. buildings, 45; docks and warehouse, 5; one tug and several other boats.

☒☒☒☒☒

When it became evident that the flames were posing a serious threat to the church building, Deacon Dobben...decided he could rescue the living Word, the pulpit Bible, from the flames, and, fairly running to the pulpit, he scooped up the large Bible, and carried it to the Ten Cate clearing a mile to the north. There that Bible was deposited and, eventually, returned to the possession of the whole church. So a book with an interesting history was preserved. That Bible, therefore, became a symbol of hope and promise for...rebuilding.

Another reason for staying and starting over soon became apparent, too. There was one little tree that had not been burned! It was still there and it was even a little stronger now! Even though the visible building was gone, so that it would have to be replaced at great personal sacrifice, yet the Church was preserved. That was the tender tree that was kept by the Keeper of His own, and that little tree had to be nourished once more. To that task, the congregation set itself with renewed faith and dedication.

The Holland Evening Sentinel, October 9, 1971

Charles Post, who fled his home in the southern part of the village as flames approached, was reunited with his family at the home of his sister-in-law.

He was told that the couple's 18-month-old baby, ill during the summer, was carried by Post's wife the entire distance. His five-year-old son, Walter, had struggled to save a wheelbarrow given him a few weeks earlier by an uncle. While fleeing with his mother, the wind had taken the boy and the wheelbarrow from the ground and carried them some little distance. But Walter did not let go of the handles although his hat was gone and his eyes were full of sand.

...In the same issue of **De Hope** was published this notice from the relief committee:

"Our attention has been called to reports of the fire at Holland, which are in material points false, and calculated to do us great injury by diverting the sympathy of the public from us.

"It has been stated that the Hollanders refused to aid in extinguishing fires for the reason that it was Sunday. It is also stated that the churches would not permit their bells to be rung fearing it would disturb the congregation, etc.

"Nothing could be more false and slanderous than these statements...Shame on those who would mock at our calamity and tell lies to deprive us of our just share in the sympathy of our neighbors."[14]

Steaming Through Smoke & Fire

Many historians claimed that the path of destruction reached from shore to shore, from Lake Michigan to Lake Huron. But this is not completely true. The effects of the fires were not contained by the shorelines. Forest fire smoke settled out over the lakes, smoglike, hanging just over the surface of the water, making navigation on the lakes nearly an impossibility. Great Lakes vessels had to light their running lamps and deck lanterns just as they would on the darkest of nights.

Shipping actually ground to a standstill on October 9, 1871 due to the impenetrable smoky darkness. Many boat captains reported their ships were oftentimes showered with sparks necessitating washing down the decks in order to prevent fires from erupting. So vast an area was literally "on fire" that this pall of smoke hung over three states, extensive sections of the Great Lakes and on into Canada.

Steaming Through Smoke and Fire

The relationship between the steamships of that earlier day was examined by a marvelous book bearing the same name as this chapter, written by James L. Donahue. Following are excerpts from Donahue's book:

The title of this book reflects the terrible fires that swept Chicago, the forests across Michigan, Wisconsin and Ohio, and the many other towns destroyed by flames during the first week of October, 1871. Many fine ships burned in port and others were wrecked because of the heavy smoke that blinded sailors.

Chicago was leveled by one of the worst fires in American history, while at the same time fires destroyed thousands of acres of forests and smaller towns in Wisconsin, Minnesota and Michigan in the fall of 1871.

Trouble With Smoke

Smoke from these fires started hampering ship navigation by mid-September. The summer had been extremely dry and the forests were burning everywhere. Some days the smoke hovered like fog on the lakes, blinding sailors even in broad daylight. Accidents began to happen:

The bark *Sunrise* went ashore on the Canadian side of lower Lake Huron, eight miles above Point Edward, Ontario, some time around Sept. 9.

The *Sunrise* was coming down the lake with wheat and was trying to make the St. Clair River. When it hit the rocky coast, the ship stove a hole in her bottom, causing the grain-filled holds to flood. The wheat started to swell, putting pressure on the wooden hull. Before salvagers could get to her, the hull split. The *Sunrise* was a total loss.

Another casualty of the smoke was the propeller *Annie Young*, which was steaming up the Detroit River after rescuing the crew of the capsized schooner *New Lisbon*.

By Tuesday, Sept. 12, the smoke was so heavy that captains had to drop anchor rather than risk their ships.

The captain of the steamer *W.R. Clinton* sent a telegram to the ship's owners from one Lake Huron port in which he said the vessel was delayed 12 hours.

Published reports said 38 ships and four strings of barges in tow were anchored at Lake Erie's Point au Pellee on Sept. 12 waiting for the smoke to lift.

The Burning of Everything

The fall of 1871 is remembered in the upper Midwest as the time of the great holocaust... It was a time of black horror for thousands of people trapped in the forests. Some who lived near the coast of the Great Lakes, or near the myriad of small lakes and streams that dot the landscape, tried to outrun the fire, hoping to escape to the safety of the water. Some sought shelter in their shallow dug wells. Others determined to stand and fight to save their homes and their towns.

They were doing all of these things when they died. Death came quickly as the flames, fanned by a gale force wind, swept down on them unexpectedly. Others miraculously survived.

No one knows how many people perished. The numbers in large tracts across Michigan and Wisconsin were relatively low because people were only just beginning to clear and settle this part of the country. Elsewhere, entire towns were destroyed. Hundreds of people stumbled out of the smoke badly burned, lacking food, shelter and clothing.

The Chicago fire was so terrible in itself, the story overwhelmed news of the other fires burning at the same time in at least five other states. To this day, history books tend to ignore the other fires, even though they were believed to have burned more square miles and done more property damage than any other single conflagration in American history.

The fires affected the ships plying the lakes.

As Chicago burned, many fine vessels were destroyed there. They included the new propeller *Navarino*, the steamer *Philo Parsons*, schooner *Glenbula* of 602 tons, schooner *Eclipse*, schooner *Butcher Boy*, bark *Va-*

letta of 407 tons, schooner *Alewick*, bark *A.P. Nichols*, bark *Fontanella,* fore and aft schooner *Christina Nielson.*

The only recorded casualties among sailors occurred on the *Alewick*, where the mate was said to have died and the captain suffered severe burns to his hands.

The iron clad propeller *Merchant* was in port, but she got up steam and escaped before the fire claimed her.

Elsewhere, the schooner *Seneca Chief* was destroyed by fire at Manistee, Mich. She was one of several vessels tied up at docks on the Manistee River when flames swept the city, burning more than 100 homes and most businesses. Other ships, including the tug *Bismark*, with three barges in tow, and a scow loaded with slabs and a pile driver, escaped into Lake Michigan.

...The Detroit *Free Press* told how shipping was stopped on Lake Huron as early as Oct. 5 because of the dense smoke. The story said the atmosphere was blinding and the situation was the worst mariners could remember.

The heavy smoke that hovered over Lakes Erie, Huron and Michigan during October was blamed for a long string of wrecks, even as far east as Lake Ontario.

Even though they were having trouble, the ships played important roles in rescue and restoration.

The steamers *George L. Dunlap*, *Union* and *Favorite* were anchored at Menominee, Mich., when the fire came. All three vessels carried hundreds of women and children from Menominee and surrounding areas out into Lake Michigan while the men stayed behind to fight the fire. The *Dunlap* brought many survivors from the fire at Menominee into Green Bay, Wis. on Oct. 10.

The U.S. revenue cutter *Fesenden* was among the ships working that week from Port Huron north into Michigan's Thumb District. She stopped at port after port, carrying burn victims out for medical attention and surveying the extent of death and destruction.

The *Fesenden* later carried supplies to the village of Port Austin, which was spared by the flames, and consequently turned into a refugee center. The first cargo to that community included ten barrels of flour, four barrels of pork, a barrel of sugar, a chest of tea, nine packages of clothing and a large quantity of crackers and cheese.

Other cargo, shipped by the Detroit Relief Committee, was earmarked for distribution at other locations south of Port Austin, but the crew complained that the smoke was so dense they could not see to make a landing. After the *Fesenden* struck a rock, her captain decided to return to Port Huron with much of the cargo still aboard.

The steamer *Marine City*, which regularly stopped at Michigan coastal towns, probably saved many lives that week by carrying people away as flames bore down on their homes.

Artwork by Doreen Peterman

The sidewheel steamer Marine City was used as a rescue vehicle for Thumb fire victims.

The steamer *Huron* brought hundreds of refugees to Port Huron on Oct. 14 and then turned back for more.

...In Michigan's Huron County, the fire was bearing down on the little settlement of Rock Falls. Two families, the Manns and the Huxtables, decided to escape to a small fishing boat around 1 a.m. Monday morning.

On board the boat were the Huxtable family, Mr. Mann and five of his children. At first the families kept the boat tied up at the small dock and boat house because the fierce westerly winds were blowing. But Huxtable said they later were forced to cut the boat adrift when the fire spread to the boat house and threatened to burn their vessel. He said they used a heavy stone to try to anchor the boat offshore, but the hurricane winds created by the fire drove them out into Lake Huron

"At daybreak the smoke and ashes were so thick that we could not see the land nor the sun, and we could not determine our whereabouts," Huxtable said.

The families were confined for about 60 hours in that small boat, without food. The children began to show the effects of their terrible ordeal on the second day.

Everybody left their homes so quickly in the night the children had no time to get dressed. They spent the time on the water wearing only their bed clothes. Their only shelter was under the forward deck. Everybody was wet from the waves which were continually splashing over the sides of the boat.

It was not until sunrise on Wednesday morning that Huxtable saw enough light from the sun to determine east from west. About that time, little Hermie Mann, age three, died in his father's arms. His last words were a request for food.

As the fire approached the town of White Rock, a few miles south of Rock Falls, the people formed a bucket brigade at the edge of town and tried to fight it.

But when the wall of fire rolled out of the thick black smoke, it came at them with such fury everybody realized their cause was lost. They turned and fled for their lives into Lake Huron.

All that terrible night, men, women and children stood together in the water, watching their town burn. The air was so hot the people were forced to stay in the water for eight hours before anybody dared to get out.

Wagons that had been partly driven into the water with personal belongings aboard caught fire and burned to the water line.

The steamer *Huron* stopped briefly on Monday. But the ship was so filled with burned survivors from other coastal towns that it didn't have room for the people at White Rock. She took on as many as could be squeezed aboard, then steamed away into the smoke for Port Huron, leaving the rest behind.

Artwork by Doreen Peterman

"Survivors at White Rock—Thumb Area," artist's rendition of the survival techniques used by the desperate people of the Thumb in 1871.

Strange Voyage of the *Moffat*

Port Huron, Mich.
Tuesday, Oct. 10.

Capt. James Moffat put his tug, the *Frank Moffat*, at the disposal of the Port Huron Relief Committee after the fire.

The tug left on Tuesday night with two barge yawls in tow, each loaded with food, clothing and medical supplies.

The expedition steamed north under the supervision of Moffat and committee member Thomas Stevens. The smoke was dense so the tug ran all night at slow speed, with the whistle blowing every few minutes. Even when dawn came, it was still impossible to see more than 10 yards in any direction. The sailors coughed from inhaling the smoke.

Moffat, a veteran Lake Huron skipper, was using every trick he knew to find his way. At 6 a.m., when he thought he had traveled far enough, he changed course toward the Michigan shore, hoping to find Lexington or Forestville docks. The tug found the schooner *Sweepstakes*, lying at anchor with her sails down. The *Sweepstakes* crew said they had no idea where they were and had not seen land in four days.

Birds, including a wild pigeon, came out of the smoke to land on the tug. The birds were exhausted and stayed aboard to rest, even though the men were only a few feet away, watching them.

At 7 a.m., land was spotted and a small boat sent ashore. The delegation landed at Purdy's place, five miles above White Rock. Purdy and three other families—24 people in all—were staying together in an old shanty, 12 by 16 feet. They said their own homes were burned. These people wanted to stay and search for belongings and friends. They were given a barrel of crackers, bread, a ham and some tea.

From here the *Moffat* steamed south to Forestville where the sailors found utter desolation. "Not a house, barn or shed was left standing. Fruit trees are burned to black, leafless stubs. Hogs, cows, chickens and other animals are lying burned to a crisp where the flames overtook them. The huge mill chimney stands alone, a solitary monument, marking the site of what three days before was a thriving village of five hundred souls," said a story in the Port Huron *Weekly Times*.

Both docks were burned, including all of the lumber and shingles stored from the mill, awaiting shipment. Survivors were beginning to arrive at the place from inland. Provisions were left with these people before the *Moffat* steamed north to Sand Beach, the early name for what now is Harbor Beach.

When the boats arrived at Sand Beach they again found ruin and devastation. The *Weekly Times* story said that "all of the village, with the exception of Mr. Carrington's dwelling and store, is entirely consumed. Mill dock, dwellings, barns and other property, Robert Erwin's residence and store with stock of goods, Pritchley's hotel and others are gone. The flames swept over a doomed village so swiftly that women and children escaped with nothing on but their night clothes."

The Carrington house was opened as a shelter for survivors and the provisions from the store were exhausted by the time the *Moffat* arrived. Many of the people there were badly burned and in need of medical attention. About ten burn victims were loaded on the boats—some of them having to be carried suspended in a quilt—for the trip back to Port Huron.

A Port Huron physician, identified as Dr. Johnson, was aboard the *Moffat*. He dressed the burns and made the fire victims as comfortable as possible as they were brought aboard.

The *Moffat* went as far north as Forest Bay, taking on more burn victims and leaving supplies. Nearly every building at Forest Bay was burned, including John Hobson's mill and home.

Because there was no firewood left north of Sand Beach for fueling the steamer, the *Moffat* was forced to turn south for Port Huron at 3 p.m.[15]

Almost every major fire year posed a threat to Great Lakes shipping in one form or another. Research files supplied by the Sleeping Bear Dunes National Lakeshore in Empire, Michigan tell of forest fire smoke hazards on Lake Michigan from just one year—1894. Below are some of the encountersvessels in this area of Lake Michigan endured:

United States Life-Saving Service Report - 1894[16]

Aug. 11 Am. str. *St. Joseph*	North Manitou Island Lake Michigan	While towing the schooner *Sidney O. Neff* during thick weather, steamer stranded on south point of island about same time as steamer *Lackawanna*. Worked 3 hours shifting cargo, so as to lighten her bow, and handling lines for tugs...then floated and in turn released her bow, which had also gone ashore.

Aug. 11 Am. str. *Lackawanna*	North Manitou Island Lake Michigan	Stranded at 1:30 a.m. during thick smoky weather. Patrol discovered steamer almost as soon as she struck and hastened to alarm crew. Rowed alongside and took master 3 miles to tug, with whose aid the vessel was floated.
Aug. 27 Am. str. *Florida*	North Manitou Island Lake Michigan	Stranded on Pyramid Point on mainland and 11 miles from station; weather thick and smoky by reason of forest fires. Started lightening load, continued working until morning of the 29th, when she was got off with assistance of tug.

Work & Casualty Chart of the Great Lakes - 1894

#32 Schooner *A.P. Grover* stranded during thick, smoky weather at South Manitou Island, August 6, 1894. Was released some time later. Estimated damage to vessel, $3,000.

#35 Schooner *James G. Blaine* stranded during thick smoky weather and some sea on northwest end of South Fox Island, August 27, 1894. Estimated damage to vessel, $2,500. Released.

#36 Steamer *Griffen* stranded on Dead Man's Point during thick, smoky weather, August 28, 1894.

#37 Steamer *Florida* stranded during dense smoke on Pyramid Point, August 27, 1894. Estimated damage to vessel and cargo, $5,100. Released.

#38 Steamer *Robert Holland* stranded during dense fog and smoke on Sleeping Bear Point, September l, 1894. Estimated damage to vessel, $5,000. Released.

#39 Schooner, *S. M. Stephenson* stranded on Sleeping Bear Point during thick, smoky weather, September l, 1894. Damage to vessel, $2,500. Released.

#40 Schooner *S.M. Fannie Neil* stranded on Sleeping Bear Point during thick, smoky weather, September l, 1894. Released. Damages nominal.

#41 Schooner *Artic* stranded during dense fog and smoke 2 miles south of Antrim Shoal, September 8, 1894. Estimated damage to vessel, $500.

#42 Steamer *City of Charlevoix* stranded 3 miles north of Charlevoix, during thick, smoky weather, September 7, 1894. Damage to vessel, $2,500. Released.

#45 Schooner *Grace M. Filer* stranded 3 miles inside of Grand Traverse Point in a gale of wind and smoky weather, September 10, 1894. Estimated damage to vessel, $700. Released.[17]

The smoke and rough seas listings that occurred on Lake Michigan in 1894 highlight the seriousness of the situation. Without a doubt, forest fires, whether they occurred in 1871, 1881, 1894, 1908, 1911 or, for that matter, in any given year; Great Lakes shipping and navigation was seriously hampered.

The Burning
Saginaw Valley and the Thumb Area

The Fire King's march to the sea took in a great deal of the territory between Lakes Michigan and Huron, destroying some two million acres of trees, leaving thousands of people homeless and scores dead.

The Grand Rapids Daily Eagle *said in its October 13, 1871 edition, "Turn which way we will, we meet the same story of woe and destruction." And a few days later—October 16th—the paper said, "The whole northern portion of the state has been more or less desolated."*

More than forty towns were totally destroyed; many more severely damaged. Sections of farm and log camp lands were decimated. Newspapers of that day did not have positive accurate death counts, so their headlines screamed in generalities—Lives Lost - Impossible To Estimate; Loss of Life Proved To Be Considerable; Hundreds Feared To Have Perished Statewide. An exact death toll was never issued, but historians consider that a figure in the 200 plus range would not be excessive, while the homeless tally was more or less established at a figure surpassing 18,000 victims.

The Burning

Saginaw Valley and the Thumb Area

On the tenth day of October, details of disastrous Michigan fires began to be known: we have already learned of the destruction wrought by the storm of fire brands and tornado-spawned fire balls—or, as they are now known: fire balloons —from Menominee County in the U.P. to the western side of the lower peninsula. The rich, lush land of the Saginaw Valley and territory northwest was reported fire swept, and fires were said to be raging in Genesee County as well as the Thumb. On the twelfth, word was received that Huron City, Sand Beach, White Rock, and Forestville had been wiped out. A number of persons had been burned to death, and approximately two-thirds of the population of Huron and Sanilac counties were homeless. On the fourteenth, fires were reported to be increasing in Newaygo, Isabella, Gratiot, and Tuscola counties, and getting worse along Lake Huron. Sixty people were said to have been rescued from the lake where they fled to escape the rampaging flames.

The disaster was most complete between Saginaw Bay and Lake Huron. An area of some 40 miles square was completely devastated and over 50 residents lost their lives—found burned to death. A catastrophe of the first order.

The fires died down in volume and size by the 18th of October. But nevertheless, as late as the 24th of that month smoke was reported as troublesome and causing problems for navigation along the Great Lakes and connecting waterways.

Section 1, Chapter 5
The Burning
Saginaw Valley and the Thumb Area

Surely more lives would have been lost had the country at that time been more thickly populated. Fortunately, it was not. But 200 lives lost were 200 more than should have been. May we never have a repetition of such tragedies again. The northern Thumb area was wiped out twice—just a decade after the first fires devastated the areas, the second holocaust finished the job, causing a terrible death toll and leaving another path of havoc in its wake.

Port Huron *Times Herald* reporter James Donahue described scenes from the 1871 Thumb Fire as follows:

> ...The 1871 fire didn't just happen in a single day. Jones wrote in his autobiography, "The fire began to run in July and August and went through my orchard and took the apples on the trees. The fire kept burning all fall. On the eighth of October, that night was the worst."
>
> Thumb historian Gerard Schultz noted in his book, "As early as Friday, Oct. 6, men were fighting a forest fire at Cato, about four miles west of Forestville. Jacob Buel, one of the men, was so busy fighting the fire that he did not have his clothes off for more than a week."
>
> The Port Huron *Weekly Times* reported that fire raged across the western parts of Huron and Sanilac counties late Sunday evening and early Monday, Oct. 8 and 9, and "fire was flying through the air like a shower of hail."
>
> The fire reached such intensity it created a hurricane force wind. A record of the fire taken from an early history of Sanilac County told how the wind unroofed buildings at White Rock "and enveloped the whole village in a sheet of flame."
>
> Survivors at Forestville told how the wind and fire "rushed in like a tornado." The town was destroyed.
>
> People banded together in bucket brigades and, using shovels and other tools to battle the fire at the edge of these towns, suddenly had to run for their lives. Most sought refuge in Lake Huron, although the high winds

created such violence in the water many people drowned, or were forced out of the water back to the fiery shore.

At Parisville, people gathered at the Catholic Church for safety as the flames roared through their farms and town. The church was spared and became one of the oldest landmarks in the area for many years. It was only recently destroyed by fire.

When the fire threatened Sand Beach, two men, a woman and nine children took refuge in a small boat on Lake Huron, according to Schultz. On Monday, high winds and dense smoke prevented them from returning to shore and so the boat with its occupants drifted across the lake to Kincardine, Ontario, Canada...one of the children died on the way.

Schultz also said a stage crowded with passengers was "hemmed in by the fire on the road between Rock Falls and Elm Creek. The driver and his passengers escaped, but the horses and the wagon were consumed by the flames."

About 70 residents of a hamlet known as Cracow, located near Parisville, grabbed blankets and jumped into a drainage ditch as the fire approached. By wetting their blankets, the people managed to save themselves when the fire passed over, Schultz wrote.

The aftermath of that fire was awesome.

The whole country north of Richmondville to Pointe aux Barques, covering most of the Thumb, was waste. Schultz said the timberland was burned over "and trees had fallen one upon another and were piled up in massive heaps for miles and miles.

"A man from Port Huron walked more than one mile on the trunks of fallen trees without touching the ground," he wrote.

Many people suffered from fire blindness, burns, exposure, exhaustion, and lack of food and water. Although it was never known how many people actually perished in the fire, estimates ran as high as 50 dead between Saginaw Bay and Lake Huron.

One unnamed writer told the macabre story of seeing a man carrying a pail filled with the bones of what had been his wife and children.[18]

In 1969 an accounting of the Thumb fire of 1871 was printed in The Saginaw *News.* It is presented below in its entirety:

Many Suffered in Thumb Area Fire of 1871

BAD AXE—"Much has been written about the great Thumb area fire of 1881 that killed 125 persons, but very little has been written about the forest fire of 1871 in the Upper Thumb," says Chet Hey, Huron County historian.

Hey said that not as many people were killed in the 1871 fire, but some of the sufferings of the people who survived kept the fire vividly in the minds of those who witnessed it.

He quoted from a report by Port Austin lawyer, banker and prosecuting attorney for Huron County, Richard Winsor, "The Great Forest Fire of 1871."

"People had their clothes burned off. Some had toes burned from their feet, while trying to escape the flames," Winsor wrote.

Winsor reported that the fire occurred during a terrific rain and wind storm. "I experienced the storm from the wagon and paint shop of Septimus Irwin of Verona Mills, east of Bad Axe Corners. (Two years later Irwin was the first settler at Bad Axe.)

"Standing on the porch I heard the terrific roar of the storm and the crashing roar of the timber. Millions of cinders were ignited and swept like feathers, floating in the storm. I felt that there could not be a human being left in its wake."

Winsor continued that the day after the fire and storm, Oct. 10, he left Port Austin with a supply train of 16 teams and wagons for Bad Axe Corners.

They followed the sandy beach to the road leading to Parisville Road.

"Timber rocked and swayed like weeds, falling in all directions, from prostrate to an angle of 45 degrees. It was falling and crashing across the road at every step."

Winsor singled out his teams and placed them 100 feet apart to give distance to make a rush in case of falling burned trees.

"A vanguard of men went ahead, cutting off and clearing timber as it fell, letting the men and teams pass. Both men and horses came through without a scratch."

Winsor's relief team returned to Verona Mills and cut its way north to Huron city the following day. It was then they saw the suffering people.[19]

Our next Thumb Fire offering arrived from Ms. Jane Miller, Secretary of the Sanilac County Historical Society at Port Sanilac, Michigan. It was a published "Sesquicentennial Spotlight" accounting:

The 1871 Fire

By Kate P. McGill

The tales of the forest fires have been told and retold, yet never lost their interest. The fire of 1871 started on Sunday night, October 8. Clearing had been going on rapidly, and fire was the only way of destroying brush. Fall was the time for this, rains were due and there was no particular danger. The fall of 1871 was unusually dry, the mid-September rains failed. The air was heated and rising from the heated ground and meeting other air currents until a wind rose that grew in velocity and fanned the burning brush heaps into whirlwinds of flame that swept the Thumb from west to east. Through some freak of nature the Cass River swamp was barely touched. During the years the country recovered from the catastrophe and small farms appeared, and prosperity seemed assured.[20]

Section 1, Chapter 5
The Burning
Saginaw Valley and the Thumb Area

Herbert Larson in *Bewabic Country* quotes a Mr. John Cockran, a resident of Houghton, Michigan who lived through the 1871 fire that rampaged through the Thumb Area of Michigan. Cockran states:

> A forest fire is a terrible thing. I know, for as a boy I went through the great Sanilac fire of the '70s down in lower Michigan (1871). To this day, if I'm in the woods and I see either smoke or fire, I get out. For days the smoke was so thick you could only breathe by lying on the ground with a wet cloth over your face. It was so dark from the smoke, you didn't know if it was day or night. When it was all over, everything was destroyed for miles in every direction. In the blackened fields, cattle lay dead on their backs, all bloated up, their four legs sticking up into the air. In one farmer's field, there was a mud hole in which the farmer and his wife survived by lying in the mud, only to find that they had to share the mud hole with a large black bear. Dead people were found burned crisp where they had fallen, trying to escape. At another farm, the whole family perished in the bottom of a well, where the farmer thought they would be safe. When they were discovered and the bodies were touched, they fell apart (steam cooked). But the most uncanny thing that happened was when a farmer in town released his blind horse. He could not believe his eyes when he returned a week later and found the animal standing alive in the barn. That blind horse had survived that terrible fire, crossed the river on his way back over the only stringer left of the burned bridge. Truly something that can not be explained.[21]

The Rev. E.J. Goodspeed wrote the *History of the Great Fires in Chicago and the West* the year they took place—1871. He himself visited many of the stricken areas and interviewed survivors. We will print several reports from this source:

> Peshtigo, Wisconsin suffered the worst blaze, but in other places fires were almost equally severe. White Rock, Forestville, Elm Creek,

Huron City, Seigal, Bingham—the list of burned villages goes on and on. And many isolated farms were burned and their owners perished.

A farmer named James Langworth lived near St. Charles, Saginaw County on a farm of 90 acres. On the Sunday of the big fire he was alone as his wife and children were visiting friends in Canada. His well had been dry for a week; his only source of water supply during that time had been what he could get by digging holes in the dry bed of a creek. During the day about a barrel of water would collect in these holes. This he used for drinking and cooking purposes.

Early Sunday morning, fire clouds of smoke were drifting across the farm causing darkness. The farmer turned his cow and several head of young stock loose on Sunday afternoon. He reckoned forest fires were burning a mile from him but were not heading in the direction of his farm. By the farm and the edge of the forest was a partially dried-up swamp nearly one-half mile wide. If the fires did turn in his direction, he was confident that the swamp would stop them. He was worried but not frightened.

Shortly before dark his farm was suddenly invaded by hundreds of wild animals—rabbits, woodchucks, squirrels—moving slowly as if dazed. When he went up to them they seemed not to notice him.

That night the farmer sat up in his farmhouse, his oil lamp a dim blur in the smoke filled room. Soon after midnight the wind changed and freshened and in the distance he could hear the roar of the flames, and the crashing of big trees as they toppled over. At 6 o'clock in the morning there was no daylight—only thick smoke billowing, and the roar of the flames roaring steadily louder. He could not see the fire, but from the sound of the flames he judged it must have eaten its way around the swamp edges and was approaching the farmhouse. He decided to leave. He made a pile of a few valuables on top of a blanket and tied up the blanket. As he was tying it, huge flames suddenly shot up from his barns and hay stacks, and a rain of burning twigs and branches swept in through the open doorway of the house. James Langworth abandoned his bundle and ran for his life.

There was a wagon road from his farm to the village and he sought this as a means of escape. Almost stifled, his throat so parched that he could not swallow, and his lungs feeling like a knife was at work in them, he stumbled forward, trying to keep ahead of the flames. And then another fire, coming from a different direction, jumped the road in front of him.

Behind him was the main fire, to the right was another sheet of flames, and trees ahead of him were burning. He turned to the left, which was still clear, though burning cinders were falling and small flames were already munching up the dry leaves which covered the ground. Several times, covering his face with his arms, he had to run in a series of leaps through small surface fires. Twisting and turning, falling into holes, stumbling over logs, he staggered on, not knowing where he was going. And at last, with his clothes almost scorched off him and his body covered with blisters, he ran into a gang of men working in the smoke to construct a fire-line around the village of St. Charles (Saginaw Valley area).

James Langworth lost everything he had in the fire, except his life and his family which were away. He was among the lucky ones.

⊠⊠⊠⊠⊠

Terrible tragedies occurred on outlying and lonely farms. When the fire was approaching, the Lamp family—consisting of Charles Lamp, his wife and 5 children—hitched up a wagon and tried to escape with some of their household goods. The fire caught up with them, and all were killed except Charles Lamp, who was horribly burned .

A farmer named Lawrence, with his wife and 4 children, tried to take refuge in a large clearing; all were burned.

Two farmers, Nathaniel May and Henry Newberry, were neighbors. Mr. May's family consisted of himself, his wife and his daughter. At the time of the fire they had friends from New York staying with them, a Mr. and Mrs. William Aldous and their 3 children.

The Newberry family farmed, between them, about a 1,000 acres and owned a mill. Different members of the family owned their own homes. One of them, a Mr. William Newberry, was a school teacher.

On the night of the fire, this Mr. Wm. Newberry heard a "great roaring," and found that fire was raging in the woods not far away. He started to go to his brother's house to see what must be done, but was driven back by suffocating smoke. In his return he found that his home was alight. He and his wife, their child and his wife's sister all fled blindly into the smoke. By the greatest good luck they came to a small water hole, 12 feet square. There they squatted, covering themselves with water, their backs to the fire. Soon the fire was racing on all sides of them; they saw the May's barn and a bridge spanning a dry creek go up in flames within a few seconds and they could hear shouting and screaming from the May's house.

They survived. In the morning, half-blinded, they staggered out of the water hole and Mr. Newberry went to look for his relatives. A short distance from the water hole he found the bodies of two men, and, farther on, the carcasses of several hogs and cows. Finding he was too blind to go on, he cut some meat from one of the dead cows and took it back to his family who cooked and ate it.

Of the 17 Newberry family members, 12 were killed. All the May family were dead (as were their guests). On another farm belonging to a man named Adnah Newton, 16 persons were burned to death. On other farms, the Doyle family and their 7 children; the Kill family of 10 people; the Spear family of 4—all perished.

☒☒☒☒☒

A Mr. Brady of Detroit was staying in the village of White Rock, Huron County, on that Sunday night. As the fire approached the village, the people turned out to try to fight the fire. Finding this hopeless, they fled into the waters of the Great Lake (Huron) and even here were not safe from the scorching air without occasional plunges beneath the surface. Mr. Brady himself was in the water for 8 hours. About him were men up to their waists or shoulders in water, holding children in their arms, and women poorly protected by their clothing from the chill of the water which was their only protection against the burning heat of the air. Huddled in the water, half-blinded by smoke and heat, they saw the fire eat up the whole of their town. In Mr. Brady's words: "Not only were their houses, fences, barns, and stock destroyed, but their furniture and clothing, and even the deed by which they held their lands, and their insurance papers."

On the Monday morning, when the fires had passed by, the exhausted villagers crawled out of the water, but there was neither food nor shelter for miles around. Later in the afternoon they were taken aboard the lake steam *Huron*, which also took the rescued inhabitants of Forestville and Cato, who were in a similar plight.

☒☒☒☒☒

John Kent and wife were living about 10 miles above Forestville and about 5 miles from the lake. For weeks the smoke in Sanilac and Huron counties has been so dense that women and children have been made sick, and every human being has been half blind. Fowls were smothered as long as three weeks ago, and the effect on cattle and horses was to render them unfit for work.

Although Kent had reason to apprehend danger to himself, wife and two children, he did as nearly everyone else did, stood by his little property in the hopes to preserve it.

Friday last he could hear the roaring of the flames and the falling of the trees from his house. At night the heavens were rendered so light that he needed no lamp in the house. His dog left him early Friday morning, and the house cat disappeared two days before, the animals seeming to have a better knowledge of Kent's farm. His children—two little girls, the youngest not a year old—were left in the house, and husband and wife repaired to the fire to try to beat it back. But while busy here, the flames crept over the dry ground from other directions unheeded and neglected. Fighting with all their strength, father and mother gave no heed to anything but the fire before them, until they were at last startled by a scream from the house. Instinctively they felt that the flames had seized it, and they started to the rescue of the children. But the smoke had settled down so thick that they ran in all directions without finding the house, and knew not its locality until the fall and crash of the roof told them that their little ones had met an awful fate.

"I tell you, mister," said Kent, "It made us crazy. The fire all around us except to the west, house gone, barn burning, hay and everything destroyed. There was only one thing to do—I got hold of Mary and plunged through the fire and smoke until we got out into the lake road and then we had hard work to keep ahead of the fire before reaching the water. It was awful, sir, to hear that screaming from those burning children, and it was dreadful to go away and leave them roasting there."

Many of the others had almost as bad experiences. While some of the farmers left the woods 10 or 12 days ago, seeing that nothing could prevent the progress of the flames, others like Kent hoped for a rain, and trusted that the fire would not advance over the cleared lands. There was a family named Cross, living about a mile back of Kent's, and when they did not see them come out, Kent was certain that every one, five in all, were roasted in the flames.[22]

In closing his chapter on the 1871 Michigan Fires, Rev. Goodspeed reported:

Many people tried to commit suicide when cut off by the flames. One man killed his whole family and then himself. A wealthy farmer shot all of his fine horses and then died with them.

Peshtigo (Wisconsin), White Rock, Forestville, Elm Creek, Huron City, Bingham, Verona, Holland, Manistee—the names read like a roll call. In an area of the peninsula between Saginaw Bay and Lake Huron, 23 towns and villages were burned out and 18 were partially destroyed. Hundreds of isolated farms were turned into blackened deserts, millions of trees became charred stumps, thousands of animals died pathetically and miserably, thousands of people were left ruined and homeless, and more than 1,500 men, women and children lost their lives.[23]

[Goodspeed's 1,500 deaths indicate the total figure taken from the Wisconsin, Illinois and Michigan fires combined]

Section 1, Chapter 5
The Burning
Saginaw Valley and the Thumb Area

Contribution to the stricken areas were received from just about every state in the Union as well as Canada and even from Europe. Some $500,000 in cash was collected as were vast amounts of clothing. Lumber companies gave out free building materials in many affected areas. Trains often delivered goods free of charge. Many people who contributed clothing or bedding supplies pinned their names and addresses on these items, in hope that some of the survivors would respond. Many did.

Below can be found a listing of Michigan relief supplies that was taken from an unknown newspaper source from the Bad Axe, Michigan area:

Salt	400 bbls.	Hardware	$4,855
Sundries	711 packages	Groceries	$13,514
Potatoes	1,100 bbls.	Ground feed	248 tons
Clothing	999 boxes	Blankets	12 bales
Corn meal	691 bbls.	Bedding	26 boxes
Drugs	3 boxes	Dried apples	75 bbls.
Chairs	159 dozen	Nails	117 kegs
Bedsteads	289	Mattresses	284
Cook stoves	345	Grain	2,160 bushels
Flour	4,313 bbls.	Clover seed	255 bushels
Beans	255 bbls.	Kitchen tables	406
Pork	462 bbls.	Lumber	455 m
Boots, shoes	109 cases	Hay	800 tons
Crockery	$1,104		

Section Two

The Thumb Fires of 1881

The Thumb Fire of 1881

Why - Where - When?

True, the Great Fires of 1871 were horrible. Yet this destruction was to virtually repeat itself in just a scant ten years time. How could this happen?

The 1871 conflagration was termed a "tree-top fire" which left in its wake a tanglement of downed and dead trees to litter the forest floor, providing fodder and fuel for the next blaze to occur when the stage was properly set with just the correct conditions. While the 1871 blaze took in more territory, the 1881 holocaust proved to be far more intense, extracting a greater toll in lives and human suffering than its earlier fiery counterpart.

This section of Michigan On Fire proves to be the most graphic. Many of the details and personal accounts may give you nightmares, but this story must and should be told to our modern-day public; basically, because it can happen again...times and circumstances are right!

The Thumb Fire of 1881

A raging forest fire.
Photo courtesy Michigan Department of Natural Resources

Why - Where - When?

A 1950 booklet published jointly by the Michigan Department of Natural Resources and the USDA Forest Service estimated that the fire of September 1881, commonly known as the Thumb Fire, burned well over one million acres, cost 282 lives, and did more than two and a quarter million dollars worth of damage. The booklet drew comparisons to the 1871 fires:

> Like the 1871 fire, the fire of 1881 came at the end of an extremely severe drought and was the result of hundreds of land-clearing fires whipped into a seething cauldron of flame by high winds. It was worse in the Saginaw Valley and the Thumb region where it burned over much the same territory that had burned over ten years before. Its severity is ac-

counted for not only by the drought and high winds that prevailed, but by the fact that the country was full of slash from logging and land clearing, and of dead and down timber killed, but unconsumed, by the fire of 1871.

No one who has not experienced a big forest fire can conceive of the appalling conditions which occur and the terror and helplessness of those in its path. The following excerpts from contemporary accounts give some idea of the conditions that prevailed:

From the *Evening News*, Detroit: Thursday, September l, 1881: "The drought all over the Mississippi Valley and throughout the northwest continues with unabated rigor. Sun spots noted...Atmosphere scorches and blisters everything...vegetation dried to a cinder, gives nothing but material for fire. Trees shedding their leaves a month before the usual time; grass brown and withered. Pastures and streams dried up. Milk scarce, butter a luxury. If it does not rain and rain hard soon, food will be scarce this winter... Buyers paying the unheard price of 18 and 20 cents a pound for butter."

Saturday, September 3: "Farmer near Stark overcome while fighting fire and burned to death."

Tuesday, September 6: "Woman burned to death while fleeing for shelter near Lapeer.., Kawkawlin in danger...terrible fires reported raging in the forests northwest and north of Bay City...air full of cinders...people suffering from heat and smoke... Fires devastating the woods around Flint.

"Saginaw: Intensely warm and smoke suffocating. East of city forest fires raging fiercely. Travel on Waterville plank road cut off...hundreds of acres afire. Fires plainly visible from the city at night...Indian settlement surrounded...Heavy fires reported in Blumefield and Bridgeport townships.

"Detroit: Heat and drought almost unprecedented. Throughout the timber regions great forest fires are raging in all directions from the Mississippi to the ocean. In many places the earth is so dry that fires have penetrated into the soil, following the vegetable fibers and moving mysteriously by this means over many miles only to break to the surface in a destroying conflagration wherever the surface vegetation furnishes fuel. (Fires) seem to break out spontaneously from the bosom of the earth.

"Port Huron: No telegraphic communications north of Croswell. Port Hope reported burned and Port Austin and Island Beach believed to be burning. Tremendous fires in Sanilac and Huron counties...Richmondville destroyed and Deckerville reported burned...Eight lives known to have been lost. Many people horribly burned."

Wednesday, September 7, 3:00 p.m.: "Wholesale devastation in Saginaw Valley and Huron peninsula. Entire townships becoming roaring furnaces and left in ashes.., Over 30 lives lost...survivors fleeing to the lake. Tyre, Deckerville, Bad Axe, Verona Mills, Elk Creek, Richmondville, and Caro burned. Forestville on fire. Railroad and telegraphic communications cut off."

4:00 p.m.: "At least 100 lives lost in Sanilac County alone. Men, women and children burned on the roadside while seeking shelter. A norther sets in, fans flames and increases havoc. Medical aid and other succor needed. Six counties (Tuscola, Huron, Sanilac, Genesee, Montcalm, and Saginaw) have suffered. Villages of Port Hope, Bad Axe, Verona Mills, Charleston, Minden, Forestville, Richmond, Anderson, Deckerville, Tyre, and Ubly in ashes. Fifty to sixty dead...more being found in cellars, wells and root houses."

Thursday, September 8: "Several hundred lives known to be lost...thousands left homeless. Principal destruction in Huron, Sanilac and Tuscola counties...fires started from burning by settlers...forest fires reported in the vicinity of Holland and in Isabella County...west wind of Monday and Tuesday changed to north Wednesday."

Friday, September 9: "The worst ever: Thirty-one townships and eleven villages swept by the flames...45 bodies found near Paris in Sanilac County...fire started in N.W. part of Sanilac County and in adjoining

Huron County from settlers burning to clear land...spread east and north to the lake shore, then west through Grant in Huron County, then south and southwest, then east across Cass River where it met another part of the fire and raged for twelve hours...500 to 600 dead, 2,000 families homeless, 15,000 destitute."[24]

A later estimate placed the number of dead at 282, of which 167 were identified. The appalling thing about this loss of life was the large number of children involved due to whole families being wiped out. A current estimate placed the property loss at two and a half million dollars, $75,000 to standing timber, fences, and fruit trees in Sanilac County alone.

Governor David H. Jerome twice sent out calls for relief and over three-quarter million dollars was raised. An interesting sidelight is that this was the first national calamity in which the newly organized American Red Cross participated as a relief agency.

A more intimate account of conditions is to be found in the story told by the Reverend Z. Grenell, Jr., of the First Baptist Church of Sand Beach (now Harbor Beach), who said: "At sunrise, Monday, September 5, the air was clear at Sand Beach. By 1 p.m. the sky was copper colored. At 2 p.m. it was so dark that lanterns were necessary out of doors to find one's way around. Darkness continued all afternoon. Many thought the end of the world was at hand. Terror heightened by the approach of flames, the stories of destruction to the west, and the arrival of charred remains and refugees. This continued until Wednesday morning, when at 8 a.m. the wind changed to north and brought relief along the shore."

A detailed account of the fires that burned in the Thumb is given in a report made by Sergeant William 0. Bailey of the Signal Corps (now the Weather Bureau), who traveled over the burned area after the fire and interviewed many of the survivors. He emphasizes the extreme dryness that prevailed, the presence of vast areas of logging slash, the debris left by the fire of 1871, the prevalence of land-clearing fires, and the occurrence of winds of hurricane force, all of which combined to produce the holocaust which resulted. There have been bad fires in Michigan since, but none as severe or extensive as the great fires of 1871 and 1881.[25]

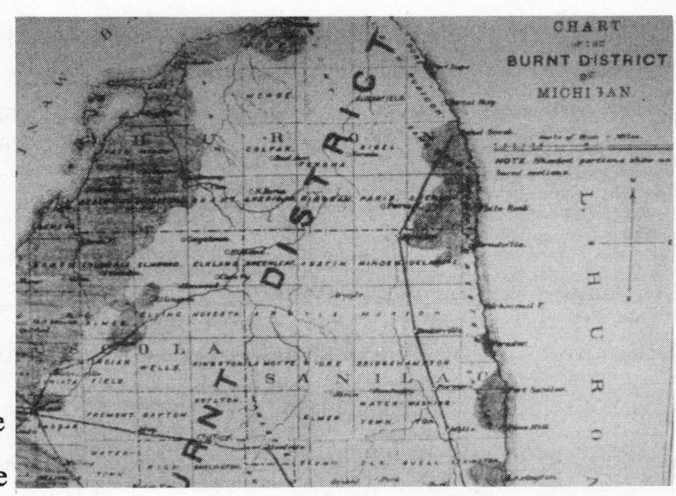

Photo courtesy Hoyt Public Library, Saginaw

A map in Sgt. William O. Bailey's *Report on the Michigan Forest Fires of 1881*. Sgt. Bailey was in charge of the Port Huron station of the U.S. Army Signal Corps (now the U.S. Weather Bureau).

Mark D. Schwartz of the San Francisco State University Department of Geography wrote a paper about the meteorological causes of the 1881 Thumb fires. Here is Schwartz's summary:

> In the summer of 1881, several months of drought, a previous fire, and careless lumbering practices combined to produce ideal conditions for a major forest fire in Michigan's Thumb area. On 5 September 1881, the warm sector of a midlatitude cyclone (following a track roughly similar to

that of the one associated with the 1871 conflagration) moved into the area, bringing strong gusts of wind reported throughout the day may have been associated with fire-intensified circulations. The fast motion, track, and strength of both suggest that they were caused by relatively short waves at 500 mb, reinforced by a trough-to-ridge (SW-NE) flow, synoptic conditions, coupled with an expanding heat wave, allowed smoke from the blaze to spread into Canada, and as far as the Atlantic Coast. The fire continued burning generally toward the northeast until extinguished by rains on 10 September. The similarities between the 1881 and 1871 synoptic situations suggest a basic Great Lakes fire-weather forecasting model, which includes a steep warm-sector surface pressure gradient as a primary component.[26]

Mark D. Schwartz's Great Lakes fire-weather forecasting model

Although the 500-mb flow patterns, and hence the complete genesis of these two systems cannot be documented, it is possible to propose a basic Great Lakes fire-weather forecasting model based on the similarities of these two surface synoptic situations:

1) spring or summer climate conditions cause vegetation to be below the wilt stage for 1 or 2 months (as described by Haines and Sando 1969-Climatic Conditions Preceding Historically Great Fires in the North Central Region);
2) high pressure forms near the United States Atlantic coast, with a storm track over the western Great Lakes;
3) cyclones develop in the Great Lakes region with large gradients of pressure and strong surface winds in their warm sectors;
4) low-level jet streaks may develop locally within the warm sector and intensify fire severity.

These jets played a major role in the 1871 fires. While there are many scattered (nonmeteorological) reports of strong winds associated with the 1881 Thumb fire, there is not enough data to confirm the existence of low-level jet streaks in this case.

One hundred years after the Thumb Fire, The Detroit *Free Press* published an article written by Doug Moreland. Selected passages of the article, "The Heavens Rained Fire," follow:

> In the flat, gentle country east of Saginaw, sugar beet farms and potato fields stretch wide to the horizon. Every few miles the highways pass through a town, some of them built along the railroads more than 100 years ago.
>
> There are few trees. Once forested with giant white pines, 150 feet tall and five feet in diameter, the countryside was logged in the early 1800s. The pine was replaced by second-growth maple, aspen and birch. Then, exactly 100 years ago this month, that second growth was destroyed by a fire of almost unimaginable proportions, a holocaust still recalled in some accounts as "the Great Fire of 1881."
>
> Starting east of Saginaw, freak hurricane winds lashed burning woodland into a firestorm that covered 1,500 square miles, destroyed 3,400 buildings, left 15,000 homeless in the face of winter, and killed well over 300.
>
> ...Said one, a resident of Minden City, speaking to a local reporter three days after the flames subsided, "By six o'clock the people began coming into Minden from the west, having barely escaped with their lives, and when morning arrived hundreds had found their way here in a half-nude condition, burned and blinded by the smoke. We then began to have a faint realization of the extent of the fire. Then we first understood that not property alone, but human lives had been swallowed up. To the west and north the roads were lined with the carcasses of horses, cattle, sheep, swine and poultry, etc., cooked and charred almost to a crisp. Then human beings, alike cooked and charred, were found. Some were still alive, with the feet, hands and face literally baked. Some had their ears and nose burned off, and their eyes almost burned out of their sockets. It is too horrible to contemplate late for a moment!"
>
> Horrible, yes. But not unprecedented.

Section 2, Chapter 1

The Thumb Fire of 1881

Why - Where - When?

[Author'Note: the article then describes other fires during previous years that hit this area. We have already discussed much of this in the previous section of *Michigan on Fire*]

...Now in the first week of September, scattered fires were burning within a 30-mile radius of Saginaw and threatened to enter the city itself. In the west, near St. Louis and Breckenridge, several farmers and a train station were wiped out. South almost to Flint, fires were burning in the swamps and brush. Forty miles to the east, as far as Marlette, several towns were threatened and one woman had died. Vassar, Mayville and Millington were in a dangerous situation. Many of the surrounding farmers had been burned out, barely escaping with their lives.

On Sunday, Sept. 5, the wind rose and began whipping these fires to life. At Cass City, 35 miles east and north of Saginaw, the townspeople anxiously awaited the approaching flames. They had already removed household goods to a plowed field outside of town, and most had spent Sunday night in the open for safety. Monday morning a heavy wind from the southwest drove a sheet of flame over the countryside and through the town. By nightfall, several houses and the bridge over the Cass River were burned. A number of people were missing and feared dead.

Farmers along the Cass River fled to the water for safety as the fire rolled over them, again and again. They saved their lives, nothing else. Cinders and ash that fell into the river formed a lye that floated on top. The water was so hot the fish died and floated on the surface by the hundreds. ...From the *Huron County News*, Thursday, Sept. 9, 1881: "With such material to work upon, it only required a stiff breeze like that of Sunday to fan these small fires and send them in sheets of flames over the country with speed, power, and fury which were irresistible by man. The intense heat caused the breeze to increase until it became a perfect gale or hurricane, capable of carrying burning brands half a mile distant and firing stacks and buildings."

The fire appeared at Bad Axe, 20 miles northeast of Cass City, a little after 1:30 p.m. Monday. The winds had begun at noon and, according to observers, trees were broken off at the stump, boulders rolled along like pebbles, and people lifted off their feet into the air. Above the wind, a strange roar was heard, the sound of the approaching flames. Shortly after 1 p.m. there was darkness, as though a curtain had fallen.

Four hundred people fled to the new brick courthouse. As they watched, building after building burned around them. Thirty men pumped water from the adjoining well and kept the walls and tile roof wet. After a few minutes they had to return inside because of the heat, and another 30 would take over. Across the street, barrels of kerosene and gunpowder ignited when the hardware store burned. The store turned dark, then blew into a bright, red glare.

Thirty townsfolk made it east to a plowed field on W.F. Thompson's farm, the fire gaining on them. They dug ditch and covered it with boards and blankets. While the women and children remained under cover, the men took turns keeping the blankets wet.

"In some places it seems as though the scenes of Sodom and Gomorra were reenacted, and that the heavens rained fire," said an observer from Sanilac County. "Survivors from the burned districts describe the scene as bordering on the supernatural. The fire did not move from building to building in the usual way, but while people were speculating as to the cause of the intense darkness, they were suddenly overwhelmed by a billow of fire that rushed upon them out of the darkness, and enveloped whole towns in flames almost in the twinkling of an eye."

...Across the lake in Canada, they, too, thought the world was ending. By 2 p.m. lamps were lit, children sent home from school and the chickens had gone to roost. It was known as "The Dark Day." The air was hot and stifling, with a greenish-yellow tinge. Ashes fell like snow, and the creeks ran yellow, like beer.

...The firestorm traveled the 20 miles from Bad Axe to the shore in two hours. The flames struck hardest five to 15 miles south of Verona and Sand Beach, where they engulfed the small towns of Paris, Argyle and Ubly.

"It grew so dark at Zinger's Hotel at 12 noon," said William T. Bope, writing from Paris, "that they were obliged to light lamps." At about 1 p.m. the wind changed and blew a hurricane from the west. At the same time the fire started all over the large clearing in small patches of blue flame. In every direction small fires could be seen starting up. By

1:30 a solid wall of flame, from 50 to 100 feet high, was sweeping from the west over Paris. At nearly every house, women and children were out in the road, wailing and wringing their hands in despair. The smoke was so dense that nothing could be distinguished 60 rods (330 yards) away. The fire seemed to burn everywhere at the same time, as though it dropped from the clouds. The sky looked like one sheet of flame.

Hundreds found refuge in wells while the flames passed over. Others survived by reaching an open field and burying their faces in the dirt to breathe. They dug holes with their hands, lay face down in ditches or waded out into a river or the lake. Survival was often a matter of chance. In Paris Township, where 23 bodies were found the first night, the fire traveled 10 to 20 m.p.h., the speed of a running man. "Horses did gallop before it, but were overtaken and left roasting," reported the *Free Press* on Sept. 13.

Many bodies were found untouched by the flames, killed by suffocation, smoke inhalation and the heat. Some survivors died later of burns and inflammation of the lungs. "The heat from the flames was so intense," said Army Sgt. William 0. Bailey, stationed at Port Huron, "that sailors at Forestville felt it uncomfortably even though the hot air had moved over the cold water of Lake Huron a distance of seven miles. It withered the leaves of trees two miles from its path. Whole fields of corn, potatoes, onions and other growing vegetables that were not touched by the flames, roasted by the heat."

Monday night the winds abated. Fires burned across the entire area from Saginaw east to the lake where the walls of flame had passed, "lighting up the heavens." Tuesday night the winds reversed and pushed the fires back over the burned districts. Heavy rains late Wednesday put an end to most of the burning, but the suffering and afflictions had only begun.[27]

Some of the reports that followed the fires of 1871 and 1881 were just a bit hard to swallow. Two such examples can be found in the pages of the *Huron*

County Illustrated History. They make clever reading. But believable? Well, I leave that judgment to you:

More Than a Pipeful

A hunter near Elkton was dressing a moose he had killed, when the fire raced toward him, cutting off all means of escape. Danger sharpens wits. This hunter crawled into the body of the large animal, whose innards he had drawn. After things cooled down, a searching party found the burned gun and the smoldering body of the moose. One of the men remarked, "I bet there ain't enough of old Jack left to fill a pipe." Imagine their surprise when they heard a smothered voice answer. "I'll bet there's enough of him left to fill the inside of a moose. Help me outa here!" [28]

Roast Pork

To escape the flames in the "71" fire, this Irish family took shelter in a culvert. The father, looking out, saw a pig roasting near the barn. At considerable risk to himself, he rushed to the barn and dragged the pig into the culvert, saying, "Begorra, an Irish family with a pig can go through hell any auld time." As serious as these fires proved to be, maybe a bit of humor was needed to push those far too vivid memories of the holocaust out of their minds. We must remember these people escaped with merely their lives and little else. Most lost family members, relatives and friends. In cases such as these...a smile, a chuckle, a laugh is worth far more than material things...they are becoming of such a victim that has indeed lost everything but his or her very life.[29]

So we have explained the "why, where and when" of the Thumb Fire of 1881. Let's end this chapter with a poem taken from an anonymous source, It could pertain to the Great Fire of 1871 or the Thumb Fire of 1881, but probably it is from the latter:

Coming Through the Fire

"Fire! Fire! Fire!"
Through the timber rang the cry;
From the fiend in red, the settlers fled,
To lake, or creek close by.

Smoke, smoke, smoke
Through wet blankets breathed the air,
All were afraid; the mothers prayed,
And God answered their prayer.

Flames, flames, flames,
To the culvert or dug well,
Whole families fled, while flames o'erhead
Gave them a taste of hell.

Faith, faith, faith, in God,
Losing all, made few depressed;
The Thumb of the Mit had plenty of grit,
Our pioneers are of the best.

Honor, honor, honor,
Our pioneers are of the best,
What they went through for me and you,
No human tongue can tell.

The Public Responds To Research Requests

In addition to my requests for information to each fire district in the fire areas, I contacted newspapers in specific areas with "open letters" written to their editors. We piqued the interest of the average citizen. Many had stories to tell from the days of their grandparents; many sent in poems or old newspaper clippings; one lady in particular called me from Oklahoma.

Fellow researcher Gerry Prich of Bad Axe helped tremendously in tracking down information for this chapter. He also helped with the previous section's research regarding the 1871 conflagrations. A part-time newspaper reporter and photographer, he knew the Thumb Area well—its people and its places. Gerry also placed "open letters" in Thumb newspapers, and he searched local libraries and historical societies. Thank you, my friend, for a job well done.

An example of my "open letter," from The Saginaw News, *follows.* News *editor Paul C. Chaffee also became intrigued by my request for fire material and not only sent past clippings from the paper's morgue, but called personally to offer encouragement and success. This book is truly a cooperative effort.*

LETTERS

Historic fires researched

Editor, The News:

I am researching the fires of 1871 and 1881 that swept through the Saginaw Valley and the adjoining Thumb area.

Should you have any of the following historical information, I would be most interested in hearing from you:

Government bulletins, newspaper clippings, fire text, historical booklets family tree booklets or centennial books (parts pertaining to these fires only), and historical photos, lithographs or line drawing sketches (copies preferred).

Whatever data you as an individual or group can supply will be greatly appreciated and credited.

Betty Sodders

The Public Responds To Research Requests

Our first presentation arrived at my desk from an anonymous person and the letter bore only a Saginaw postmark. Obviously, it came from one of the area newspapers, perhaps the Saginaw *News*. It was dated September 9, 1963 and was written by Neil Smith. It follows in its entirety, except the accompanying photograph of Charles Dondineau, retired 87-year-old farmer:

Retired farmer recalls fire

Threshing bee was interrupted

BAD AXE—It was 82 years ago last Thursday, on September 5, that the historic forest fire of 1881 spread its terror and destruction across the Thumb area. One who can still remember the day is Charles Dondineau, Bad Axe, a retired Pinnebog farmer. Now 87, Dondineau was only a boy, 5½ years of age, when the conflagration raged across his father's farm, two miles southwest of Pinnebog, but he still has a vivid memory of the day.

"It was a day to remember," he says, adding, "I can close my eyes and still see the flames as though it were yesterday."

There was an old fashioned threshing bee in progress on the Dondineau farm when the fire was sighted, approaching from the southwest. Dondineau recalls that the men knew it was a big one and immediately departed for their homes.

The Dondineau family—at that time the parents and three youngsters although there were 11 children later on—sought safety on the bank of the Pinnebog River which cut through the farm.

Dondineau remembers the family took all of their belongings to the river, where because of some green timber and cleared land everything was saved. It was hot and smoky and the family was showered with sparks but the flames swept past them. Strangely, the Dondineau log house also escaped.

Searching his boyhood memories, Dondineau recalls seeing the flames race through the forest, "40 rod away." He can still see the old cedar rail fence as it burst into flame from the intense heat and remembers that the barn across the road disappeared in a burst of fire.

When the Dondineau's barn burned, so did all of the grain that was threshed earlier that day. There were no more threshing bees in the district that fall because there was no grain left to thresh, Dondineau recalls.

On the river bank Mrs. Dondineau kept the children playing in the river while she herself kept busy wetting down the bedding and furniture with river water to keep it from being ignited by sparks.

Dondineau, who was eager to start to school that fall, had to wait three years. The schoolhouse burned and was not rebuilt until 1884. He spent his first day in school when he was eight.

Before the fire reached the farm, Dondineau's father drove his span of oxen to the riverbank, pulling a wagon piled high with the last load of wheat not yet threshed. "That load gave us flour for the winter," Dondineau remembers.

He also recalls that a field of potatoes roasted in the ground from the intense heat and the crop was spoiled. A field of turnips, surrounded by a clearing on one side and green timber on the other, escaped unharmed so the family had turnips instead of potatoes.

Two cows were also saved by driving them into the river. They furnished fresh milk.

The fire is one of Dondineau's earliest memories. "I have never forgotten the place where we lived on the river bank for five days. I can show it to you today," he says.

After the fire had passed, other neighbors who had found shelter began dropping in. "Everyone wondered what they were going to do," Dondineau remembers as the chief topic of conversation.

Many of the homes and barns were burned but the immediate area had no fatalities. Histories of the fire estimate that some 70 persons lost their lives as the fire swept across Huron County. Dondineau recalls that a girl by the name of Turner, living four miles away, was among those who died in the fire.

The great fire is rated as one of the major fires in the history of the country. Dondineau, in looking back, remembers that the blaze was a landmark in time, a fixed point by which to date happenings. He also says, "It doesn't seem long ago!"[30]

A reader of the Huron *Daily Tribune*, Linda (Finkel) Siewert of Bad Axe, sent a family history she received at a family reunion. In her cover letter, Siewert said the piece "tells of our ancestors and what they were going through in the fire of 1881."

In the Beginning

This is a brief history of the Finkel family and when they immigrated from Germany to the United States on April 30, 1873. Ferdinand Finkel, born January 19, 1838, left Germany at the age of 35 years and 3 months. Henrietta Finkel (nee Friese) was born January 23, 1840 and left Germany at the age of 33 years and 3 months. They brought their four boys and one girl with them: August, 14 years, 8 months; Emil, 7 years, 8 months; Amanda, 5 years; Carl, 2 years, 8 months and Wilhelm, 6 months. Two of the children died in Germany within a day of each other from diphtheria and were buried immediately.

The Finkels arrived in Wyandotte and stayed there a few days at a cousin's who had come here some time before the Finkel family arrived. Mr. Finkel was unable to find work in Wyandotte, but had heard of the lumbering business in Port Hope and went there with his family.

They moved in a house that had no floor in it. They bought a stove, and with cooking utensils and bedding brought from Germany, they set up housekeeping. They had $1 left of their money. They applied this on a land contract for 80 acres of wild land 2 miles northwest of Port Hope.

Mr. Finkel worked at odd jobs. One was at Grindstone City for 50 cents per day. Later he obtained work at Stafford's salt block at $1 per day where he worked 14 years. The first year they lived almost solely on field peas and turnips, which they bought from William Pochert who had a little land cleared and some crops. They bought some bacon from the store to fill in. While working at the salt block, he also built a log house on the land he purchased. He cleared more land to build a barn.

Then, in 1881, a forest fire came. The sky became very dark in the early afternoon. The ashes and sparks were flying like snowflakes. Two children, Bertha aged 6 and a brother, ran to a neighbor who already had a wagon hitched. The family, with the Finkel children, quickly gathered some food and bedding and drove to Port Hope all the while fighting spark fires on the wagon and clothing.

One of the other children, Charlie, ran to an aunt's home in another direction. He, with his aunt, uncle and their children and grandmother, went out on the lake on a raft. Mrs. Finkel, an expectant mother, remained by the house carrying all the food stuff (having baked earlier) into the cellar, which was framed by boards and then covered with a door of boards, as an entrance to the underground cave-like structure. But it all burned. She had gathered the children's shoes in a baby buggy, which burned. She had to leave finally with the bedding on a wagon and found refuge in a plowed field.

Mr. Finkel remained by the buildings chopping the board fences away from the buildings, drawing water from the well and pouring it on the house. Hastening back and forth, in his desperation, he dropped on his knees and prayed. The clouds opened up and light shone through.

Although the barn burned, the house was spared. The fire died down by the next day. The family and several other wagon loads of people came to Mr. Finkel's house and remained for some time, as it was the only house left for some distance around. Some people who had dropped their bedding and belongings in wells found everything burned. One man, Mr. Brining, was found dead in a well. All the water was dried out. The trees were toppled over, burned off at the roots. From the debris, the people had them sawed into boards and rebuilt their homes and barns. Mr. Finkel's family was all safe; but Mrs. Finkel was blind for 6 weeks.

...Mr. Finkel died June 11, 1933 at the age of 95 years, 4 months and 23 days. Mrs. Finkel died January 31, 1923 at the age of 83 years, 8 days.[31]

Another letter arrived from Mrs. Robert French of Gilford, Michigan. Her letter follows:

July 14, 1992

I was interested in your article of July 8, 1992 in the *Tuscola County Advertiser*, requesting information on fires that ravaged the Thumb Area years ago.

My mother was one of six children born to Duncan and Catharine Sherman Cameron. They came from Tilsonburg and Norwich, Canada and settled eventually along Sucker creek (1882) in Wells Township on a 40-acre farm in Section 28—southeast of Caro, Michigan. Grandpa built the shanty they lived in until they were finally able to build a more livable house several years later.

Mother wrote a book of their early years in which she told of a fire that swept through the area just after they moved into the new house. Perhaps this wasn't one of the "big" fires of the Thumb. The new house was built about 1898, if mother's memory was correct.

In her book she wrote: "It wasn't too long after we moved into the new house until one day we smelled smoke. On investigation we found someone had started a fire west of and across the road from us. It was all virgin pine. We were so frightened it would burn our house for if it got into those tall pines there was no stopping it. And, it did. The fire would run up those trees like crazy, with such a crackling noise, and when it burned one of them, off it went down with a bang and the sparks would set many more on fire. So, we stayed up all night and they loaded what furniture we had on the wagon. Pa set pails of water on the roof to put out the sparks. But when morning dawned the house was still there. We were all so grateful and moved right back in. That house still stands and is lived in on Rossman Road."

If any of this is of any interest, you may use it in your book.

Yours truly,
Mrs. Robert French
Gilford, MI
(Retta Robinson French)

Mrs. French also included a copy of a poem written by her mother, Stella Cameron Robinson (1889-1983). This, too, was found in the book her mother had written regarding their personal fire. While this neither pertains to the 1871 or 1881 great fires, I deemed it important enough to include in this section, for we must also remember that during this era, forest fires were commonplace and each and every dry season had its fair share of runaway blazes.

The Big Fire

One-thing I'll remember
As time grows old,
Seeing the fiery blaze flashing
Thru' the tall pines so bold.
In horror we watched it
All thru' the dark night,
Fearing our new home would vanish
Before morning light.

At last, the house built
But not finished inside,
We quickly moved in
With great joy and pride.
It was 'home sweet home' for
Which we waited so long—
With nice painted floors
And built good and strong.

They were now really living
Their dreams had come true.
Out of the old board shanty
Into a house nice and new.
The smell of the new wood,
A well and a cistern
No more water to carry,
More time for fishing.

My folks worked so hard
Thru' the hot summer days
To build a real home
Which stands there today.
Dad cut logs, had them sawed,
Huge lumber piles made;
Three cornered he made them
In which we kids played.

With a fancy bay window
And Flowers inside,
And too—several bedrooms
My mom fixed with pride.
She sewed rags for carpet
For the living room floor,
My dad bought an organ
Who could ask for more?

Then all of a sudden,
We saw smoke curling round,
Not long till we heard
A crackling sound.
Someone started a fire
In those tall virgin pine
Across the road, and we only
Had one thing in mind.

But when morning dawned
Our house was still there,
We all were so grateful
It's blessing to share.
So back in we went
And the furniture, too,
From out the old shanty
Into our home so new.

Then we all were rejoicing
It was one happy day,
Our home out of danger
So we moved in to stay.
To go on with our planning
One room at a time,
Building hopes for the future
And enjoy life's sunshine.

Another letter came in, from Joan Kennedy of Oklahoma City:

July 23, 1992

Since I subscribe to the *Huron Daily Tribune*, I read your article here in Oklahoma.

My mother was Evelyn Slavir, Bad Axe; father, John Livingston, New Greenleaf.

I have a chair that the American Red Cross had given my great-grandparents after the fire. This was supposedly the first time they helped Michigan residents.

Originally it was a table and 4 chairs. My great grandparents resided in Sigel Township in 1881 (Flora and George Patterson). Mother died in 1986 but many times as a young girl I had been told of some accounts her grandmother had relayed to her. On my fathers side, great grandfather, Neil Livingston succumbed a year later from smoke inhalation damage. He is buried in Cass City. I imagine you'll find many headstones in cemeteries in the area dated 1881-82... victims or indirect victims of the fire.

I understand that both sets of great-grandparents survived the fire by dousing themselves with water and going into the storm cellars until the fire passed.

I hope this small bit of information will be of some help to you.

Joan Kennedy

P.S. By the way, since people were much shorter in stature in those days, my 1881 "Red Cross" chair is much smaller than of today's manufacture.

Photo courtesy Joan Kennedy

A chair given to 1881 fire survivors George and Flora Patterson by the American Red Cross.

After hearing about Ms. Kennedy's chair picture, Saginaw *News* editor Paul Chaffee sent this 1951 newspaper clipping describing just such an artifact:

1881—That's how Thumb residents recall great fire

CARO—A battered wooden chair on display at Caro Red Cross headquarters serves as a reminder of the great fire which swept through the Michigan Thumb 70 years ago.

The Public Responds to Research Requests

Connie McNinch, 13, of rural Caro poses with the chair which Red Cross gave to a Thumb family which lost all its possessions in the great fire. Connie's great-grandfather lived in the area at the time.

The chair was given by the Red Cross in 1881 to one of 3,231 families whose property was destroyed in the fire. It was passed down from generation to generation and finally given back to the Red Cross.

Since receiving the chair, Mrs. Gerald O. DeBoer, executive secretary of the Tuscola County Red Cross, has compiled much of the story of the great fire.

According to Mrs. DeBoer, the fire destroyed a major part of Tuscola, Huron, Sanilac, and St. Clair counties. Three hundred persons burned to death in the fire. It consumed 1,531 houses and 1,480 barns and outbuildings, and left 14,448 homeless.

One of the prime sources of information about the fire is George S. Spencer, 83, of Deford. He was living with his parents on a farm near the point in Tuscola County where the fire is believed to have started.

Sept. 5, 1881, was a dry, windy day. No rain had fallen for weeks. Ponds and swamps had died from lack of moisture.

No one is sure just how or just where in Tuscola County the fire started. It was the time of year when people used to burn brush piles and other debris left by lumbermen and those engaged in clearing the land. Many people think the wind may have whipped a brushpile fire out of control.

Flames leaped to treetops and raced along on strong winds. The fire raced northeastward to the lake shore at the tip of the Thumb. Then winds shifted to the west and the fire spread eastward through Sanilac and St. Clair counties.

By late afternoon great smoke clouds darkened the sun over parts of Canada to the east.

Mr. Spencer recalls how farmers in the Deford area (at the boundary of Tuscola and Sanilac counties) saw the fire coming and thought the end of the world was upon them. He tells of how minutes before the fire reached his parents' farm, and while the wall of flame was more than a mile away, a large stump in the middle of a cleared field suddenly burst into flames.

Wild animals took refuge in buildings with humans. Men put women and children into wells. Some people escaped by wading into rivers and covering their heads with wet blankets. Those who lived near the lakeshore took refuge in the waters of Saginaw Bay and Lake Huron.

Mr. Spencer recalls that a neighbor's team of oxen came through the fire alive but lost their hooves; that another neighbor turned six hogs loose and never found a hair of them...but did find six large grease spots a few rods from where he released them.

The fire acted queerly, it seemed to those early Thumb residents. Flames would engulf one building and suddenly extinguish themselves while destroying other buildings nearby. Mr. Spencer insists the community church was untouched except for one burned plank on the front steps.

Mrs. Allah Schreder of Caro remembers hearing her grandfather, Chris Binder, tell of the great fire. Mr. Binder was one of the first settlers in the community of Ruth in Huron County. His farm, with about 60 acres of cleared land, became a mecca for neighbors trying to escape the fire. Buildings on the Binder farm were not harmed by the fire.

Mr. Binder used to tell about one neighbor who was sure all would be lost in the fire. This man boarded up all openings to his barn, then slit the throats of all his livestock and ended his own life with a shotgun. He was found later, after the fire passed by and left his buildings untouched.

Mr. Binder has told how the area was darkened by smoke for days; how neighbors tied ropes from building to building to guide them in walking about.

The fledgling American Red Cross was quick to respond to the need of relief in the Thumb area. From New York, Clara Barton dispatched all the money, food and clothing the organization could raise.

Three Red Cross centers were set up in the area. One, at Bay Port, was operated by Michael O'Brien, great-grandfather of Connie McNinch, who presented the chair to Tuscola Red Cross.

For a year and six months the Red Cross continued to dole out supplies to families hit by the fire.

Besides clothing and food, the Red Cross brought in supplies of furniture. The chair handed down from generation to generation originally was given by the Red Cross to a Sinclair family near Port Austin at the tip of the Thumb. [32]

And so we have it. Not the tale of two cities, but the tale of two chairs, both part of a huge relief consignment of the fledgling American Red Cross organization.

The next historical document presented arrived from Virginia Gottschalk of Hemlock, Michigan. She photocopied it from the 58-page *Centennial History of Port Crescent*, written by June Nelson and published in 1968. Gottschalk's husband John grew up in Port Crescent and is one of the little boys pictured on the front cover of the book.

The booklet's segment on the Thumb fires is reproduced here:

From These Flames...Spring 1882

Ten years had passed since the county was recovering from the first of the Great Fires. Now again Spring came to a people still stunned from a much greater holocaust.

In late summer the *Huron County News* had printed items that were portents of the awful days that were to come. In August, after a long spell of dry weather when every brush fire seemed hazardous, the readers received the following warning of disaster:

"Looks like '71!" "Local Insurance Agents Tremble!"

Then on Sept. 2, 1881:

"FOREST FIRES again became very threatening in several sections of the county this week. On Wednesday much anxiety was felt at Bad Axe and Huron City.

"The rain falling today will doubtless remove present danger and it is not likely to become so dry again this fall."

It was a false hope however, as the headlines of the next week proclaimed:

FIRE! DEATH! DESTRUCTION!!! The Horrors of '71 surpassed—Bad Axe, Verona Mills, Huron City, Tyre and other places Burned. AID URGENTLY NEEDED!

"To realize how these fires could be so destructive and extensive one must understand the condition of most of the unimproved land in Huron County. The fires of 1871, which were so general, converted a great portion of the green woods into windfalls.

"All of the timber (consisting largely of pine, hemlock and cedar with some hardwoods) on thousands and thousands of acres fell down and were piled and interlocked in every shape in impenetrable masses. It has been a common remark that there would yet be another fire greater than the one which caused these windfalls before they could be gotten rid of. During these ten years something has been done towards cleaning them up. Large quantities of cord wood and timber has been taken from them.

"Settlers came in these places because it was easier to clear. These settlers set fires to get rid of the tangled fallen trees often saying that a big burn was what they needed.

And a BIG BURN was what they got when "Sunday a stiff breeze fanned these many small fires and a conflagration was started." Port Crescent and Port Austin were fortunate to escape with little damage although a bridge up the Pinnebog River was burned and also some barns and grain. "The fires broke through from Lake and Hume townships about on a line with the lowest range of the sections. These townships border on Saginaw Bay and the winds coming from the water toward the heated and rarefied air on the shore, naturally held firmly in the west without any oscillations toward the southwest. Therefore the fires near the southerly limits of Lake and Hume were held in check by the moist westerly winds. They were driven back from Hume by the north wind about 2 o'clock Monday.

"The village of Port Austin was threatened from one to half past three, when the wind changed to northerly. It blew a gale at first and continued to blow a fresh breeze all night."

In spite of the horror and devastation brought to the inland portions of the county, an optimistic item appeared in the Caseville locals—no doubt read with some bitterness by those who suffered in the fire:

"Although bringing misery to so many, we can hardly realize at present the great benefit the country will derive from the fires in the near future by rendering the land more available for settlement. Everything will progress with rapid strides. Railways will be pushed through; a tide of immigration will pour in; farming and pasturage will be largely engaged in and in ten years from now the country will be 50 years ahead."[33]

The above text furnished yet another point of view from those much earlier times. Yes, many believed the fires—as bad as they were—supplied a much needed boost to the local economy. Small satisfaction, indeed, to the many who lost their lives or suffered horribly from the burns they received.

Two *Sesquicentennial Spotlight* pieces were supplied by Jane Miller of the Sanilac County Historical Society. Here is the balance of the article titled "The Fire of '71" by Kate P. McGill [the first portion was printed in Section l]:

...The fall of 1881 was very hot and dry. The air was full of smoke, and one heard of small fires here and there. On Sept. 4 I had an errand to the Sam Wilder place in Lamotte. Driving east from Lamotte little patches of fire were unnoticeable in the woods that lined the road. Traveling along at a brisk trot my horse suddenly snorted and wheeled around in the road. Looking ahead I saw flames of some size. By the time I had reached open country the little patches of fire had become a general fire in the undergrowth. Next day, Sunday, Wm. Ronald lost his life near that spot and Monday, mail carrier Humphrey was burned to death at the spot my horse turned.

The fire of 1881 swept from Marlette to the Huron shore, leaving the country as bare as burned-over prairie. Cattle, horses, chickens lay roasted beside the smoking ruins of farm buildings. Apples being roasted on blackened boughs of once thrifty orchards.

No sooner had word reached the outside world than relief poured in from every quarter of the United States. Food, clothing, seed grain, money with which to buy stock, lumber for buildings, poured into the committee on relief. Headquarters were at T.E. Hough's wareroom, and all who needed help were cared for. There were some funny as well as many tragic happenings. On opening a box from a distant city carefully packed, were ball gowns, slippers, fans, men's silk hats, white vests, etc. However, beneath there were warm and serviceable garments in abundance. What a showing of brotherly kindness the great fire brought out.

In the end they proved a blessing as the land was easily cleared and the great barrier of the Cass River swamps ceased to exist. From their suffering the people winning a great victory.[34]

The next piece, the author of which is unknown, was passed on by Lois Johnson of the Marlette Historical Society:

The 1881 Fire

It was my privilege to grow up a neighbor of two life-long Marlette residents, Mrs. Anna Hurd-Newell and Mr. Harold Keys (both deceased) who still resided in the houses they were born in on their family homesteads.

Over the years I was fortunate to be told many colorful stories of rural Marlette life of many years ago and was also told about "The Fire," as they simply called it, and how both families weathered it.

Mrs. Anna Newell was the granddaughter of Thomas and Ellen Ross who lived on the dead-end section of Mayville Road, east of Germania Road. The Ross family had seven children. Mrs. Newell's mother, Ellen, was a small child in 1881. To escape the fire, the Ross family pulled a farm wagon to the center of a plowed field and covered themselves with water-soaked quilts. When the fire had passed over and they were able to come out, they found everything had burned; but they were not without food. They ate apples baked on the trees and potatoes baked in the ground where their garden had been.

Harold Keys was the grandson of James Keys who lived four miles east of town on Marlette Road. James Keys stayed on as the fire approached from the west, hoping to save his buildings. He soon found his fight futile, as flames all but surrounded him. His last action before fleeing to the Cass River, one-half mile east, was to kick away a burning log which was leaning against the west wall of his house. He was as surprised as anyone when he found his house untouched by flames upon returning.

The house of James Keys was replaced long ago by a larger and finer Keys home on the same site. (4364 East Marlette Road), but the maple trees James Keys planted later still line the road in front of the house. [35]

There were many, many more people who wrote and called, offering text or information. Several even ran down leads for me. One man used part of his upcoming vacation to travel from Saginaw to Oscoda to check out a story there relating to the Au Sable-Oscoda Fire of 1911. All of these contacts gave your author a good feeling, one that indicates people simply do not forget the tragic happenstances. They care for our Michigan past just as much as they are concerned about our state's future. Human nature, with all its failings, is a wonderful untapped source of caring and concern. My special thanks to all the folks who contributed, large and small, throughout this publication.

Excerpts From *The Flaming Forest*

One of the most interesting, thorough and factual publications put out about the Thumb Fire of 1881 was published by the Tuscola County Advertiser *as a Historical Publication titled,* **The Flaming Forest**. *The* Advertiser *was a fledgling newspaper of 13 years' experience when the Great Fire of 1881 occurred. This paper had been founded by Henry G. Chapin, a young printer, who learned the trade at the Dansville, New York* Advertiser, *located in the home town of Clara Barton, founder of the American Red Cross. The Thumb Fire was actually the first nationwide test for this comparatively new organization.*

The Flaming Forest *preserves the haunting memories of this former era. Much of its text was written many years ago by Miner Chipman, an early Bad Axe resident. Additional input also was acquired from newspapers and magazines of more recent times that recall other details of the fire. The staff at Caro that publish the Tuscola County* Advertiser *stated, "Gruesome, horrible and awesome though it is...The Great Fire of 1881 is a part of the Thumb's heritage...and through it we more fully appreciate the agony and the suffering by which this great area was tamed and brought into flower."*

Excerpts From *The Flaming Forest*

Photo courtesy Michigan Department of Natural Resources, Greg Lusk Collection

Sketch of the State Historical Marker near Bayport honoring the Thumb Fires of 1881, from *The Flaming Forest.*

Located between Sebewaing and Bay Port is a small roadside park on highway M-25—the shoreline highway that virtually circles Michigan's Thumb area. Here stands a small historic marker placed by the Michigan Historical Commission and registered as Site #141 in the state's registry of historical markers. This emblem of the Thumb's past calls attention to the Great Fire of 1881 and reads as follows:

Section 2, Chapter 3
Excerpts from The Flaming Forest

Small fires were burning in the forests of the Thumb, tinder-dry after a long, hot summer, when a gale swept in from the southwest on Sept. 5, 1881. Fanned into an inferno, the fires raged for three days. A million acres were devastated in Sanilac and Huron counties alone. At least 125 persons died, and thousands more were left destitute. The new American Red Cross won support for its prompt aid to the fire victims. This was the first disaster relief furnished by this great organization.[36]

Today, this marker is shaded by tall trees and surrounded by the soft green grass. The surrounding countryside is mainly agricultural. The sign reminds us of another day, not so long past, when the grass was not green and when trees—instead of giving cool shade—fueled a fiery inferno.

Following are some of the unique descriptive pieces found in the Tuscola County *Advertiser's* Historical Publication from the collection of "The Flaming Forest" stories of 1881:

***Detroit Evening News*, Sept. 6, 1881:**

LAPEER—Mrs. Richard Elliott of Five Lakes, in this county, was burned to death in the woods last night while fleeing from her house to that of a neighbor, she having been driven out by the forest fires which raged around her home.

EAST SAGINAW—An anxious day has nearly passed. The thermometer has ranged from 90 to 98 degrees and the atmosphere is like a furnace. There is no rain in sight.

Heavy fires are reported on the Otter Lake branch of the Flint & Pere Mar-

Photo courtesy Michigan Department of Natural Resources, Greg Lusk Collection

The cover of *The Flaming Forest.*

quette Railroad. At French's Crossing this afternoon a train was on fire. Between Bridgeport and Birch River fires are bad and the village of Clio was threatened. This afternoon a fire engine was telegraphed for from Clio and one was sent from Flint, as none could be spared from Saginaw.

EAST SAGINAW—The fires are doing considerable damage between this city and Midland, and many miles of fences have been destroyed.

The village of Freeland is threatened, but owing to the excitement and terror of the people it is difficult to obtain definite information.

Since 7 o'clock this evening telegraphic communication has been cut off between this city and Vassar and three miles of fire are reported along the road.

EAST SAGINAW—Telegraphic communications between this city and Vassar was cut off tonight and three miles of fire is reported near Seidens, burning fences and timber.

It is reported that a large force of men at work on the road bed of the Saginaw, Tuscola & Huron Railroad were driven off by the fire.

Another day of horror is anticipated tomorrow.

First News From Port Sanilac

Special dispatches to the Detroit *Free Press*:

PORT SANILAC—There are families in this part of the country burned entirely out, leaving the majority of them with only the clothes they had on. many families had to go to the lake to escape the fire.

It is reported that Richmondville is entirely destroyed.

PORT SANILAC—The whole country is burning up. The fire is raging terribly two miles west of here with a strong west and southwest wind blowing. In the township, yesterday, and last night, about a dozen farms were cleaned completely of buildings and as many other barns were destroyed last night.

Section 2, Chapter 3
Excerpts from **The Flaming Forest**

Terror reigned supreme in all hearts, many people not going to bed. In Forester Township the fires were worse. A belt two miles wide was completely stripped of everything and a number of persons are reported lost, though the only one positively known to have perished is a lady named Birch.

Richmondville, ten miles north of here, is completely destroyed, only one building remaining. Seven lives were lost and one other person badly burned. John Lee, wife and mother, and Abram Thornton, wife and son are lost; the two latter jumped into a well.

Two girls named Sharkey and Winters and an old man named Winters can't live because they are burned so badly.

Anderson Station, on the Port Huron & Northwestern Road, was completely destroyed. Much livestock was lost and great damage done north of Anderson. I know of fifteen farms completely devastated.

Persons coming from Sandusky yesterday came through solid flames. On the line west of this place nearly every family has its goods packed up ready to move on a moment's notice. Eight buildings south, and six north, of Sandusky were burned yesterday.

As I write a report comes from Forestville that the whole village is destroyed.

Trains have stopped running on the Port Huron & Northwestern Railway, yesterday's mail train being unable to get above Deckerville.

PORT SANILAC—The news is getting worse and worse. We are in no immediate danger of being swept away, but are ready to go into the lake.

Mrs. Deebert and four children were burned southwest of Sandusky. The Dennison family is reported missing. A family of nine in Forester, named Wilson, are all burned.

McClure's schoolhouse, Elk Creek Mill and all the buildings and Elk Creek Bridge, all south of Sandusky, are gone.

Everybody is moving to the lakes.

The fire west of us is coming, but we hope to keep it down and save the town, but God help us if it doesn't rain soon.

VASSAR—The fires continue to rage. The fires are within two miles. The whole country on the east side of Cass River is in flames and the wind is southwest. A family residing on Houghton Creek were compelled to seek shelter in a well and remain there for six hours. At one time twenty-four women and children were crowded in one well. No one can at present estimate the terrible loss in this county.

VASSAR—The fire is still raging within three-fourths of a mile of Vassar. If the fire can be kept out of the corporation Vassar can be saved. All the mills and foundries have been shut down and the citizens are out in force fighting the fire. Destitute families continue to come in from burned districts.

CARSONVILLE—A general conflagration has swept over this entire county spreading death and desolation in its track. Twenty-five families have been rendered homeless, and have had everything they possessed in the world consumed.

Two entire families have been burned alive, one that of a farmer named Deebert consisting of wife and four children. All burned to death in Watertown Township and their charred bodies were left upon the bare and blackened ground. Another entire family, named Dennison, is reported burned and still the whole horrible truth is not half told. The mail carrier from Marlette to Bad Axe is also reported to have perished.

LEXINGTON—At present the fire is nearing Croswell and they apprehend great danger unless the wind subsides. It is said the roar of the fire may be heard at the distance of a mile.

No Telegraph Service To Port Austin

The *Evening News*, Wed., Sept., 7, 1881, front page, continues:

The best efforts of the Western Union telegraph employee to "get a hole through" to Port Austin, etc. has failed today, and up to 3:30 p.m. nothing has been heard from there, the wires being destroyed by fire. There is yet no confirmation of the reported burning of Sand Beach and Port Hope, and there are good grounds for hoping that as yet such fate has befallen them. There is no danger at Harrisville or, at least such was the case this morning.

A special to *The News* from Lansing says that the woods north and west of there are all afire, and the city is filled with smoke. Such a drought has not been known for years.

PORT SANILAC—The fire equals in destruction that of 1871, and is not done yet. It is raging for miles west of here, and as I write a large gang of men have gone to fight it back from buildings of a man whose whole family is sick in bed, himself included. I have heard of many families being missing, and as many as 10 are known to be burned to death.

A party has gone to Richmondville with relief. Seventy-eight farmers were burned out west of Forester this morning. The smoke in not as dense now as it has been. There is no news from the north as the telegraph line is burned down above Forester.

Many persons will perish unless they have medical aid soon.

EAST SAGINAW—The wires are down between here and Vassar, and nothing can be heard from that district.

Trains are running to St. Louis but 20 miles of telegraph line is down and the damage along the road will total $50,000 up-to-date, and no telling where it will stop.

Ten Bodies Found, Bad Axe Burned Up

LEXINGTON—The wind on Monday spread the fires in an easterly direction, burning houses, barns, stock and crops. Many lives have been lost in this county. Caro, Richmondville, Carson burned and reports of the burning of Bad Axe and the destruction of Verona Mills.

Haywood Vale, part of Port Hope, including the mill and dock, and Huron City are all burned.

Ten bodies were brought into Sand Beach, and others are hourly reported, while the dead bodies of men, women and children, horses, cattle, sheep and hogs are found in some sections too numerous, in the general horror, to occasion remarks and probably not less than 100 lives have been lost in all. The weather continues dry, a high wind is prevailing and the fires are still raging terribly.

***The Detroit Post and Tribune*, Sept. 7, 1881, in a dispatch from Lapeer:**

Two miles northeast of Five Lakes, Richard Elliott resided on an 80 acre farm, 10 acres of which were cleared. Here he was trying to lay the foundation of future prosperity; but the wave of destruction rolled that way and leaping 20 rods across a corn field, the blaze gathered in his dwelling, hurrying the inmates, his wife, Christina Elliott, aged 39 years, a little son, and Mrs. John Frederick, a neighbor, out into the road for safety. Mrs. Elliott got together a quantity of clothing and followed Mrs. Frederick and the child in their flight before the fire. Blinded and suffocated with smoke and heat, the women struggled on with the child, her companion urging Mrs. Elliott to drop the bundle that impeded her progress, which she neglected to do and was soon left behind the others, who escaped. About this time Mr. Elliott started for home on horseback from Five Lakes, fearful that the fire might reach his clearing, but after going about a mile was compelled to abandon the horse on account of the burning logs and timber. He soon found he could not follow the direct road even on foot, and so went north, approaching by the rear, and found all his improvements, including house, barn, fences, drops—everything a mass of smoking ruins. Frantic with the disheartening sight he started down the road in the track of destruction and met a neighbor who informed him that his wife and child had gone to Mrs. Brown's for safety. He struggled on and soon fell to his knees, overcome with the smoke and heat, but gathering strength, arose and groped onward until he had got about sixty rods from the smoldering ruins of his home, when he came upon the charred and lifeless remains of his wife. She had been caught by the fire, and died alone amidst the wreck and ruin that surrounded her.

Feared Loss of Life is Frightening

***The Detroit Evening News*, Thursday, Sept. 8, 1881, 2:00 o'clock edition:**

Every telegram, letter and human being coming from the devastated districts in Huron and Sanilac counties shows that the loss of life and property has been fearful, far surpassing that occasioned by the great fires of 1871. Tongue cannot tell the full story of the trouble that has come upon the poor people on whom the wrathful flames have wreaked their fury. It is now very clear that the first dispatches, telling of the terrors of Monday, which were almost hoped to be exaggerations, have in fact fallen short of the state of affairs.

In Detroit, Chicago and New York people were reading of the great fire in southern Michigan. As the printers in the newspaper offices in Detroit worked type cases setting up the latest dispatches from Saginaw, Flint, Bay City, Sand Beach...the people of Bad Axe went unconcernedly. Communication was slow. The telegraph lines were down...but what of it. The fires, somewhere far, far away, had felled a pole or two.

On Thursday, September 8, 1881, Rev. Z. Grenell, Jr., pastor of the First Baptist Church of Detroit, arrived in Detroit from Sand Beach. He came down on the narrow gauge and the Grand Trunk and arrived at noon. On his way to Port Huron by the narrow gauge railroad, it was noticed that in some places the track had proved an effectual barrier to the flames, which did not find fuel in the gravel road bed. In other places it burned the ties and twisted and destroyed the rails, which had to be replaced.

As the Rev. Grenell looked from the car window he saw "a burned desert of ashes and smoldering embers, without a sign of vegetation or animal life...a country abandoned by God and man, and to which it was impossible to imagine anyone returning."

The telegraph poles had all burned and the wires had been reset upon any stick that could be found, and for long distances were merely laid along the ties beside the rails.

Rev. Grenell continues: "The scenes of horror in the woods were too frightful for any pen to portray. The dead were found everywhere, very rarely recognizable, and in most cases indistinguishable human remains.

"Many had thought the end of the world was at hand and were filled with terror. The horrors of the imagination were soon intensified by the approach of the flames, the stories of the universal desolation to the west of them, the dread that they were fated to a frightful death, and then by the arrival of the charred, blackened and shapeless remains of the poor victims. This awful condition continued all along the shore until Wednesday morning."

He (Rev. Grenell) then goes into a minute description which in this day of yellow journalism, would be considered unprintable.

Mail Carrier is Burned to Death

Wm. Humphrey, the mail carrier from Argyle to Elmer, started on his route Monday, September 8, 1881. He was stopped by the flames. He unhitched the horse from the wagon, made a saddle of the mail bags and mounting the beast turned back at a gallop. This is what the people of Argyle thought happened. The horse arrived at Argyle without rider or mail bags. Believing the worst had happened, they tied a mail sack on the horse and turned him back on his route. The poor beast followed the habits of his daily work and dashed over the road into Elmer. Humphrey's burned body was afterwards found in the wilderness in one place, the mail bag, half consumed, in another, and the wagon in another.

A Cry For Help is Issued

On Thursday, Sept. 8, 1881, Mayor Wm. C. Thompson of the city of Detroit issued this proclamation:

To the Citizens of Detroit:

Reliable information has been received that numerous villages in this state have been totally destroyed by fire and their inhabitants rendered homeless and destitute and that a large number of farmers have been driven from their homes by the flames which have destroyed their houses, barns, stock, leaving them without shelter and in want.

The sufferings of these homeless and destitute people, our own fellow citizens, appeal to the humanity of the country and especially to that of Detroit. It is an imperative duty to afford them liberal and instant relief.

From Port Sanilac came the news that Abel Thornton, son and wife were burned to death. That Sarah Sharkey and John Mohan were burned at Richmondville.

Six were Found Dead in a Well

In Marion Township six were found in one well and seven in another. There were many reports of death in the northern part of Forester Township...but the names of the dead had not as yet been ascertained. The village of Bridgehampton was burning...but no details. All the roads leading to the lake were lined with fleeing refugees. An old man named Cole, living northwest of Port Sanilac, was burned to death.

Two men of Port Sanilac returned with news from Richmondville. Stephenson's mills were burned and all the surrounding houses. The people were suffering for want of food.

Dr. E.A. Hoyt of Port Sanilac braved the flames and with medicines and bandages made his way into the country north and west of the village. He reported many burned fatally. He found seven dead bodies at the Ridge schoolhouse.

A correspondent to the Detroit *Free Press* writes from Port Sanilac: "Upwards of three hundred persons perished in the flames. There was no escape for them. In many instances I found men, women and children lying on the ground on their faces, just where they had been overtaken by the fire. I found the bodies of children, burned to a crisp, on top of logs where they had climbed for safety. There was no finding each other when once separated. Many took refuge in wells and root houses, thinking to escape, but in almost every instance they were suffocated. The details of the disaster in Huron County are as bad as here. I believe that when all returns are in one thousand persons will be found to have perished. In Marion Township the family of one Richmond, six in number, were found dead in a well. And another family...name unknown. Rev. W.E. Allington of Port Sanilac found sixteen dead bodies near Deckerville. There are only five buildings left between there and Minden. In Paris Township, the wife of John Flytewager and his seven children were burned alive. Fifteen others burned to death near Parisville. The Day family...and Morris Clifford and his wife and child. A man and woman were found dead on the road between Donner's mill and Tyre. Mr. Paine, of Sibley, was burned to death. Fifteen families were burned in Moore and Argyle. Five hundred families are reported at Minden as having been burned out. A woman burned to death a half mile from Tyre. We need help immediately. Medicine and medical assistance."

NOTE: The Richmond family above referred to were near neighbors of the present publisher of the Tribune. The whole family dove into a new 12 foot deep well with about two feet of water in the bottom. They hoped to escape the suffocating smoke and heat and flames which swept over them from their burning buildings. The top of the well was covered with boards and planks. These caught fire and while burning dropped down on the father, mother and five children. The baby, less than a year old, was drowned in the water. The father's head was partly burned off. All were dead when found the next day. The Richmonds, however, lived in Delaware Township instead of Marion. The family consisted of the father mother and six children. The oldest boy, 12, was away at a neighbor's and was the only member of the family left alive. —Editor, Rudy Petzold, *Tuscola County Advertiser*, Caro.

The Detroit papers of the 8th began printing "eye witness" reports of those who had come down by boat or rail from the burning areas. *The Detroit Post and Tribune*, Thursday, Sept. 8, 1881 contained the following dispatches:

One of the most intelligible accounts of the condition of things was related by Mr. J.W. Barry, of McClure's Express. He said: "At Sand Beach when we left they had worried all day, but did not consider the town in danger for they have a good system of water works. Verona Mills is gone, clear burned up. We got people from there and brought them down. Then at Bad Axe, the next place, the fire has swept everything, but the courthouse. Reports stated Paris, a Polish settlement, was burned out. Everything was swept away, not a house remains standing and a clergyman who came from there said there were in the road the bodies of sheep, hogs, horses and people caught by the falling trunks of trees as they fell, suffocating them by the smoke."

"So far as you could learn, what was the estimated loss of life?" was asked Mr. Barry.

"It is impossible to fix any figure. Mr. Jenks at Sand Beach says 100 lives will not begin to cover the loss. The dead are found all through the peninsula and those who live are separated by miles of burning trunks and heated ashfields."

Special Dispatch to the *Post* and *Tribune*:

SAND BEACH—The fires in this county are still raging. Bad Axe, our county seat, is all burned up except the courthouse, one store and a few small buildings. Verona Mills, 12 miles west, is all burned, except the hotel and church. Huron City and Forest Bay are entirely destroyed. The dock, mill and other buildings are burned at Port Hope. The fire is now about two miles from here and our firemen are doing their best to save the village. There is no immediate danger. There have been 20 bodies found burned in Rubicon, three in this township, and there will undoubtedly be more. Reports from Paris are that the township is all burned. Wires down, send this by steamer.

Some Eyewitness Tales of Disaster

Later: Several men arrived here this evening (Port Huron) from the burned district. Geo. McDonald of Minden, Sanilac County, tells a harrowing tale. Over 200 families are homeless in that section and suffering from want of food and clothing. Mr. Haviland from the same place tells of a large number of lives known to have been lost. John Ballentine of Verona Mills says that 53 lives were known to be lost in the neighborhood of Sand Beach. The fire suddenly reached Verona Mills on Monday and the town was soon wiped out. The wind was so strong that Mr. Ballentine and wife were picked up and blown 15 or 20 yards. A woman and her husband were found lying against a tree dead, the woman being partly delivered of a child. In the vicinity of Richmond and Western Forester and Marion Township, reliable information leads me to say that upwards of 300 persons perished in the flames. There was no escape for them. Persons who have been through the terrible ordeal say that in 10 minutes from the time the fire struck there would be no vestige of a house left.

An unknown informant says: “I have just returned from a trip through the burned district and a description of the sights I saw would make the reader’s blood run cold. In many instances men, women and children were found lying on their faces in the road dead just where they had fallen when overtaken by the fire.”

The Hurricane Rush and Roar of Flame

Through the welter of news dispatches pouring into the metropolitan papers; the rumors, the guesses, the panic, the appeals, I begin to realize the magnitude of the "Fire of 1881." Contradictions, corrections, personal impressions, fragments, hear-say stories...but back of it all the rush and roar of a hurricane of flames.

...I see the sun hidden, and the twilight of hell...and the darkness. I hear the screams of men and children as they flee along the fiery paths of burning forests. I see the burning muck tossed high into the air and carried like meteors on errands of destruction. Beneath an ocean of smoke I see dimly through the haze the burning home, the blazing barn, the straw stacks, the world aflame. Along the roads leading to the lake I see men, women and children, horses, cattle, in a mad rush for safety.

Husbands dragging wives, mothers dragging children...fire behind them, fire on all sides of them, fire in front of them. I see them stop overwhelmed by heat and smoke gather, huddled in the center of the roadway, and a million voices of death whistling about them. I see love and devotion...a timid wife gazing momentarily into the eyes of a husband...the flare of a flame..I hear the fearful cry of a child in the wild bewilderment of disaster...I hear the fitful gasps of one more breath of life...and I see them sink into a shapeless mass...and consumed in a breath of flame.

...I see men, women and children seeking safety in the cooling depths of wells, but the fire pursues them, strangling them, throwing them down in tangled masses of humanity at the bottom. I see them seek shelter in root cellars..and die horribly in the darkness. I hear the curses and the prayers, the screams of pain, the awful sound of children battling with a choking death.

I see men coming into Sand Beach, hatless, shoeless, faces blackened with the smoke...bewildered, confused. The end of the world. Husbands fighting a burning road to reach a home somewhere in the wilderness...to reach a home... perhaps already devoured in the wild orgy of death.

I fall and stumble over the body of a mere boy...dead, face down on the road.

A farmer, name unknown, has been burned to death in Arbela Township, and in the Cass City region nine miles square was burned over. Nine lives are known to be lost and there is great destitution.

...George McDonald, of Minden, Sanilac County, said that smoke and darkness came on about 10 o'clock a.m. and by noon they were obliged to light up for dinner. At 3 p.m. lanterns in the streets were necessary. Minden is on the Port Huron and Northwestern Railroad. He described how they found whole families four miles west of Minden burned to cinders, and others shockingly burned but still alive. Richmondville claimed sixteen bodies in one field. Railroad communications were cut off, but on Wednesday, a construction train passed over the railroad line and provisions had been sent from Port Huron for immediate relief.

...The country looks as though the destroying angel had waved his sword over the land and carried death and destruction on every side.

People Left Helpless, Destitute

SAND BEACH—The condition of the people in Huron County and the destruction caused by the fire have not been exaggerated in the reports sent to the *Post* and the *Tribune* during the past few days. I have just returned from Bad Axe, 18 miles above here, and the scenes I have witnessed today convince me that the story has only been half told.

...The fire was peculiar in many respects. It left nearly every oat field, in some instances burning on all sides of grain in shock, and seldom running over the stubbles. In places it went in streaks and the houses located on hilltops have nearly all escaped in the region I have traveled through.

The amount of stock that perished cannot be estimated. On the road today I counted 12 head of cattle, sheep and three hogs that had been driven out of the woods by the heat and had perished. One mammoth ox sought shelter under a bridge but that caught fire and the beast burned to death beneath it. Parties of men have been out burying the animals for two days past. I met one gang at 4 o'clock this afternoon and was told they had buried over 150 head in Verona Township and were not through yet.

Langdon Hubbard of Huron City lost over 100 head of cattle. The stock that is left has little to live on.

Many families living back from the main roads are suffering for want of provisions. It was reported to me this morning that some of the sufferers were eating the dead cattle, but upon investigation I was only able to find one man who had made use of the carcass of a dead steer. I had filled my traveling bag with crackers and dried beef before leaving Detroit, for myself in case of an emergency. On the road, I overtook a 16-year-old girl, exhausted and scarcely able to walk. I invited her to ride and when questioned about her condition, the tears came to her eyes and she confessed that she was traveling in search of something to eat. When I placed my lunch before her, she devoured it with the eagerness of a half starved lion. "This is the second fire I have gone through," she said, "and may God spare me from another."[37]

Remembering...

As the years passed after the second disastrous forest fire literally wiped out the "Thumb" area, this section became known as the Michigan Heartland. True, the once great pine forests were forever gone, but now, due to an act of God, the land was cleared for farming...so, in essence, all was not virtually lost...but an enormous price was paid both in loss of life and property in the process.

A special section of a recent issue of the newspaper at Harbor Beach showed a painting at their newly dedicated community center building. The clipping read as follows:

The Great Fires 1864 - 1871 - 1881

1864 Fire—The first forest fire to devastate this section to the thumb occurred in October 1864. The mill, first school house, homes and other buildings were completely burned out.

1871 Fire—The second fire occurred in November 1871. Its aftermath left several dead, many homeless and an enormous amount of property damage. Homes, barns and livestock were destroyed and many residents sought shelter in Lake Huron.

1881 Fire—The September 1881 fire was by far the most wide spread and destructive holocaust in the history of the thumb. Entire villages were burned out. Some sought shelter in wells and were saved, others were suffocated by smoke when the direction of the fire changed. The survivors moved in to search for victims lost in the burned rubble. Over 1,520 homes were destroyed, 3,230 families were burned out, the value of the property destroyed was $2,347,000.00

Furthermore, this little gem of information was forwarded by Mrs. R.H. (Ginny) Steele, Secretary of the Newaygo County Society of History and Genealogy, White Cloud, Michigan: "Reports of heavy damage from forest fires in 1881 originated all over the county, especially north and east. And as a bit of sarcasm, the (Newaygo Republican) quotes, 'that the fire department consists of 50 fire buckets.'"

So now may we present a series of related news articles describing the events of this historical period...

Remembering...

After a disaster, those involved often attempt to exclude the horrors from the past as far from their minds as is humanly possible. Perhaps this is part of the total healing process. Perhaps it is the only means for one so involved to retain a vestige of sanity. But regardless for the need of a proper explanation, sooner or later, after the healing time is completed, the person recalls the events once again that were earlier impossible to cope with. My personal reasonings on this phenomenon remain that once a victim's spirit, soul, mind and body have been restored, he or she can then accept the truths of the unfortunate experience. The dead are buried. The homes rebuilt. Business places restored. Remembering is the last step of acceptance.

The stories presented here are those of "remembering." Many were found during research from area newspapers. Some are written interviews with senior citizens who survived the Fires of 1881 and strongly suggest that their memories and sense of recall will be carried with them to their graves. We, too, must remember these disastrous events, tragic as they may seem, so that history will not ever again repeat itself.

Great Fire Of 1881

...Local histories all speak of the great fire starting shortly before noon on Sept. 5, a Monday.

Section 2, Chapter 4
Remembering...

Robert Warner of Cass City was seven years old that day. He remembers the fire. He had gone into Cass City with his father, a justice of the peace, in a horse and wagon to get supplies.

By noon, he recalls, the air was thicker than usual with smoke. By two o'clock a strong southwest wind began to blow. A black cloud had blotted out the sun, and kerosene lamps were lighted in stores and homes. Fearful for his wife and other children on the farm, Judge Warner started home. Near the Cass River bridge the horse balked. As Judge Warner was trying to whip the horse ahead, a man stumbled out of the ditch, a blanket wet with river water about him.

"Go back!" the man yelled. "The bridge is burned out."

Judge Warner left Robert with friends, and then tried it alone on horseback. He made it, found his family safe, but Robert didn't know that until three days later when he returned home.

But at the same moment the fire threatened Cass City, flames broke out near the Huron County Poor Farm, Bad Axe. By two o'clock the wind was blowing fiercely, the sky darkened, and flames rolled over the entire area.

Suddenly everyone was frightened, but there was no place to hide. Some sought shelter in plowed fields, digging holes in the earth in which to bury their faces to escape the suffocating smoke. Meanwhile, the fire burned their clothes and blistered their flesh. Some sought safety in the rivers, submerging their heads to escape the flames, coming up only when necessary to breathe. The river water became so hot that fish, trapped in the shallows, were cooked.

Wild beasts became tamed with fear and herded with domestic animals in the field. The bodies of one family were found in a cornfield. Nearby was the carcass of a bear, which apparently had sought the company of humans in its desperate bid for safety. Another man leaped into Lake Huron and found himself side by side with a big bear, as docile and submissive as a dog.

The heat withered leaves on trees two miles from its path. Fields of corn, potatoes ,onions and other vegetables not touched by the flames were roasted. The unnatural became commonplace.

The heat caused strange growth and pear, apple and other fruit trees burst into blossom.

The speed and power of the fire are incalculable. Sometimes the flames advanced with the roar of a tornado, the fire whirling in a giant cylinder. Other times they rushed forward in great sheets a hundred feet high that would lift into the air, skip whole areas, then swoop down to the ground to consume everything in the new spot.

As the storm came it uprooted trees, blew down buildings, carried roofs through the air, lifted men and women from their feet and threw them back violently to the ground. Through the blackness great balls of flaming punk fell into the villages and fields, and fires would burst forth.

There was no running from the flames. Some tried and died as the inferno overtook them. The people prayed and while they prayed they fought with every tool at their command.

[Authors note: Some of the bodies that were found were in a kneeling posture as if that victim was in prayer. In one such case the charred remains of a mother and her five little children were found in this manner...she in a kneeling position, with the hands of her children in her lap, all burned to a crisp!]

...Those who have studied the Thumb Fire of 1881 say the only other fire that could compare to it was the great Chicago fire of 1871. The Thumb fire didn't result in as much property damage nor affect as many persons as the Chicago fire. But for the area covered and the ferocity of the storm, the Thumb fire ranks as one of the worst disasters by flame this nation has experienced. [38]

The next several articles come from a 1958 issue of the Saginaw *News*, which was a special edition published in remembrance of the Fires of 1871 and 1881:

The Oldest (102) And Youngest (77) Survivors of Great Thumb Fire of '81 Are Mother And Son

Remembering...

CASS CITY—Oldest and youngest survivors of the Thumb's great forest fires of 1881 are the Osburns of Cass City and Kingston. Mrs. Martha Osburn—she'll be 103 March 5—is the oldest; her son, James Osburn, 77, is the youngest.

The flames roared through Huron, Tuscola and Sanilac counties, leaving more than 100 persons dead, thousands homeless and countless acres blackened. The date was September 6, 1881. James, now supervisor of Kingston Township, Tuscola County, was born August 29, 1881.

The Osburns talked over the great fire yesterday at Stevens Nursing Home in Cass City, where Mrs. Osburn has made her home for four years. Her son lives on Mushroom Road, near Kingston, about a mile from the home in which he was born.

Mrs. Osburn recalled that her mother-in-law, Mrs. Margaret Osburn, had come from Ontario to make her home and help with the new baby. That morning of Sept. 6, as she got up and looked out a window the sky was gray with smoke, the sun a dull red ball.

There was no choice whether to run or try to save the home. There was no place to go.

Andrew—Mrs. Osburn's husband—and his mother hauled water from the well and soaked the house. Bed clothes were also soaked. There was no help from neighbors, they had their own problems.

When sparks landed on the Osburn home, Andrew and his mother squelched them with water-soaked clothes. Later when Margaret Osburn returned to her Ontario home, she took with her the dress and apron she was wearing that day.

"She was proud of the holes burned in them," Jim Osburn commented. "Many families gathered at the old White School," he said. "They started a backfire and cleared an area they shared with bobcat, bears, deer and other wild animals.

"Not too much livestock was lost. There wasn't much. The Whites had a team of oxen. We had nothing but the home and small field.

"Many settlers threw bedding into the wells and jumped in. That saved many lives in the Kingston area."

Some of the families had survived a fire in 1871 and knew what to do, Osburn said. A small log barn—then a cabin, which survived the great fire—stands on a farm about a mile from the Osburn home.

Mrs. Osburn, despite her 102 years, has a good memory and the great fire which threatened her home and her first born stands out among the many experiences which were hers as she helped pioneer a new country. [39]

☒☒☒☒☒

Marion Woman Recalls Great Fires In Thumb

An 88-year-old Marion woman is in the thinning ranks of persons who lived in the thumb when devastating forest fires swept across the area in May 1881. She is Mrs. Bertha Chadwick, widow of a pioneer barber in Marion, a community in Osceola County.

Mrs. Chadwick was a child at the time of the Great Fires. She lived in Sanilac County, where her parents, Mr. and Mrs. James Hill, owned a prosperous farm. Her father was a Singer Sewing Machine Co. agent who had made a buggy trip to Bay City the day of the fire. He could smell smoke in Bay City and worried about his family and farm.

And worry he should, for the fire roared over the farm. His wife, Mary, fled with her children to the home of a cousin in a low area out of the path of the flames.

The farm buildings were destroyed. All livestock except one cow was lost. One hundred baby ducklings were burned. Mrs. Chadwick's mother did manage to save a goose-down feather-bed, a wedding gift. Mrs. Chadwick years later converted it to pillows, which she still uses.

The family moved near Croswell to make a new start. The Red Cross—which in Michigan dates to that time—sent the family a huge box of relief goods. Mrs. Chadwick recalls that the box was so big the Hill children used it as a playhouse.[40]

☒☒☒☒☒

Tuscola County Areas Twice Ravaged By Forest Fires

The Tuscola County Townships of Elkland, Novesta, Ellington, Vassar, Millington, Indian Fields, Janiata, Elmwood, Arbela, Almer, Wells, Gilford, Freemont, Tuscola, Koylton, Denmark and Kingston suffered much during the fire of I881. And the most damage occurred in Elkland, Novesta and Ellington townships.

On Monday, Sept. 5, it was a day of general conflagration. The county was swept by a storm of fire. Of this, the U.S. Signal Service reported as follows:

"The course of all the fire which together made the great conflagration, was mainly toward the northeast. How the fires ran racing over the four counties has been told, but the story gives no picture of the terrible fury of the storm of fire, and wind that destroyed the property and lives of the farmers and settlers.

"The heat of the flames was so intense...that birds, escaping from these terrible flames, were carried far out into the lake, and dazed and blinded and finding no resting place, were drowned.

"Several witnesses gave an account of a curious phenomenon, illustrating the intensity of the heat. A peculiar blue white flame would sometimes burst forth from ignited tree stumps, flicker a few seconds, and then the strong wind would suddenly extinguish it. It resembled a lighted candle.

"Sgt. Baily says, 'oxygen and carbon will ignite at temperatures of 400 degrees centigrade and as the old tree stumps were badly charred by the fires of 1871, they were essentially a carbonaceous substance. The air was highly charged with gasses, and the temperature raised 400 degrees or over, the causes of the phenomenon can, I think, be traced to these conditions.' The phenomenon attracted attention in several places. Even the earth in some places took fire.

"The speed with which the flames and wind traveled, and the tremendous powers they exerted, are almost incalculable. The conflagration is described as roaring like a tornado and as giving forth loud, explosive sounds that were terrifying. As the storm advanced, it uprooted great trees, blew down buildings and threw people down with such force as to injure them. "The flames literally raced through the country, licking up villages almost in an instant. An anonymous writer says: 'Dark and gloomy swamps, filled with pools of stagnant water, and the home for years of wild cats, bears and snakes, were struck and shriveled and burned almost in a flash. Over the parched meadows, the flames rushed faster than a horse could gallop.' Horses did gallop before them, but were overtaken and left roasting on the ground."[41]

The theme of this chapter is "remembering." A September 22, 1981 issue of the *Detroit News* follows this thought with a headline that reads:

1881 Fire Still A Vivid Memory

PARISVILLE—Raging fires all but destroyed this crossroads hamlet 100 years ago this month but residents still talk about it as though it were yesterday.

The September 1881 holocaust started in Lapeer County when small fires set by farmers to clear fields were whipped out of control by gale force winds. The fires burned more than a week.

More than a million acres of forests and farmland were charred, hundreds of homes, churches and businesses leveled and at least 125 people perished—22 of them in Parisville, the highest toll for any community.

But the hardy descendants, who began their research of the destruction two years ago, estimate it may be 1982 before they complete restoration work on a museum holding artifacts and paintings of the fires.

"Even after 100 years, the anniversary kind of overtook us," said Stan Rutkowski, whose great-grandparents survived the curtains of fire which swept across Huron, Sanilac, Tuscola and Lapeer counties in Michigan's Thumb area.

The consuming flames triggered the first national response from the then fledgling American Red Cross, established by Clara Barton.

"We hoped to pinpoint all the locations of the deaths," says Rutkowski, who heads the small historical society that has turned one of the buildings that survived the flames into a museum. "But it will be another year before we get everything done."

Photo by Gerry Prich

Lemanski Memorial of 1881 fire, erected by the Lemanski family and others from the Parisville area to honor their dead.

Visitors stopping at the square-logged structure, built in 1871, can view vivid paintings of the fire done by Rutkowski's wife Marilyn along with newspaper accounts of the disaster and such artifacts as a silver dollar melted into a mass of twisted metal.

Or they can visit the graves of victims in the cemetery alongside St. Mary's Church, which has been destroyed four times by fire. It is believed to be the oldest Polish community in the nation, which has personal accounts of the tragedy passed down through generations.

One farmer trying to scamper down a well was asphyxiated when flames swept over it. Another hung perilously for two hours by his fingertips only to discover, after daybreak, that the well's bottom was dry and less than two feet below his feet.

Flames fed on crisp vegetation—no rain had fallen for two months—and cuttings from logging operations when white pines and stands of lush hardwood covered much of the Thumb.

But the fires danced a crazy path wiping out entire families in some homes while sparing other buildings.

Several of those structures survive today, including a hotel that is now a bar and an old home which Rutkowski says, "probably was the best built home in Parisville," even though its porch is sagging.

While the holocaust forever ended the logging era in the Thumb, it opened up the land for farming.

The region today ranks as one of the most fertile crop producing areas in Michigan. [42]

Yet another eyewitness report came from an out-of-state newspaper, the *Times Record* of Valley City, North Dakota. Part of this article is reprinted below:

> Fire disasters which swept the state of Michigan back in the early '80s and the founding of the Red Cross at that time are recalled by Mrs. James McCully, 103 Beeman Block, known to her many friends in Valley City as "Grandma McCully," 83 years old.
>
> Though an invalid, caused by an accident three years ago when she slipped and fell on a downtown walk fracturing her hip, she enjoys her radio and all the news it gives, and keeps up with the times. Her daughter, Mrs. C.A. Fritch, lives with her.
>
> Mr. and Mrs. James McCully came from Deckerville, Mich., in 1905, and while on their farm near Deckerville, in 1881, the second big fire swept Michigan and Mr. and Mrs. McCully took refuge in their potato field and saved their lives by lying down and burying in the sand. Though they kept throwing sand upon themselves, Mrs. McCully was severely burned and for months had lost her voice.
>
> One of her saddest memories is that her neighbor's daughter, Sarah Sharkey, 16 years old, had run from her own home to the McCully's home and during her flight had inhaled so much smoke and was so frightened that it caused her death. She died in Mr. McCully's arms and the irony of it was that the Sharkey home was not burned. Mr. McCully had the

experience of living through the two big fires of 1871 and 1881 without receiving even a burn. He died at his home in Valley City in February 1930, and was 77 years old.

They were given aid in 1881 through Clara Barton...[43]

The rest of the above article proved to be mainly repetition of earlier reports. You may or may not have noticed, however, that the young girl mentioned above, Sarah Sharkey, appeared earlier in this section in two other instances. Her name and death were mentioned in several reports, merely under the guise of statistics. Cold facts. I somehow felt better after discovering the news clipping from North Dakota, because now Sarah is not simply a number—easy to forget. Now she is a person that, in our minds, lived and breathed, had neighbors who were friends. Yes, it was a useless death, especially since her very homestead was spared from the oncoming advance of the flames, but now she's not a nameless, faceless human being. We can sense her extreme panic. We can feel her shortness of breath—even that last final gasp for fresh air as she lay in Mr. McCully's arms. Sad, yes, but she won't be easily forgotten.

Remembrances!

Our next accounting is taken from a 50-year anniversary article in the Huron County *Tribune*:

Flames Swept County Just Fifty Years Ago

Saturday, September 5, 1931, marked the 50th anniversary of the fire which laid Bad Axe in ashes. Monday afternoon, Sept. 5, 1881, but 21 buildings, large and small, remained standing after the dreadful afternoon of flame and smoke.

My mother, Mrs. Chipman, and myself and sister, Gale, were saved with more than a hundred others in the dear old courthouse. My father was in Harbor Beach, then Sand Beach, to try a suit. At 1:30 the case was dismissed because of the darkness. People lighted lanterns with which to light the way along the street. My father and Rev. Vertican, Pastor of the Bad Axe Presbyterian Church, went to the harbor and sat on a stone pier that was under construction for the breakwater and there consoled one another. Miss Mary Morgan, accompanied by her brother, Will, had gone to Sand Beach that morning where she was to teach. The school was dismissed a few moments after calling to order after dinner, because of darkness.

Saved Law Books

Attorney Wm. T. Bope had gone to Paris to attend a suit. Using a small cart I saved my father's law books, which were in an office used also by Lawyer James Skinner, that stood on the Skinner block. After father's books had been safely stored in the vault of the register of deeds (my mother had secured the consent of Mr. Carl Heisterman, the county register of deeds, to put them there). I immediately went to Mr. Bope's office to save his books. Those I placed in the judge of probate's office. For two nights they served as my bed.

How well do I remember all the events of that memorable day. How the men tried to quiet the fears of the women and although having barrels placed on the roofs of the two hotels, and on the platforms in front of their stores and filled with water, the owners would say, "We are just doing this to be on the safe side, I don't think there is any danger."

Hay Spread Flames

At one o'clock a sudden gust of wind quickened the blaze west of town which had been quietly eating its way from the McDowell neighborhood, along through the underbrush and dry grass on the south side of the road. The fire ignited a haystack at Mrs. Elvin's at the extreme west end of town. In a moment the great fire of 1881 was on for Bad Axe. Armsful of blazing hay were carried by the breeze, each moment growing stronger, across the town. One lodged in the belfry of the Baptist church, another was drawn into the haymow of the Cole barn, on our street, Hanselman. In a half dozen places simultaneously, buildings burst into flames.

At 11:30 mother had gone to Mr. Cary's home to see Mr. Heisterman about putting the law library in the vault. The family was seated at the dinner table...Mrs. Cary never cleared the dinner table, the fire was on, the old courthouse standing on the same block, was on fire.

Ran to Courthouse

People grabbed valises, boilers, tubs, anything they could fill with clothing, precious belongings, etc. The cry, "Run to the courthouse" rang out. Terror stricken women and children ran for their lives. The courthouse yard was fenced. Many a woman and man dropped their trunks, feather bed or bundle of clothing inside of the gate, that they might help their children hustle into the courthouse, the haven of safety. The belongings burned, the families were safe.

During that afternoon of terrible experience, men pumped water from the courthouse pump, fortunately on the east side of the building, until they would drop exhausted and men who were carrying water throwing it onto the sanded wooded surfaces of the building to cool it, would pause long enough to carry in the fainting or smoke blinded men.

The many colors of the fire caused by explosions of chemicals in the drug store, gun powder in the hardware, 36 barrels of Robert Philps' kerosene, were terrifying in the extreme: red, green, copper, blue, black and purples would follow one another in the colors flashing across from the courthouse.

Watch House Burn

I remember Mrs. C.E. Thompson watching her house burn while standing in the clerk's office. Mr. Thompson was one of the county officers.

I recall hearing Mrs. Wm. Rapson tell how near her child came to burning. The Rapson brothers owned the "old courthouse." When the children were told to "run to the courthouse," they, of course, thought of their courthouse, and ran into the one across the street. It wasn't easy to find them, as they ran from room to room in their fright.

I remember Mr. Sep Irwin coming in at the front door of the courthouse carrying some small grips. In a loud voice he cried, "Is my wife here?" "No," came an answer. "She went east with Dr. Deady."

Doctor Deady had a gig. He started east sharing the gig with his landlady. Farther down the street, Mrs. Irwin relieved Mrs. Erehenberg of her infant a few months old, and took it with her.

Flames Leaped 100 Feet

Through flames leaping nearly a hundred feet in the air, the Doctor drove towards Verona. Thirty-six of the refugees reached Billy Thompson's place east of town, I think a mile and a half or two miles. There the men dug a trench, put the women and children into it, threw wet strips of rag carpet over all. Mr. Irwin and Nettie (Mrs. Morgan) reached the Thompson farm.

On our street was the Baptist and Methodist Protestant churches: Rev. Bettes, the M.E. pastor's home, George [Author's Note: last name not clear enough to print, due to condition of newspaper clipping] residence and Cole's barn. Mr. Strudwick's and my father's houses were left standing with our chicken coop in that end of town.

I remember several thought it was the end of the world and that when the smoke would clear away the star of Bethlehem would surely appear.

Father walked nearly all the way home from Harbor Beach. He carried a ham and a 25# sack of crackers, expecting many to be hungry, but McLean's, Odell and C (rest can't be read) and the Morgan stores were still standing.

I hope to attend the Pioneer Picnic at Caseville, Day. I wish that the survivors of the 1881 fire in Bad Axe might have a reunion. I know there are not many left. But we are celebrating the 45th anniversary of our new building in Bad Axe, Sept. 1, 1886 today.

With best regards and wishes to old friends, I am yours truly,

Winnie Chipman

Note: There was an editor's note on the above written piece: (On the occasion of her 45th wedding anniversary, Mrs. Winnie Chipman Walker, editor of the Unionville Crescent and former resident of Bad Axe, had her attention called to the terrible fire of '81, the anniversary of which is the same as that of her marriage. When these events were recalled she was reminded of the old days in the town of her birth, Bad Axe. She writes above in an entertaining fashion some of the incidents of the great fire. —Editor)[44]

Stop and consider for just a moment that the casualty list would have been extremely higher had that brick courthouse that housed the town's women and children not been saved. Almost the entire population of the village of Bad Axe were assembled at this one building. If it had not been for the valiant efforts of the men, I'm sure the courthouse would have been destroyed. In etchings that I have seen, this municipal brick building appeared to be three stories tall and men were up on that roof with pails to keep it watered down. One accounting stated that the wind was so extremely strong that men carrying water buckets had to be pushed ahead by others from their backs. Imagine that. This was a holocaust, a flaming tornado, a fiery hurricane all wrapped up in one unique special delivery package—a package of death.

Michigan's "Sore" Thumb
First Disaster Relief For The American Red Cross

Dan Fishel, of Graphic Arts Press in Roscommon, described the Great Michigan Fire of 1881 that swept the Thumb Area as follows: Three days of brush fires burned off the entire thumb of Michigan. Heat could be felt several miles out into Lake Huron. Fire considered worse than Chicago Fire.

In this chapter we will learn of Clara Barton, founder of the American Red Cross and how Michigan became a teaching station for the handling of disasters. It serves as a fitting conclusion to this section on the Thumb Fire of 1881.

Michigan's "Sore" Thumb

First Disaster Relief For The American Red Cross

Courtesy American Red Cross

"Help, or I perish!" A drawing of the famine situation following the September 1881 Michigan forest fires, the first disaster in which the American Red Cross sent relief supplies to the victims. The drawing appeared in *Leslies Illustrated Weekly*, October 1881.

Most of us are well aware of the Red Cross, an organization that we have come to expect as a helping hand at disasters of all types. In this next excerpt, the founder of the Red Cross, Clara Barton, refers to not only the organization's birth, but its first assignment as well—the Michigan forest fires:

The Red Cross In Peace and War

By Clara Barton

...A meeting was held in Washington, DC, May 21, 1881, which resulted in the formation of an association to be known as the American National Association of the Red Cross.

...Dansville, Livingston County, N.Y., being the country residence of Miss Clara Barton, president of the American Association of the Red Cross, its citizens, desirous of paying a compliment to her, and at the same time of doing an honor to themselves, conceived the idea of organizing in their town the first local society of the Red Cross of the United States...Thus we are able to announce that on the eighteenth anniversary of the Treaty of Geneva, in Switzerland, August 22, 1864, was formed the first local society of the Red Cross in the United States of America.

Almost immediately following this occurred the memorable forest fires of Michigan, which raged for days, sweeping everything before them...man, beast, forests, farms...every living thing, until in one report made of it we find this sentence: "So sweeping has been the destruction that there is not food left in its track for a rabbit to eat, and, indeed, no rabbit to eat it, if there were." Here occurred the first opportunity for work that the young society had found, and again I give without further note their report:

"Before a month had passed, before a thought of practical application to business had arisen, we were forcibly and sadly taught again the old lesson that we need but to build the altar, God will Himself provide the sacrifice. If we did not hear the crackling of the flames, our skies grew murky and dark and our atmosphere bitter with the drifting smoke that rolled over the blazing fields of our neighbors of Michigan, whose living thousands fled in terror, whose dying hundreds writhed in the embers, and whose dead blackened in the ashes of their hard-earned homes. Instantly we felt the help and strength of our organization, young and untried as it was. We were grateful that in this first ordeal your sympathetic president was with us. We were deeply grateful for your prompt call to action, given through her, which rallied us to our work. Our relief rooms were instantly secured and our white banner, with its bright scarlet cross, which has never been furled since that hour, was thrown to the breeze, telling to every looker-on what we were there to do, and pointing to every generous heart an outlet for its sympathy. We had not mistaken the spirit of our people; our scarce- opened doorway was filled with men, women and children bearing their gifts of pity and love. Tables and shelves were piled, our working committee of ladies took every article under inspection, their faithful hands made all garments whole and strong; lastly, each article received the stamp of the society and of the Red Cross, and all were carefully and quickly consigned to the firm packing cases awaiting them. Eight large boxes were shipped at first, others followed directly, and so continued until notified by the Relief Committee of Michigan that no more were needed. Meanwhile the hands of our treasurer were not left empty, some hundreds of dollars were deposited with him. A most competent agent, our esteemed townsman and county clerk of Livingston County, Major Mark J. Bunnell, was dispatched with the first invoice of funds and charged with the duty of the reception of the supplies, their proper distribution and of making direct report of the condition and needs of the sufferers.

"The good practical judgment of the society led them to consider the near approach of winter and the unsheltered condition of the victims, bereft of every earthly possession, and warm clothing and bedding were sent in great abundance. Our cases were all marked with the Red Cross and consigned to Senator Omar D. Conger, of Port Huron, who led the call of the Michigan committee and to whom, as well as to his kindhearted and practical wife, we are indebted for many timely suggestions.

"...We hope our report may be satisfactory to you, and that our beautiful little valley town, quietly nestling among the green slopes of the Genessee Valley, after having offered the first fruits of the Red Cross to its own countrymen, may always be as prompt and generous in any call of yours for suffering humanity."

Michigan's "Sore" Thumb
First Disaster Relief For The American Red Cross

> These were the first steps of the American National Association of the Red Cross in relief work and in the organization of auxiliary societies. The completion of this work, which may have seemed premature and preliminary, left the association free to continue its efforts with the Government of the United States on behalf of its accession to the treaty.[45]

In the onset, the Red Cross basically provided clothing and household goods to these 1881 fire victims. Food was distributed through Michigan charities with the exception of some non-perishable bulk items that were furnished by the Red Cross. We earlier learned of this organization sending tables and chairs to families who lost all their belongings. The group also sent building supplies—not for permanent dwellings, but rather temporary shelters, for winter was fast approaching. Ms. Barton recognized that these displaced fire victims needed a sense of stability in their lives—a place to hang their hat, so to speak, a place to sleep, a place to cook a meal. In this manner dignity was somewhat restored.

Actually, it appears that the long-range Red Cross plan was one of self reliance: Provide shelter. Equip that small dwelling with basic furniture. Give its occupants enough seed to sow next year's crops.

This proving ground for the American Red Cross granted both the Congress of the United States and the U.S. citizenry knowledge that the organization could serve the country well in times of disaster as they so ably did in wartime.

When Clara Barton raised her white flag with the red cross emblazoned in its center, here in the Michigan Thumb Area, it was the first appearance of this now familiar symbol. These Red Cross volunteers worked until cold weather set in and during the course of their stay food, clothing, medicine and building supplies were distributed to countless thousands of fire victims. Money also was collected—actually, $80,000 was donated by this infant group known as the

Courtesy American Red Cross

Relief supplies at Cass City.

American Red Cross. This sum was relatively small in comparison to the huge sums collected by other relief groups and individuals in New York City and Detroit. For example, New York contributed $138,052 while Detroit raised some $207,294 for the disaster areas. These were indeed considerable sums of money for the late 1800s.

Michigan's "Sore" Thumb
First Disaster Relief For The American Red Cross

Certainly the American Red Cross put down deep roots in our Michigan Thumb Area. But had this devastating fire not taken place, they may not have proved their national worth for some additional years. So, in essence, Clara Barton's new organization needed the Michigan tragedy just as much as the fire victims needed the help of the Red Cross. This humanitarian organization proved its worth in the raising and disbursing of relief money and the rehabilitation of persons suffering personal losses during times of disaster. And, yes, Michigan was just such a disaster area with 70 townships burned, 1,521 houses destroyed, 220 dead and over 14,000 people in need of assistance.

Many newspaper articles related the Red Cross story during the Thumb Fire of 1881, but a short accounting found in a May 21, 1981 copy of *The Detroit News* sums it up fairly well:

Crucible Of Fire Puts Red Cross To The Test...

Good sometimes does come from evil, though it certainly didn't look that way in the fall of 1881 when forest fires were burning the entire Thumb area of Michigan to the ground.

What good from that sort of evil, you ask?

Well, the fires in the Thumb were a testing ground for a newly formed organization called the American Red Cross, which celebrates its 100th birthday today.

The fires of 1881 originated in the Sanilac Valley in Lapeer County, where new immigrants from Europe were using fire to turn what had been lumber land into farmland. It hadn't rained for two months. Everything east of Lapeer was as dry as tinder on the last day of August. High winds began to fan the smouldering fields and swept flames up the valley into Sanilac County.

By early September, the entire Thumb area was aflame. The toll of dead probably never will be known. But at least 169 names of victims were recorded. By the time the fires died out, a million acres of farm and forest land, 44 townships and numerous villages had been devastated.

Here's how eyewitnesses described the disaster of 1881 in the Thumb:

- The heat was so intense, sailors said it made them 'uncomfortable' in ships seven miles offshore on Lake Huron.
- Winds pushing the fire were so strong they rolled big boulders along the ground 'as though they were pebbles,' uprooted trees, blew down buildings, lifted men and women off their feet and 'threw them back violently on the ground.'
- Four days after the fires were out, peach and apple trees far enough away to survive burst into unnatural bloom.
- Many of the immigrants died because they made the mistake of trying to hide in wells, not realizing smoke would settle there and smother them.

What good could come from such a tragedy?

Clara Barton, who fought her way into the slaughterhouse hospitals of the Civil War to improve conditions for the wounded and dying, had founded the American Red Cross on May 18 of that same year.

The new organization looked for a way to prove itself to the public and the devastation in Michigan's Thumb area provided its first chance.

The infant Red Cross rushed volunteers to the Thumb, collected money, purchased food, clothing and shelter and distributed all these things. It was hailed for saving lives and lessening the suffering of thousands of destitute survivors of Michigan's great fire of 1881.

That was the first rescue effort but far from the last great errand of mercy of the American Red Cross.

Naturally, the Red Cross was there again in 1908 when the next great Michigan forest fire, the so-called 'Metz Fire,' swept the Alpena area, taking 44 lives.[46]

Michigan's "Sore" Thumb
First Disaster Relief For The American Red Cross

Courtesy American Red Cross

A relief party searching for sufferers in the wake of the stream of fire.

In 1961 the Sebewaing *Blade* & Unionville *Crescent* newspapers printed an article which, at the end, reports on the efforts of the Red Cross:

Disastrous 1881 Fire Anniversary Recalled

...The violent wind-driven fire had burned unchecked for three days when a heavy rain began which finally ended it on September 10. The Michigan Conservation Department estimated that it left 282 dead. Thousands of survivors were completely destitute, huddled in the homes of neighbors and strangers with nothing to call their own and a Michigan winter approaching. Into this scene to join the efforts of local relief committees came the American Red Cross on its first mission of mercy for the victims of disaster.

One of those who remembers it well was John Paganetti, a founding officer of the Macomb County Red Cross Chapter who lived in Mt.

Clemens at the time of his death five years ago. He often recalled that when "Clara Barton's Red Cross" appeared on the scene he was personally fitted with a pair of shoes by one of the workers so that he could assist her in providing relief to the disaster sufferers. Charles Quay recalls that a few days after the fire "word came to the little village of Forester that the United States revenue cutter *Fessenden* would call at the Forester dock with a load of relief supplies that had been collected by an organization, 'Clara Barton's Red Cross.'"

The assistance supplied through Red Cross was small in comparison with the help provided through relief committees organized in Port Huron and Detroit, representing only $80,000 of a $700,00 relief effort. What the Red Cross did then, however, was the beginning of the greatest voluntary disaster relief and rehabilitation program in the world. Clara Barton's one-chapter "American Society of the Red Cross" has become the American National Red Cross with over 3600 chapters chartered by the U.S. Congress to perform duties which include that of carrying on "a system of national and international relief." [47]

During my research I came across two interesting Red Cross articles that pertained to their first efforts during the Michigan fires from this era. You may find them interesting or wish to follow up on some of the requested data. The first piece was printed in The Saginaw *News* July 29, 1980:

Red Cross Seeks Relief Effort Details...

The American Red Cross, which will celebrate its 100th anniversary next year, is seeking documentation of its first relief effort—the great fire of 1881 that raged across Michigan's Thumb.

Through its Huron County chapter, the Red Cross is seeking photographs, diaries, medical records, written accounts, artifacts or even handed-down recollections of its relief effort following the three-day blaze. Clara Barton, the group's founder, later wrote that the organization might have died a quiet death if the Michigan fire had not given it an opportunity to prove its worth.

Although numerous news and eyewitness accounts mention the Red Cross assistance, specific details are lacking. It is known the group helped provide at least a portion of the hundreds of thousands of dollars in food, clothing and money that poured in from across the country after an appeal for help was issued by the governor.

"We're looking specifically for the site or sites of the Red Cross relief camps," said Patricia Mroczek of Bad Axe. She said some accounts have the Red Cross using a trainload of lumber to build a relief camp. One unverified story mentions camps in Cass City and Bay Port.

Anyone with information can contact Nora Engler at Towne and Country, Pat Mroczek at the Huron Daily Tribune, or Donna Detmer at Tim's Market, all in Bad Axe.[48]

The next small article appeared in a September 23, 1961 copy of The Saginaw *News*:

Red Cross Using Thumb 1881 Fire Sketch

A sketch made at the scene of the disastrous forest fire in the Thumb area in 1881 is being used as the picture of the week by the American Red Cross to show the organization in action on its first disaster job.

The sketch, made available through the *News* files, was used throughout the country in magazine and newspaper stories. The illustration, along with a description of the fire written by a *News* reporter, were offered to the American Red Cross by Miss Susan M. Blackney, executive secretary of the Saginaw County Chapter.

The sketch used in the poster shows forest fire refugees collecting supplies at a Cass City store. The disaster brought some $800,000 worth of funds and supplies to Michigan from the Red Cross, which had been organized only a few months before the fire.

The fire began on Sept. l, 1881, and raged for 10 days before rains dampened the woodlands. The death toll reached 125 and property loss was $2 million. [49]

It is fitting that this national organization mark and remember the first disaster that it responded to. Throughout these first two fire sections, discrepancies can be found. Perhaps we will never actually know how many people were killed in either the 1871 or 1881 fires. Most likely, historians will never determine which holocaust was the worst. What we do know is that both fires were listed among the worst blazes that ever ravaged this nation. Both left victims behind. But only one of the two was helped by the newly created American Red Cross. This is the important difference between these two great fires that occurred but ten years apart from one another. From that point on, history would never be the same. No matter what the disaster proved to be—fire, flood, earthquake, tornado, volcanic eruption—the Red Cross was on the scene quickly to assist the hurt, the troubled, the homeless, the ultimate victims of disaster.

Section 3

Over The Years: U.P. Forests Blackened

A Chronology Of U.P. Forest Fires

The Upper Peninsula of Michigan is a very special, unique place and hopefully always will be. Forests, lakes, streams, hills and valleys abound. Wildlife is bountiful. A place of quiet and peace where souls are soothed with a fish pole in the hand on a summer's day.

Forest fires have always proved a threat in this well-timbered country; today, yesterday and beyond. Oftentimes, naught but blackened stumps were left after a rampaging fire swiftly struck a district. Here you will learn not only of the fires themselves but also the deaths and damages that resulted.

A Chronology Of U.P. Forest Fires

Photo courtesy Michigan Department of Natural Resources, Greg Lusk Collection

Example of a typical turn-of-the-century Upper Peninsula town.

Almost from the very beginning of time the lush, green, pristine beauty of the Upper Peninsula of Michigan has been put at risk by raging forest fires, turning the rare beauty of this land into blackened, charred stubs and stumps. Fires occurred during prehistoric times, according to the examination of fire-damaged remains of ancient trees found in sub-carboniferous sandstone formations, coal deposits, peat fields and glacial scourings. Fire scars that were still visible on extremely old trees provide additional indications that forest fires repeatedly happened since the establishment of our present forests.

Section 3, Chapter 1
A Chronology of U.P. Forest Fires

Forest fire data as far back as the 1600s, when explorers and the Jesuit missionaries were traveling the Canadian and Michigan territories, shows lightning strikes were the main cause of these fires. Amer-Indians were also responsible for many early fires due to their personal needs—driving game, burning off bogs for better berry crops and as a means of harassing their enemies.

But many, many other factors entered into the total picture as well, as sections of the land became more settled. Land clearing caused blazes to race out of control. Loggers, hunters and fisherman often proved to be careless in the woods. Trains, before spark arrestors and other modern-day equipment, were a chief cause of forest fires along their rights-of-way. It was imperative that their bridges and trestles be protected from runaway fires, so the railroads hired men to walk the tracks to check fires before they raced out of control.

But in these much earlier days, there were many times when fires swept through U.P. countrysides unrestrained, leaving in their wake blackened wastelands with small villages wiped out and people by the score left homeless. There were also many occasions when cities themselves felt fears of forest fires invading to the very edges of their civilization, and had there been but a mere shift of wind direction, little could have been done to save their homes and businesses.

Most of us probably regard the forest fire season as taking place during the hottest part of the summer, basically the months of extreme heat and dry conditions found in July and August. But the month of May actually is the most dangerous, just before green-up occurs when hot weather often follows the snow loss.

Following, you will find a partial listing (from 1847 to 1950) of many of the fires that devastated the Upper Peninsula at the topside of Michigan. In later chapters we will delve more fully into individual forest fires. We will cover in some depth small and large conflagrations that swept this peninsula from DeTour to the far east and Ironwood-Bessemer at its western extremity, then on northward to Isle Royale and southward to Menominee County.

U.P. Forest Fires

1847 Isle Royale

1871 Menominee County—50,000 acres burned.

1877 Fires reported at Michigamme, Marquette County, L'Anse, Republic, Ishpeming, Palmer.

1883-85 Forest fires in the Newberry area.

1891 Fires reported in most of Chippewa County.

1894 Fires near Ishpeming, Iron Mountain, Norway, Salisbury Location, Sagola, Deer Lake and Ewen.

1896 Ontonagon—344 buildings burn. 228,000 acres burned with fires reported at Trout Creek, Bessemer, Rockland, Greenland, Ewen, Sidnaw, Thomaston, Munising Junction and Yalmer Siding. Additional fires burned on Isle Royale in the vicinity of Chippewa Harbor and 64,000 acres burned between Ishpeming and Big Bay.

1906 Forest fires ranged from Newberry to Bessemer—a distance of 250 miles—as well as at Iron Mountain, Quinessec and Marquette County.

Section 3, Chapter 1
A Chronology of U.P. Forest Fires

1908 Fires in the Copper Country and Isle Royale. Calumet and Houghton suffer losses.

1913 Houghton County reports many fires, especially near Chassell.

1914 Many counties report damage from forest fires including:

Baraga County	8,131 acres
Gogebic County	2,598 acres
Houghton County	13,890 acres
Iron County	8,930 acres
Keweenaw County	5,400 acres
Ontonagon County	14,120 acres

1917 Total acres burned in the U.P. was over 75,000, with fires occurring mainly in the western end of the peninsula.

1918 100,021 acres burned in the Upper Peninsula, with a total of 194 fires.

1919 Large fires reported in the Newberry-Trout Lake area with additional acreage burned in the western counties of the U.P.

1920 Another bad fire year, especially in the western counties. Total acreage burned: 140,000.

1922 Only 7,750 acres burned across the U.P.

1923 Silver City in Ontonagon County suffered a 50,000 acre loss. More fires reported in the Copper Country, Republic, Michigamme, Ishpeming, Yalmer Siding and Big Bay.

1925 Fires at Champion, Keweenaw Bay, Baraga, Kenton and Sidnaw areas. Eastern U.P. on fire. Western counties suffer damage too. Central U.P. reports fires in Alger, Iron and Schoolcraft counties. Mackinac County reports over 5,000 acres burned.

1926 Fires in Dickinson, Marquette, Baraga and Houghton counties.

1930 Mid-peninsula on fire from Seney to Menominee County. Two large fires on the rampage in Mackinac County and one in Ontonagon County.

1931 Fires reported in Iron, Ontonagon, Schoolcraft and Keweenaw counties.

1933 50,000 acres burn in U.P. in Delta, Ontonagon and Gogebic counties.

1936 Schoolcraft county has huge blaze in Green School district taking in 10,000 acres. Isle Royale on fire with CCC workers fighting the blaze.

1942 Marquette County has some forest fires reported.

1943 Marquette County reports forest fires.

1947 Fires at Presque Isle and Little Girl's Point - Gogebic county. 248 fires burning in the Keweenaw.

Michigan Forest Fires—1871 - 1949

Calendar Year	Number of forest fires reported	Acres burned	Damage (in dollars)
		Fragmentary Data	
1871		2,000,000	
1880	267	238,270	985,980
1881		1,000,000	2,300,000
1896		228,000	1,250,000
1908		2,369,070	2,570,450
		Official Record (compiled by U.S. Forest Service)	
1911	191	156,480	3,465,860
1912	139	40,170	66,100
1913		(No statistics available)	
1914	935	408,765	97,714
1915	632	157,622	155,113
1916	497	283,300	33,103
1917	479	193,934	102,368
1918	704	238,122	114,183
c1919	862	418,359	406,856

Calendar Year	Number of forest fires reported	Acres burned	Damage (in dollars)
1920	560	76,445	405,991
1921	1,028	283,641	296,390
1922	538	38,483	35,265
1923	1,336	466,474	534,811
1924	1,936	242,956	149,766
1925	3,887	733,750	475,115
1926	1,524	145,060	101,730
1927	2,394	94,720	71,050
1928	1,340	67,150	59,970
1929	2,457	51,920	54,230
1930	4,690	290,300	279,160
1931	4,282	284,940	189,690
1932	2,635	40,840	17,990
1933	4,721	205,370	173,870
1934	3,300	54,680	34,500
1935	1,696	19,280	18,300
1936	3,010	97,790	2,827,220
1937	1,564	19,500	41,870
1938	1,561	20,970	41,960
1939	1,566	48,330	271,030
1940	1,072	18,442	33,008
1941	1,658	11,054	28,970
1942	1,080	17,875	59,318
1943	909	19,795	61,499

Calendar Year	Number of forest fires reported	Acres burned	Damage (in dollars)
1944	1,758	24,672	79,705
1945	1,124	36,816	181,208
1946	2,263	44,328	249,017
1947	1,804	26,900	162,267
1948	2,094	18,071	118,470
1949	1,964	24,974	128,708

Table showing Michigan forest fires and the damage they inflicted. Reproduced from *Forest Fires and Forest Fire Control In Michigan*, by J.A. Mitchell and D. Robson, Michigan Department of Conservation / U.S. Department of Agriculture - Forest Service, 1950.

Forest fires were serious business. Lives were lost, property and holdings destroyed. The lumber and logging industries were especially hard hit. By the early 1900s, companies were posting signs warning of the seriousness of the fire situation. An excellent example follows:

A Chronology of U.P. Forest Fires

500 PEOPLE KILLED!

FIVE MILLION DOLLARS WORTH OF PROPERTY BURNED BY

FOREST FIRES!

Lower Michigan and Ontario will never fully recover from the Fire Losses of July 1911. These FIRES DESTROYED LIVES and PROPERTY; BURNED HOMES and TOWNS; Caused FEAR and PANIC; Threw THOUSANDS of WORKMEN out of WAGES and out of FOOD; Created POVERTY and DISTRESS everywhere. What caused these fires?

Carelessness! MARK THE WORD! **Carelessness!**

CARELESSNESS IS RESPONSIBLE FOR FULLY 90 PER CENT OF ALL FOREST FIRES AND FOREST FIRE LOSSES. When CARELESSNESS becomes general it often results in DEATH. Who, then, is responsible? Would you like to feel that a fire STARTED by YOU or NEGLECTED by YOU had made a clean sweep of lives and property? Would you fire your friend's house knowing that his children were within? We are but children--often--helpless in the path of a raging forest fire.

What Can You Do? BE CAREFUL!
What Else? PUT YOUR CAMP FIRE OUT!
What Else? HOLD THAT MATCH UNTIL IT IS OUT!
What Else? LOOK FORWARD TO WHAT MIGHT HAPPEN!

If the property is NOT yours, PLAY FAIR! BE FAIR!
If the property IS yours, PLAY SAFE! BE SAFE!
THE TIME TO PUT THE FIRE OUT IS WHILE YOU CAN!
THE PREVENTION OF FOREST FIRES IS EVERY MAN'S DUTY.

For help, in case of fire, call upon the wardens of the

Northern Forest Protective Association

MUNISING, .:. MICHIGAN

A 1911 fire warning poster. Reproduced from *Forest Fires and Forest Fire Control In Michigan*, by J.A. Mitchell and D. Robson, Michigan Department of Conservation / U.S. Dept. of Agriculture - Forest Service, 1950.

[Author's Note: early in this publication we covered the disastrous fire that jumped the Menominee River into Michigan after it ravaged nearby Peshtigo, Wisconsin. Though this was a U.P. fire, I did not include it in this section because I felt that it belonged in that specific time slot, where it fully added to the length and breadth and magnitude of that 1871 total holocaust, which in turn destroyed Chicago, wiped Peshtigo, Wisconsin off the map and ravaged Michigan from the shores of Lake Michigan to the dunes of Lake Huron. They were, indeed, the Great Fires of 1871.]

The Ontonagon Fire Of 1896

The Ontonagon fire could have made an excellent movie for you have a plot of greed played out by a powerful lumber interest against a town in need of corporate assistance after fire literally swept away their village. Without destroying the proposed plot, I will merely pique your interest by stating that the good guys triumph in the end with the local sheriff confiscating a trainload of logs that the bad guys had other plans for.

Remember, this was a time without unions or workers' benefits in a very poor land—a place where truly the worker "owed his soul to the company store."

The Ontonagon Fire Of 1896

The summer of 1896 proved to be unusually dry, especially in the entire Upper Peninsula. As early as August 25th, *The Detroit News* reported that "forest fires have gained terrible headway in the vicinity of Trout Creek." On the 29th of August, the towns of Rockland, Greenland and Bessemer were direly threatened. On September 12th, the town of Ontonagon, with its sawmill and immense lumberyard, was devastated—wiped out! For two weeks fires had been burning unchecked in the swamplands near the village. On the 12th, winds freshened into a near gale from the southwest at approximately 40 miles an hour and within a few hours everything in the town was reduced to ashes. The blaze entered via the vast lumberyard and during its rampage left 1,500 residents homeless.

There had been a great deal of anxiety in the area for weeks previous to the final destruction, as several minor fires had continued to burn unchecked. Fortunately, however, just before the town itself was consumed and before the telegraph wires went down, messages had been sent to railroad headquarters for assistance. Special trains were dispatched to the area to bring residents out and food and clothing in.

While only one life was reported lost, there were any number of estimates on the damage done by the Ontonagon fire with figures ranging from a million to three million dollars. The huge Diamond Match Company mill and yard lost some 65 million feet of lumber, adding to the total devastation.

The Ontonagon Fire Of 1896

The above paragraphs offer the sum and substance of the Ontonagon fire, but as with most stories, other factors are often at stake.

By the year 1890, the western sections of the Upper Peninsula were well into the business of logging. At one time, the Ontonagon valley was certainly a sight to behold, resplendent with towering white pines as far as the eye could see. Early accountings from this period indicate that the "pine barons" employed wasteful practices, leaving forest debris behind as the forests were systematically denuded of the great pines. However, we must also bear in mind that the Ontonagon valley was comprised basically of virgin timber—a great deal of it proved to be ancient and dead or dying trees. Many had simply rotted and lay where they fell, offering forest floor fodder to fuel the flames of any forest fire, whether started by an act of the Almighty God or man himself. After the loggers passed through a given area, additional tops and branches were left behind, taking some seven years to decay. But foresters agree that rarely did this woods litter actually decay, for usually these dead branches became tinder dry and within the short span of a few years, these cutover lands provided a breeding ground for forest fires.

To the west of Ontonagon was Matchwood, which acted as the local headquarters for the great Diamond Match Company. In the early 1890s, this company made an intensive search for pine timberland in the western section of the U.P., acquiring some 100,000 acres in Ontonagon County. Much of this timber was in the watershed of the Ontonagon River.

But fire hastened the decline of pine as the "blue ribbon" crop of the northern forests. As early as 1871 fire swept to the borders of what we now know as the Ottawa National Forest. Additionally, terrible fires again devastated the region in 1891, 1894 and 1896 (the latter date being the year of the Ontonagon fire). In summation, Ontonagon's populace proved to be the first Michigan citizens to "see the future." Through over-cutting and disastrous forest fires, King Pine was at its turning point, swiftly entering into its decline. And somewhere down the road its final death scene was imminent.

The fires of 1893 and 1894 were devastating, destroying thousands of acres of standing timber. In order to salvage the fire-damaged logs, John H. Comstock, who was the Ontonagon manager for the Diamond Match Company, received applications from 250 jobbers, and let twenty contracts to cut 130,000,000 feet over and above the wood from their own camps. During 1894 and 1895 a total of 48 camps were operating that winter on Diamond Match Company lands. By the end of March 1895, 160,000,000 feet had been cut with 22 camps still cutting. The greater share of these logs were to be transported down the main branch of the Ontonagon River to Lake Superior.

A high water level was needed to float this enormous amount of cut timber downstream but the snow melt and spring rains simply failed to materialize. Jam-ups were common. The spring of 1886 proved to be one of the largest river drives ever on the Ontonagon, even though that particular winter the Diamond Match Company had done no logging whatsoever. The rains came and a two-year supply of logs jammed the river. From Lake Superior as far up the river as the eye could see was nothing but thousands upon thousands of logs—an estimate of 50,000,000 feet of logs was recorded.

Just before the disastrous fire of 1896, the Diamond Match Company's huge mills at Ontonagon were operating at full capacity. The river held logs aplenty, giving not only the matchstick mills steady work, but also keeping busy the shingle and box plant located on the river island.

Barges and ships regularly entered the harbor to load sawed lumber and other supplies. Wood was everywhere—many reported lumber stacks were piled as high as three-story buildings. Ontonagon was a house of sticks, and soon the fire-wolf would be blowing their house down.

The town was a bustling one. The Bigelow House was the grandest of the local hostels. Ontonagon sported a newspaper called the Ontonagon *Herald* and today this publication is still in operation with a 100-year plus operating record. The editor on that fateful day in September of 1896 knew as soon as the fire really took hold that his building soon would follow suit. So before closing up shop, he had the forethought to telegraph immediately an order for new presses.

The fateful day of the fire began with the dawning of a bright red sun reminding one and all of the old sailor's saw—"Red at night, sailor's delight; red in the morning, sailor's take warning." The swamps to the west of town had actually been burning for weeks, even months until most had been rendered into dry, mud-caked bogs. A pall of gray smoke had hung over Ontonagon for days, but on Tuesday afternoon of the 25th day of September a wind freshened from the southwest and a snake of fire encroached closer to the mill.

For days, mill crews had gone out putting out small blazes, but this one seemed stronger. Just after one o'clock the mill's fire whistle blew and all millhands turned out to fight fire. The women and children were urged to reach points of safety and with the winds fast increasing to gusts of up to 75 miles per hour, a dozen buildings were quickly consumed.

Next was the West Side mill and adjoining lumber yard. Attacked by ravenous tongues of flame, fire leaped high into the sky and jumped the river where it fed its monstrous belly on piles of waste sawdust. The mill itself became a roaring fiery furnace—an inferno spewing masses of fire and cinders toward the main part of the town. The hurricane-force winds actually picked up blazing boards, hurling them off in all directions to ignite additional blazes.

And...the fire spread. Within two hours little was left but ashes and ruin.

As in all fires from an earlier era reported throughout this book, much of the destruction was blamed on the town's bad element, from brothels to saloons. Newspapers later reported that when it proved imminent that the entire town would be surrendered to the fast approaching fire-god, without pretense of a battle the menfolk stormed the bars and broke out kegs of whiskey instead of seeing to the safety of their loved ones. Perhaps these accountings were the *National Enquirers* of that period. Later, reports of further carousing during the hard- scrabble times directly following the fire were also written up in the papers of that day. It was said that wine and spirit kegs were dug from the rubble and much drinking took place. Hearsay, perhaps; rumor, perchance.

Section 3, Chapter 2

The Ontonagon Fire Of 1896

After the firestorm crossed the Ontonagon River the large four-story frame Bigelow House was the first structure to catch fire. Townsfolk at the lower end of the city fled for their very lives toward Rockland and Greenland. Others sought refuge in the river and Lake Superior, but the rage of winds whipped Old Mother Superior into a frenzy, making escape by water extremely hazardous.

By three or four o'clock in the afternoon the winds took a dramatic shift into the northwest, resulting in such a devastation that man and animal alike had no further choice but to literally run for their lives to escape the flaming firebrands and walls of flames that ignited everything in their path. Everyone fled in abject terror—men, women, children, horses, cows, pigs!

By the end of the day 345 buildings were forever gone. A bank, four fine churches, the courthouse, the jail, two hotels besides the Bigelow House, 12 shops and stores, 13 saloons, two excellent newspapers, three schools, the Diamond Match Company's two mills and their company store, Gorgan's Opera House, two fine iron bridges spanning the Ontonagon River, a barge—the *City of Straits*—that was tied up in the harbor and most of the town's private dwellings were gone, all gone!

While several deaths were reported, only one was actually substantiated, that being of an elderly German lady, a Mrs. Pirk, who had lived with her daughter in the lakeshore section of the city. Her daughter, Mrs. Geist, vainly tried to rescue her mother and was severely burned in the attempt. Several days later, the charred remains were found in the ruins of their house and were interred in Ontonagon's Evergreen Cemetery.

Many, many domestic animals panicked and perished in the holocaust, with reports of burned bodies of horses, cows, pigs, dogs and cats, as well as hens, ducks and roosters strewn all about the fire district.

The demon fire-god had done its work well, for the disaster scene took in well over a square mile of ruination. Only about 12 buildings remained standing and usable, offering some form of shelter to the townspeople remaining in the city proper. The town's power house that held the electric plant and water works was spared, as was one of the hotels, The Superior House. Moving from the lakeshore area over to the other end of town, 12 more homes remained standing.

Ontonagon's hey-day was finished.

Photo courtesy Michigan DNR, Greg Lusk Collection

A forest fire at its peak—awesome, devastating, frightening.

Almost immediately, appeals for aid were sent out to surrounding cities. Fire relief committees were formed. The Chicago, Milwaukee and St. Paul Railroad granted five-day free passes to anyone who wished to leave the area. Additionally, all freight sent into the distressed village was also shipped free. Railroads during times of dire disasters were the relief lifelines of the doomed community. The role they played cannot be forgotten. Big business had a soft heart!

The military sent in 150 tents and a tent village was immediately erected at the fairgrounds, which the forced inhabitants dubbed as "White City." A detachment of 30 state militia arrived from Calumet and Houghton to maintain order. The first nearby town to answer Ontonagon's calls of distress was Baraga, which sent supplies in by boat on a wind-tossed Lake Superior.

A relief station was established on the road to Rockland where people could receive household goods, food and building material—all donated and brought in by rails and waterways. Money and valuables removed prior to the fire from the bank were placed under guard at the horse barn on the premises of the County Poor Farm. Many of the town and county records were burned up in the path of the firestorm, for the courthouse was gutted. School records also were lost. The state Legislature appropriated a sum of public money, and insurance companies paid out large sums to those fortunate enough to have adequate coverage.

But basically the general population—the average low-wage earner—had little or nothing to look forward to other than a bleak, bitter winter fast approaching with little shelter, food or clothing.

The era of pine logging was over. Diamond Match Company refused to rebuild its mill facilities at Ontonagon, for most of the standing timber had been ravished either by forest fires or logging. It was time to cut your losses and run and be damned by the workers who had toiled so hard over the decade in their ultimate behalf. The heads of the company—the decision makers—did not reside locally or even within the boundaries of the state. They might as well have lived in a foreign country, for they sat in their board rooms discussing the fate of a village located in a remote section of the Upper Peninsula as though it had no heart or soul. Money, not morals, set their standards.

There were still millions of feet of logs lying in the Ontonagon River, and officials wanted them to offset their mill fire losses. The local populace already felt the mills would not be rebuilt but they were simply not prepared to sit calmly back and watch the corporation's hired hands pull log after log from the river jams and place them on flat cars forming a train of considerable length. The town's governing body sent telegrams off to their headquarters at Green Bay in hopes of stopping the log train. Their urgent message read: "But see, our town is burned, we must rebuild it. You are leaving our families here stranded, destitute, with no work for our men. We have schools to build. We have our streets and roads to be kept passable. We cannot move away; most of us have no place else to go. You have cut off and removed our only taxable resource, the only thing that represents wealth in all this country."

The company replied, "What do you expect us to do about it? Of course the grass will now grow in your streets!"

James K. Jamison described what happened next in his book, *This Ontonagon Country:* "A long train of cars loaded with pine logs backed down to the end of steel to get a running start that would carry the load over the grade out of the river flats. Steam shrieked through the safety valve of the panting locomotive. There were two long blasts of the whistle. The engineer nursed his throttle. Here was the first train load of logs out of the Ontonagon country. The locomotive took hold of the load, gathering steady momentum. They were pounding up out of the river bottom when a huge man swung agilely aboard the engine. He laid his hand on the engineer's shoulder. 'Back her down to the station, brother,' Sheriff O'Rourke ordered. And back down came the train. The sheriff exhibited a tax warrant on the logs. But it was a gesture too belated." [50]

The Great Ontonagon Fire that swept through that community during the afternoon of September 25th, 1896, left over 2,000 people homeless in a matter of a scant two to four hours time. Shacks were erected. Many people left town to seek help and home with relatives.

The town gradually regrew—slowly—and it never reached its former glory. The Diamond Match Company pulled out forever, resettling its mills at Green Bay, Wisconsin. The village of Ontonagon was forced to start over from scratch.

But what lesson is to be learned from all this? One, perhaps, of corporate greed? Upon examining the record of this out of state industry, we readily find indications that this company had placed its own key men in top political offices—such positions as Township Supervisor and President of the town. Once the corporation moved to Green Bay and resettled its vast operation there, petitions were filed in court to oppose local taxes assessed against its remaining Ontonagon properties—both land and timber holdings and logs still residing in the jammed-up river.

The Diamond Match Company offered a classic example of corporation greed both before and after the huge conflagration that destroyed everything of value in this small port village. Notoriously, they showed their true colors of domination over a community—a near monopoly of the unskilled labor market, owners of a huge company store offering little or no sales competition, placing its own officers in key political positions and finally blatantly voicing its loud opposition to just taxation. What it all boils down to is right is right and wrong is wrong. And they, serving as "big business interests" were definitely wrong! The boom or bust days of the western end of the Upper Peninsula were gone. King Pine was dethroned!

Newspaper Clips & Eyewitness Accounts
Ontonagon Fire Of 1896

The power of the press. It is always evident when disasters are reported. People respond. Disaster relief is forthcoming. Without the graphic descriptions displayed in an earlier press, we modern-day folk might never have come to realize the dangers and hardships that existed along these Michigan frontiers. True, life was simpler, but it was also dangerous.

In this chapter we allow the ghosts of the past to relate their individual accountings of the Ontonagon Fire of 1896.

Newspaper Clips & Eyewitness Accounts
Ontonagon Fire Of 1896

All throughout this publication I have chosen to present news clippings from state and outstate newspapers to graphically describe these scenes of disaster shortly after they actually took place. Downstate newspapers either sent reporters north on the train or often had staff writers stationed at the larger U.P. towns and they would telegraph their stories back to Detroit. In that manner, people down below were kept abreast of what was occurring in the far flung areas of the U.P., where just as it still is today, many people from the lower peninsula had relatives in the North Country. By the year 1896, with better forms of communications and travel, Michigan was shrinking and news from near and far, both good and bad, traveled comparatively swiftly. Readers of several Midwest newspapers learned quickly of the fires. Examples of these bulletins and dispatches begin with an August 27, 1896, article in *The Detroit Evening News*:

DESOLATE

SCENES IN STRICKEN ONTONAGON VILLAGE
ONLY A FEW FISH HOUSES MARK THE SITE
WILD SCENE IN THE SALOONS DURING FIRE
DRUNKEN MEN LAY SENSELESS IN THE STREET
FATAL DELAY IN FIGHTING THE FLAMES
CURIOUS INCIDENTS OF THE GREAT CONFLAGRATION

ROCKLAND, MICH., Aug.27—A scene of ruin presents itself to the visitor at what was once the thriving village of Ontonagon. The only buildings left are a few fish houses on the lakeshore, a few residences on the outskirts and the power house.

Only ashes and twisted iron make up the site of the big Diamond Match Co.'s saw mills, dry kiln, store and box factory; the four beautiful churches, the courthouse, jail, town hall, land offices, schoolhouses, the Bigelow House, Centennial, Paul and Cottage Row hotels, the Miswald brewery, Masonic Hall, the fire department buildings and depot, and even many rafts of logs along the river were charred and ruined.

The only thing of real value left in the entire town was Manager J.H. Comstock's collection of coins valued at many thousand dollars—one of the best in the world.

The only life known to be lost was that of a man who entered one of the mills just before the boilers blew up.

The scenes in the village when the fire first began to rage were indescribable. Barrels of liquor were rolled out of the saloons and freely drunk. Many men were lying around drunk, leaving their wives and children to shift for themselves or be cared for by others.

Animals Went Mad

One fine trotting horse broke loose and ran into a network of hot wires, singeing the hair from its legs. Then it started down the street at a furious pace, without a break in its trot, until it ran into another net of hot wires and turned a somersault into a cellar full of coals.

In the Bigelow House yard, pigs were roasted alive, and some can be seen today, standing erect but burned to a crisp.

W.C. Cameron, who had charge of the Diamond Match Co.'s mills, while Manager J.H. Comstock was out of town, is being criticised. The fire had been spreading in the swamp on the west side for several days. When the wind sprang up, it is said, many prominent citizens went to Cameron and warned him of the danger and begged that he shut the mills down and send the crews to fight the fire. He scouted their fears, and the mills were not shut down until the west side mill caught fire.

A timely effort by the mill's crews, it is thought, would have prevented the catastrophe.

The poor farm, under J. Crooker, four miles out on the Greenland road, has been turned into a hospital. James Mercer and R.D. Francis, neighboring well-to-do farmers, are caring for others in need.

Several women were hemmed in on the streets with blazing buildings all around them. They were all saved, and are receiving the best care possible.

The railroad people are doing all in their power for the people. Supt. Minturn of the railroad, and Supt. Fry of the telegraph company, are on the ground, and trains and wire services are free to fire sufferers.

Thrifty Merchant

While the fire was the hottest, one merchant who had been doing a big business and had a large stock heavily insured in town, stopped a team loaded with women and children and tried to hire the driver to turn them out and haul three boxes of goods which he had just rescued to Rockland, saying: "They will burn sure if I don't get them out, and I have no insurance on them." The driver gave him a cut of the whip for sympathy.

Provisions and supplies are arriving in every train, and the people will soon be provided for.

It is thought the town will not be rebuilt, although the Diamond Match Co. may put up a small mill, as it has several millions of logs in the river and much timber standing, but the company may sell its holdings. In that case but very few buildings will be erected.

The power house and water tower are intact, and men are cutting off all broken services as fast as they can be reached. The water will be turned on as soon as fuel for the engines can be secured, and the ruins drowned out. This will take some time, and until then only rough estimates of the total loss can be formed.

Graphic Story

The story of the fire, as told by, one eye-witness, is as follows: "Smoldering forest fires had burned in the swamp south of the Diamond Match Co.'s big mills for two weeks. At noon the wind freshened. At 1 o'clock the first mill caught fire, despite a fire department creditable to the town, and of the special firemen and apparatus of the Diamond Match Co. The west side mill speedily became a seething mass of flames. The automatic sprinklers deluged the whole interior with water, but the gale from the southwest drove the flames into the lumber along the river, where 60,000,000 feet of pine lumber was stacked in piles as high as a three-story building.

"The fire leaped across the river from the lumber and attacked the second mill, the planing mill of the Match Co., and the towering lumber piles stacked along the eastern banks. From there on it was a race for life. Quickly the flames spread. The firemen were compelled to abandon their apparatus and flee for their lives.

"Blazing shingles and fire brands were carried hundreds of feet high by the irresistible current of hot air to fall a quarter or a-half mile further on to fire the buildings that they lit upon. The flames from the lumber blazed two hundred or more feet high and the dense smoke and brands of fire made the scene a piteous and frightful one.

"During the fire the sky was brilliantly lighted for miles around, but as night began to settle over the burned district the situation became a startling one. With the hope that the flames had attracted attention in some of the adjacent towns, the men and women wandered aimlessly over the black heaps which once had been their homes while their little ones, frightened almost to death clung to them, crying for food."[51]

☒☒☒☒☒

Ontonagon No More
City Completely Destroyed

Special to the *Chicago Record*

GREEN BAY, WIS., Aug.26—At 9 o'clock this evening the following dispatch was received by trainmaster Elderidge from Supt. Minturn of the Chicago, Milwaukee & St. Paul; who is at the burned town of Ontonagon, Mich: "All mill and lumber docks except the government dock are destroyed. There is nothing of any kind left standing on the west side of our main track and everything on the east side of the track is burned except a fringe of small residences around the outskirts of the town on the hill. The waterworks, electric light plant, jail, county buildings and every business house is burned. We have taken about 350 people to Rockland and beyond, last night and today. A cold west wind is blowing. The tracks are burned out and kinked from a point 1,500 feet south of our coal sheds northward. All our buildings are destroyed except the water tank, and that too will go if the wind changes. No one is known to have perished, although a few are yet unaccounted for. The total loss outside of the railroad property will amount to over $2,000,000. The Diamond Match Co., loses about 25,000,000 feet of lumber, well insured. Ten to fifteen millions of feet belonging to other parties is also destroyed."

Help Sent To Fire Sufferers

In response to the appeal of J.H. Haight, president of the burned village, a special train loaded with provisions was sent from the city at 8 o'clock this morning and the supplies were added to along the route.

MILWAUKEE, WIS., Aug. 26—A special...from Houghton, Mich. gives particulars of the fire which destroyed Ontonagon. The fire originated in a swamp just south of the Diamond Match Company's mills. A forty-mile gale swept the flames before it and the flaming mills, box factory and immense dry els of the match company were soon reduced to ashes. The flames then descended on the business and residence quarter of the city and finally lodged in the sawed lumber on the dock. The destruction of the village was complete, barely a dozen houses in the suburbs remaining standing. The onslaught of the flames was so sudden that barely one in twenty succeeded in saving any of their effects.

There are about 1,800 men, women and children without food or shelter. Many are insufficiently clothed, and they suffered severely last night.

The Diamond Match company lost two fine sawmills having a daily capacity of 450,000 feet and other mills and buildings, worth in all $2,000,000 and lumber worth nearly $1,000,000. Insurance to the extent of $75,000 was carried. The loss on the balance of the village will foot up about $2,000,000, with about $300,000 insurance.

The Heaviest Losers

Besides the Diamond Match company, other large losers are:

Sargent, Gennings & Gilkey of Oconto, lumber loss	$100,000
Louis Heideuger of Marquette, lumber on dock	25,000
James Norton of Ewing, lumber on dock	1,000
Wm. McFarlan of Bruce's Crossing, lumber on dock	10,000
Lowe house, four-story hotel	10,000
Centennial Hotel	5,000
Paul house	5,000
John Hawley's big store, total loss	20,000
Bank of Ontonagon	5,000
Chicago, Milwaukee & St. Paul depot, post office, courthouse jail and schoolhouse	50,000
James Mercer's large warehouse, dock and coal sheds	50,000

Also the government breakwater and waterworks and 500 residences.[52]

Hoodlum Element Rules
Authorities At Ontonagon Decide To Call On Governor Rich For Troops

Lives Of Peaceable Citizens In Jeopardy
Fires Break Out Again Near The Village But Are Finally Fought Back
Town Of Rockland Threatened With Destruction

The Situation Is Serious

ONTONAGON, MICH., Aug 28—A fierce wind has sprung up and the surrounding country is again in flames. Over two hundred men have been sent out to fight the fire and save the remaining houses about the village from destruction.

The Fire Is Driven Back

MILWAUKEE, Aug. 28—Dispatches received from Ontonagon tonight say the fires which broke out this afternoon were fanned by high winds and threatened to destroy the temporary buildings and tents, as well as the few structures that escaped the conflagration of Tuesday, but that several hundred men finally fought them back.

The situation outside of the destitution and suffering is described as serious. In digging in the ruins of burned saloons large quantities of liquor were found and scores of men became intoxicated. Today this element ruled affairs with a high hand, putting the lives and property of other citizens in jeopardy. The hoodlum element interfered with the distribution of relief and the relief committee has determined to call on the governor for troops to do guard duty.

Fires Threaten Rockland

At midnight a telegram was received saying that Rockland, a village south of Ontonagon, from which the relief work at the burned town has been directed, was threatened with destruction by forest fires. A large force of men is fighting it. The remains of Mrs. J. Pirk were removed from the ruins last evening. It is not believed more than three or four perished in the fire.

The bank at Ontonagon opened for business this morning. The records were found in perfect order, and the bank's loss by interruption of business was more than by the fire.[53]

The Hoodlum Element Rules piece featured above came to us from the Milwaukee *Journal*. It must be noted that the western parts of Michigan's Upper Peninsula are actually more akin to the states of Wisconsin and Illinois than lower Michigan, and many of the residents of this area are more loyal to the Milwaukee *Journal* and the Chicago *Tribune* than the Detroit *Free Press* or *Detroit News.*

The next report comes from the Detroit *Tribune*, dated August 27, 1896:

INSTANT AID!

Needed By Ontonagon Fire Sufferers

2,000 ARE HOMELESS

Gov. Rich Issues a Relief Proclamation.

U.P. TOWNS ARE HELPING

Work of the Flames Was Not Exaggerated
Loss Is Now Estimated At Almost $2,000,000

MARQUETTE, MICH., Special Telegram, Aug.26—The accounts of the annihilation of the village of Ontonagon by fire, published in the *Tribune* this morning were not exaggerated. On the contrary, the loss of property and destitution is even greater. The damage to property is estimated at about $2,000,000. It is difficult even at the present time to get accurate information from the stricken city, as the ruins are still blazing and means of communication are cut off. There is only one wire in the county leading direct from there, and it is loaded with train orders, making it almost impossible to send out press dispatches.

Those who were forced out of the town number nearly the entire population, and they have been left absolutely homeless and penniless. The number of such is estimated at 2,000. It is stated that only 15 buildings, mostly residences, have been left standing, All the rest were swept away. The fires in the lumber yards and sawdust piles are still burning, making it too hot to allow anyone near. Even the saw logs in the river were partly burned, so fierce were the flames.

Few families saved anything from their homes. The course of the flames was so rapid, that the people were content to escape with their lives. The water in the river became heated to an unbearable point and the storm upon Lake Superior precluded taking refuge there. The people fled in all directions and families were divided, while a few are still missing. It is not certain that they have perished and it is hoped when the scattered people are again gathered together all may be found.[54]

⊠⊠⊠⊠⊠

The next clipping is taken from the Houghton *Gazette* but no date is provided:

ONTONAGON FIRE

2,000 People Homeless and Starving

Many Lives Supposed to Have Been Lost

Section 3, Chapter 3
Newspaper Clips & Eyewitness Accounts
Ontonagon Fire Of 1896

Mr. Christ Cain, one of the Ontonagon fire sufferers, who came into town this morning on the tug *Colton,* told the *Gazette* the following relating to the fire, which burned that town Tuesday afternoon of this week. He said that a fire had been started in a huckleberry swamp about half a mile from the town. No attention was paid to this fire, until about one o'clock in the afternoon when a gale of wind started which carried the flames into the Diamond Match Company's houses, lumber piles and mills and swept everything before it. The fire then crossed the river catching other lumber piles and then sweeping the village until now only about six houses remain standing.

He said that the suffering there is something beyond description. People were taken to Rockland as fast as possible but that town being small the necessities were soon gone. Members of families scattered from each other, and many are now supposed to have perished in the flames and died from exhaustion. Communication is cut off from one side of the river to the other as the bridges are burned and there is no means of getting supplies from the west to the east side. Mr. Hawley had his tug *Tramp* all of Wednesday and that night hauling in nets of fish and no sooner would the fish be brought to shore that they would be taken by the people and devoured about half-cooked. The tug *Colton* left Baraga yesterday afternoon with provisions and arrived there last evening which relieved the wants of the people temporarily. There was a terrible sea running on Lake Superior and fifteen barges and vessels were lying in shelter at the canal, but Capt. Brassau ventured out with his boat, with waves dashing over her, and having 2½ feet of water on her decks all the way up. She returned here again this morning with several families on board, leaving some of them at Hancock and Houghton and taking the remainder to Baraga.

The following telegram was received by Village President H.M. Hoar Tuesday A.M.:

"Ontonagon, Michigan, burned entirely out. Fifteen hundred to 2,000 people homeless. We need provisions, clothing and shelter for them. Help us out all you can."

J.H. Haight,
President of the Village[55]

As the years passed, the horrendous fire that swept Ontonagon that late day in September of 1896 was not quickly forgotten. From time to time, eyewitness accountings were recounted in the pages of the Ontonagon *Herald*. We now present two such pieces, as they offer an actual addressing of that day their city burned down, rather than second-hand tales received from the skeptics and gossips of that time. The first small article appeared in the Sept. 21, 1956 edition of the *Herald:*

Disastrous Ontonagon Fire Of '96

Recalled By Pioneer Woman

On a balmy 25th of August, 1896, the little town of Ontonagon was virtually swept off the Upper Peninsula by fire. The huge Diamond Match Co. mills burned and many of the high piles of timber, potential match sticks, were leveled as the flames spread during a high wind.

One of the persons who still lives in the Ontonagon country was living not far from where the fire started. She is Mrs. Richard Henry, a stalwart pioneer of the Ontonagon - Lake Superior area.

Mrs. Henry was 29 years old at the time. She recalls the blaze as having originated on the property now occupied by the pulp mill. Then, 60 years ago, it was the site of the Diamond Match Co. mill.

Men had worked all morning at the mill. The day was warm and accompanied by a strong westerly wind. At one o'clock in the afternoon, a mill blaze started. Soon the building was a roaring inferno with sparks wafted about like light feathers under the impact of buoyant zephyrs.

Town Was Ablaze

Soon the sparks ignited many flimsy business houses, homes, boat houses and allied structures across the river. In less than two hours the town was afire.

Mrs. Henry, the former Miss Katherine Schramm, recalls a number of deaths in the flames. She remembers the awful happening as one of horror, something like a Hades on earth.

Mrs. Henry describes a fascinating golden mass following the blazes. Adhering to a much melted 20-dollar gold piece were five fused silver dollars. A jeweler in the area later looked it over and indicated it as being one of the finest mementos of the fire he had seen.

Mrs. Henry became a resident of the Ontonagon country through the location of her parents there. Mrs. Henry easily recalls the site of the house of James Kirk Paul, founder of Ontonagon. It was next door to the home occupied by one of the Ontonagon country's widely known school teachers, Miss Ann MacAdam.

Mrs. Henry says she will never forget the first night after the fire. A Mrs. Paul Francis, on the Greenland road, helped her by providing her family with a dozen eggs and a feather pillow. This gesture of kindness has left an indelible mark on her memory, "especially when most folks had so little," she reflects.

The group spent the second night on her father's farm. They continued to use his facilities for a few weeks until her husband Henry could provide his brood with something more substantial. [56]

The second eyewitness account also appeared in the Ontonagon *Herald,* on August 26, 1964. Of all the stories published regarding the Ontonagon fire, I fully believe this one is by far the most interesting, exciting and fascinating:

Woodbury Tells Of Ontonagon Fire

Sixty-eight years ago next Tuesday the Village of Ontonagon was leveled by a disastrous fire that destroyed everything in its path and left hundreds of persons homeless.

E.O. (Del) Woodbury, 85, a distinguished Ontonagon pioneer, has entertained many audiences over the years with his recollections of the events of August 25, 1896, and during the Upper Peninsula History Conference here July 24 he held officials and members of the Historical Society of Michigan spellbound with his eyewitness account of the Fire.

Because only a limited number of persons have had an opportunity to hear Mr. Woodbury's description of that eventful day in Ontonagon's history, the *Herald* feels that his remarks, condensed slightly here, should be published in order that future generations will have a permanent record of one eyewitness' experiences.

August 25, 1896

"When we went to work the morning of the fire it was about 70-75 degrees, I would say, and we had been bothered by smoke for, oh, a number of days. The sun was just a red ball up there and since we had no covered roads then—just dirt roads—why, when a ripple of wind came which was strong enough, everything was dust and dirt.

"The mill had started up at 7 o'clock. I was loading logs with the big chain up in the mill. Everything went along fine that morning. I went up to the mill to talk to the men there after dinner, and as the mill started up again we all went back to where we belonged. Little did we think then, that when the sun went down that night the mills would be shut down, never to run again, and everyone would be burned out and have nothing left but what they wore on their backs.

"As the fire swept closer to town after the alarm at 1:15 p.m., they were already urging people to cross the river. I said I'd better get home, since my father wasn't there, and when I got there I told my mother that this looked like an awful bad fire and if the wind should change or anything, why, we'd have no chance at all.

"So I started digging a hole, and my mother put a lot of things in it and my three sisters kept bringing a lot of things out of the house and we buried quite a lot.

"There's one little thing that happened that day, sort of a dramatic affair that happened in the jail that I'd like to tell you about.

Section 3, Chapter 3
Newspaper Clips & Eyewitness Accounts
Ontonagon Fire Of 1896

"The Sheriff of Ontonagon County (Cy Corbett) was out of town that day, and there were two prisoners in the jail, Redpath and Beveridge, both in on a murder charge. The jail was right in the line of the smoke when the fire started, and it would get the first wave of the fire. When it had burned close to them, those fellows became pretty alarmed. Mrs. Corbett was there and she couldn't find the key, so they pounded on the door and they even went to the bars on the window and tried to loosen them. One of them said, 'My God, are you going to let us burn in here like animals in a cage?'

"Then, out of the clear sky a little white haired lady with blue eyes and a white face appeared. She said to Mrs. Corbett, 'Ain't you gonna open that door, ain't you gonna let my husband out?' It was Mrs. Beveridge.

"The two women looked for the key and found it, and the two men went out, along with Mrs. Corbett and her two children and her aged mother, and Mrs. Beveridge.

"The fire was right there, almost at the jail, by that time. They went east, by the courthouse and the Episcopal Church down the hill where there's a swamp. When the road got to the swamp it ended, but there was a little trail there. Mrs. Corbett missed the trail, and now the fire was behind her and the swamp was on fire ahead of her. Cinders and smoke were all around her and with her two children and her aged mother, she was getting bewildered.

"Then out of a clear sky a firm hand grabbed her by the arm and said, 'Mrs. Corbett, don't worry any more, we'll see you out safely.'

"It was Beveridge, one of the prisoners. Her mother was taken care of by Redpath, and they took the family out to safety, beyond the fire lines. The next day those fellows said that 'it was their duty' when they saw the first beginnings of the fire out there to wait and see if those women were safe or not. That's just one of the little incidents that took place that day.

"I was home, digging away and when I'd look down towards the fire it was just a solid black cloud, and all at once that would bust open and, whew—just like a sheet of flame up there. You'd reach up here and lift your hat and paint your hair down again, so you could put your hat back on.

"When those things happened it was a problem for me to know whether to take the family and leave then, or wait until the wind changed, if it did. Well, about 3:30 the wind changed. We got just one little breath of cool air ahead of that. Then there was no stopping. We went.

"Another little incident took place that day. A Mrs. McDermott was living farther below in the town, and her home would be enveloped in the change of wind—the fire had driven her from her house. About 20 minutes before the fire alarm that day, the infant baby died, and, of course, when she had to leave her home she took her baby in her arms.

"On the way up the hill by the Methodist Church a neighbor came along who knew her predicament and he said, 'Mrs. McDermott, we'll put the baby in the church.' The Catholic Church was right there, so they put the baby up on the altar. When they came out the flames were eating at the church. The baby was cremated in that church.

"My family and I had to go to the east side of the ball park to get over on the Greenland road and when we got there, I don't know if anybody could explain the scene. It was full of people, and the smoke and wind were terrible. There were some little baby cabs and these little red wagons that the boys had and some push carts and there was a horse or two with a wagon, and the likes of that. But there was one thing about it. I don't recall that anybody said one word. And I don't think anybody was crying. It was just something that you didn't know what was going on.

"We just kept on going—where we were going at the time we didn't know, because the smoke was so dense right there. But we went up the road and when we got by Eddie Barsheau's—that's the home of Miss Catharine Breitenbach now—we were out of range of the fire but the smoke still hung over everything.

"It just seems though, folks, that there was something in front of that fire to feed it and nothing could stop it. Some buildings a hundred feet from the line of fire didn't burn. Down where Mrs. Mitchell lives, down there where Wolfe's live, those were all buildings that all burned, but just across the alley it didn't burn.

"We kept going, and before we got to the Mercer farm—that's the Willman home now—word came that the train was going to take people to Rockland. We had never thought of Rockland, although my mother's parents lived there.

"Well, I grew about four inches when I heard that, because I knew then that if we ever got there the family would be safe at least. So we went up to Spellman's Crossing, where there were two coaches waiting and a lot of people. They filled the coaches, and we were feeling happier than we did earlier, and later in the day, sort of congratulating ourselves at getting out of the fire, when a kind of shudder went through all of us. What would have been our fate if this had happened at night?

"The train went to Rockland with two coaches loaded with people. The Rockland people had their arms, doors, gates and everything else open to us, welcoming and taking care of the victims of the Ontonagon Fire. We went to Burns'—that was my mother's home—and I asked grandma to wake me up when grandpa got up to go to work at the National Mine at 6 in the morning. I was going to go down to Ontonagon.

"So I came that day with the Miswalds. They had bought the old Catholic Church and turned it into a brewery, and spent $12,000 on remodeling and machinery. They just got going when they were burned out, and were covered with about $6,000 insurance.

A Wisp Of Smoke

"I got out of that wagon that morning and walked up by where the Methodist Church is now and I looked around. I had to wink and blink my eyes before I could believe that what I saw was true. Where the day before stood a hustling, bustling little village, a beautiful big store, two sawmills, forty million feet of pine lumber, and more, what do you think I saw now? Just a little wisp of smoke—and the rest was naught but ashes.

"That afternoon, about 3 o'clock, the St. Paul Railroad brought up three sleeping cars and the telegraph man wasn't long getting hooked up to the wire so Ontonagon was again connected with the outside world.

"That evening Joseph Haight, the village president, called a mass meeting up at the Haing store—that's where Davison's Market is now—asking everybody who possibly could to go to relatives or friends to ease up the situation that they had, until the officials could 'get the smoke out of their eyes,' as he termed it, and see how they could take care of everybody.

"There was one bright spot there. No matter where you went, all you had to do was have a ticket that said 'Fire Sufferer' signed by the village president, and the St. Paul would take you to Sidnaw or Omaha or wherever—anywhere on the St.Paul—and that worked for five days. And the same arrangement was in effect for freight coming into Ontonagon. No matter whether the car was loaded at Chicago, Green Bay, Milwaukee, Marinette, Menominee, Escanaba, Iron Mountain, it all came into Ontonagon free for those five days. Nobody in the world knows how much that meant, except those that saw it.

"First we had a 'Gimmie House,' where you went down and they gave you stuff. They had to have a house, of course, to cover up all the things that came in. Then the soldiers, about 30 militia, came in, and put about 150 tents up. The idea of the 150 tents was to centralize the population so they would be easier to take care of. They were there for quite a while. They also put up a tent for eating. I believe that the first food that was cooked there was pea soup. That soup was only for a day or so, because right away there was ham and eggs and bacon and everything. The morning I came in with the Miswalds they had their wagon loaded with stuff that Rockland had sent down—all kinds of food.

"As time went on things began to ease off a little. Everybody that had a lot was getting a little lumber once in a while and I know I was down to the Gimmie House one day and one of the fellows in the office said, 'Del, go and get your dad and come on and unload some of this lumber. Take enough home to build your tarpaper shack.' I did. Glad to get it.

"I don't know how long the soldiers were here, probably 3 weeks. When they left they just took their tents. They didn't take any equipment with them, but left everything for the fire sufferers. But all through those trying times I don't believe that there was anybody that really went hungry. Maybe some fellows had to sleep out in a field for a night or two, but not many. I don't know how many hundreds of sleeping car blankets the St. Paul brought in.

"At the meeting that night, Mr. Haight appointed several committees, each to take care of its own little area. They'd let a farmer's team go down if they loaded with blankets and stopped at every house to see if that house had blankets. If you and your wife only had one blanket, you'd get two blankets. The St. Paul was wonderful. They did everything they possibly could to help us.

"The insurance adjustors had their rooms up in the old Corvillion home on the old Rockland Road. If you had insurance and needed adjustment, you went and got one of those fellows and they fixed you up.

"Doc Jordan's office was in tent six and Doc Nitterayer had a room or part of a room in Tom Stapleton's house in south Ontonagon.

"The Gimmie House, as time went on, commenced to wane as people got fixed up with furniture and stoves, lumber, clothing, and a lots of grain, like Gold Medal. A whole carload of flour came in. The fellows who had committees would take a load of flour and stop at every house.

"I was down there one day when just this one car came. We opened it up and here's all these little boxes, which probably retailed for about three or four dollars. They were a wonderful thing. They could heat the house that you were building or they could also do the cooking for you.

"We had these tarpaper shacks up you know, and we could move our family into them. It was our place to sleep, and you knew that's where you could get something to eat. Those three words—'Home Sweet Home'—meant a lot. We put it up over the door.

"That night our first meal was supper. And when we sat down to eat we bowed our heads in a moment of silent prayer for the outside world being so generous.

"And all of these things helped us to put our shoulder to the wheel, to rebuild our stricken village."

At the conclusion of his remarks, the 85-year-old pioneer received a standing ovation from the 120 members and guests of the Historical Society.[57]

I found it just a bit ironic that, indirectly, the Diamond Match Company—the manufacturer of matches, the cause of many an accidental or arson fire—proved to be so unsympathetic to the needs of these fire victims who had spent almost a half a lifetime working in their best interests. Yes, corporate greed at its worst.

On the other hand, the Chicago, Milwaukee & St. Paul Railroad showed ultimate compassion for the people of the fire-ravaged town, providing unending support and supplies. In a later chapter in this section on U.P. Fires, we will more carefully examine the role played by trains, their crews and the men that owned them.

U.P. Fires

Region #1 - 1891 To 1949
Region #2 And #3 - 1863 To 1943
Region #4 - 1877 To 1947

This chapter presents recorded data from the four fire zones or sections found across Michigan's Upper Peninsula, each of which has had more than its fair share of historic forest conflagrations. Here you will find fascinating stories, from women boarding a rescue train while their clothes were catching fire to an accounting of a team of horses wading knee-deep through ashes after a flash forest fire passed through their area.

You will also learn of a deadly rescue of two lighthouse keepers, including problems due to rough Lake Superior seas.

U.P. Fires: Region #1—1891 to 1949

The Upper Peninsula of Michigan is divided into four Department of Natural Resources fire districts. Region #1 takes in the counties of Keweenaw, Houghton, Baraga, Ontonagon and Gogebic at the far western extremity of the U.P.

To better understand this frontier land, we must realize that by the year 1890 the lumbering of pine was this area's chief industry. The great valley of the Ontonagon river proved to be one of the most bountiful sources of white pine in the entire midwest. But history also records that the pine barons used extremely wasteful logging practices. Fire, followed by insect infestation, further hastened the decline of pine. As early as 1871, the now famous Peshtigo Fire actually swept fringe areas of the present-day Ottawa National Forest, threatening this region. However, the worst fires of the great pine era occurred in 1881, 1893, 1894 and 1896.

During these times, the Bergland and Ontonagon districts were hit extremely hard. Nestor and the Diamond Match Company both suffered huge timber losses. The 1894 forest fire swept across the entire western U.P. just two days after the Hinkley, Minnesota blaze. Here in Ontonagon country, settlers had their bags packed ready to flee the flames if required to do so. The *Diamond Drill* (Crystal Falls) reported in a September 8, 1894 issue that smoke and intense heat were so bad that the Chicago and North Western Railway suspended operations, as ties were catching on fire and rails had warped. Furthermore, a September 8, 1894 issue of the Ontonagon *Herald* stated that an engineer for the

Chicago, Milwaukee and St. Paul line tried to run the gauntlet through the blazing forest, and paid for this daring with his life, as the train of log cars dashed into a cloud of smoke and fire in which the engine overturned and the man was killed.

Near the junction of Gogebic and Ontonagon counties were the mines. Frontier towns sprung up like mushrooms after a warm spring rain:

Bruce Crossing—Founded in 1888 by D.M. Bruce of Ontonagon was originally called Military Road. The Duluth Southshore and Atlantic Railroad changed its name in 1889.

Calderwood—This village was named by a group of Minnesota lumbering men whose operation was known as the Calderwood Lumber Company. It was located 9 miles from Trout Creek, settled in 1900, and had a population of 100 people by 1915. It died when the mills pulled out in 1930.

Ewen—This 1888 community grew by leaps and bounds and contained several sawmills, hotels and boarding houses, brothels and saloons. It was named after a railroad surveyor, Ewing. During a short span of five years, Ewen rivaled Ontonagon both in population and growth rate. By this time, the town also boasted of churches and an organized fire department and a water system.

O'Brien—This small town that grew from the humble beginnings of a lumber camp was founded in 1893 and located in McMillan Township, 24 miles from Ontonagon. Population was listed at 50. The town was made up of a post office, general store, lumber mill and a scattering of houses. In the early 1900s O'Brien was listed as Nestor.

St. Collins—Located a mere stone's throw from O'Brien and two miles to the east of Ewen, this small village served the needs of the Nestor Logging Company and was also known as a "whistle stop" on the Duluth Southshore and Atlantic Railroad.

Matchwood—To the west of Ontonagon was Matchwood, which was the center of activity for the mammoth Diamond Match Company operation in the south end of Ontonagon County. Logs were shipped by rail from this point for processing elsewhere. Established in 1888, it sprouted a population of 100 residents by 1893. Business establishments included a hotel, grocery, sawmill, depot, general store and a saloon. Fires in 1891, 1893 and 1906 destroyed much of the town.

Trout Creek—Started as a mill town in 1891, Trout Creek grew to include a bank, telephone company and an electric plant.

All of these small communities were at one time or another directly in the path of forest fires that devastated the area.

A Ewen newspaper known as *The Cloverland Press* featured a column called "The Matchwood Minutes," which in 1891 said, "Fires raged in the area around Matchwood with no rain having fallen for most of the summer. The entire town was burned up. A special train was sent from Ewen to save the people. While they were running to get onto the train, the flames were raging on both sides of the track and some of the women's skirts were in flames. No lives were lost."[58]

In 1893 the entire eastern section of Matchwood Township was lost to fires. These were mainly cut-over pine barrens that were tinder dry. Once again, the town of Matchwood was destroyed. In due course, the Diamond Match Company built a new warehouse and residence for their superintendent and gradually the town was rebuilt, containing two stores, a school, hotel, saloons and a sawmill.

Matches, that today play a villain's role in many a forest fire, also were—through the Diamond Match Company—at the center of blazes during the turn of the century which destroyed so many communities from Ontonagon to Ewen.

An accounting from the *Ewen Centennial Book - 1889 to 1989* offers another example of this grave situation that took place in this fire country around Matchwood:

> The air around Ewen had been full of smoke during the late summer of 1893. This was an annual occurrence and no one paid particular attention. Settlers burned slashings for hay meadows and it was rumored that some fires were deliberately set to provide work.
>
> Rain hadn't fallen for weeks and the pine slashings were explosively high. Then it happened. A hot southwesterly wind began to blow. Smoldering fires became alive and the smoke thickened. Several small fires quickly expanded and soon ten miles west of Ewen a wall of fire began sweeping eastward. Burning embers were carried hundreds of yards by the wind, setting new fires.
>
> In green pine timber the fire crowned and advanced at express train speed. There was nothing that could be done by man except to get out of the way. According to old residents, people in Ewen were loaded on flatcars and taken to Bruce Crossing, five miles to the east. When the fire burned itself out the damage was appalling. The town of Matchwood was completely in ashes. Lumber camps and miles of corduroy roads were burned. Thousands of acres of what was once beautiful white pine were burned or left standing naked. (The losses by lumbermen were enormous.) Rudolph Stint told this writer that he could see all the way to Ewen from Matchwood, a distance of five miles, and not a tree was standing. Ashes in places were two feet thick. He could drive across country with the ashes reaching the horse's knees and in places wagon-axle deep. The town of Ewen, what was left of it, was untouched. Only weeks before, a fire starting in a hotel had wiped out most of the town.[59]

The fires of 1893 and 1894 were devastating. Thousands of acres of standing timber were destroyed. The following report came from the pages of the L'Anse *Sentinel*:

> The past week has been prolific of forest fires throughout the northwest, especially in the developed portions of the western Upper Peninsula. O'Brien, the headquarters of the Nester Estate logging operations in Ontonagon County, is wiped out, including camps, stores and logging outfits.
>
> A 500 foot long bridge on the DSS&A railroad near Bruce Crossing is destroyed. In consequence, one train on this road had to be abandoned for several days last week, the other train transferring baggage and passengers at the burned bridge. All along the Duluth division of the DSS&A, the fires are doing more damage to timber and property. An experiment farm conducted by the Ayer Estate six miles south of Kenton was in imminent danger on Monday. The general agent, Mr. Manning, telegraphed for men, and a small crew started out Tuesday. We have not heard yet if any damage has been done or not.[60]

Another small town plagued with fires during the late 1800s was Ewen. The peak of Michigan's lumber era arrived in 1890 with 2,124 sawmills in operation across the state. The cut was 4,245,177,000 feet of lumber valued at $83,000,000. Michigan led the entire country in lumber production. Ewen made her worthwhile contribution toward the above figures. Estimated timber in the 1880s from Ontonagon County alone stood at some four billion feet, and here Ewen occupied a front row, center stage seat because of her location.

Section 3, Chapter 4
U.P. Fires
Region #1 - 1891 To 1949

In discussing Ewen's fires, we could call this section "Save The Mills And Let The Town Burn." For in essence, that is more or less what took place. Once again the descriptive accounting is credited to the *Ewen Centennial Book*:

> On July 20, 1893 Ewen was reduced to ashes. At 1:30 p.m. a blaze was discovered at the rear of the Snyder House. The flames soon spread to adjoining buildings and despite all efforts to stay the march of the fire, by 6:00 p.m. every business house was a heap of ashes. The only buildings north of the railroad tracks left standing were Hargrave's general store, the depot, water works building, a church, railway tank and a few new buildings at the outskirts of the town. Following is a list of places destroyed and losses sustained:

Louis Danto, general store	$12,000	Insured
Lepsett & Harrison, general store	8,000	
G. H. Smith, dry goods	7,000	Insured
J. H. Scott, hardware	4,000	Insured
E. B. Hulick, liquors	4,000	Insured
J. Laisure, liquors	3,500	
Snyder House	7,000	
Conover House	8,000	
Raymond House	2,000	Insured
Mrs. J. McConner, millinery	3,000	
American House	7,000	Insured
James McConry, liquors	3,000	
Clark, Farnam & Co., general store	8,000	
Ewen Weekly Recorder	1,000	
Marquette House	3,000	
James Horton, grocer	4,000	Insured
F. B. Osborne, drugs	4,500	
Ewen Exchange Bank	3,000	
W. Triplett, jeweler	5,000	Insured
A. Wood, barber	500	

H. G. Hubbell, bakery	1,000	
J. P. Rossman, market	4,000	Insured
Finch Building	2,000	
Union Hotel	2,000	Insured
Jack Garvin, groceries	2,000	Insured
Stephen Johnson, liquors	1,000	
J. Sleedy, market	1,000	
R. Urban, law library	700	
Dr. George McElveen	1,000	

In addition to the above listed losses, other losses reported include: Stewart Bros. $5,000; Esh and Connolly $5,000; H. Kind $1,000; John Garvin $2,500; Steve Johnson saloon $4,000; J. Sladler $4,000; W.D. Hatfield $4,000; Railroad House $5,000; F.J. Hargrave, moving $2,500.

L. J. Chamberlain of Bessemer was in town at the time of the fire and wired to Bessemer, Ironwood, Ashland and Ontonagon for aid. The railroad company responded promptly and immediate relief was afforded.

At 6 o'clock all efforts of the citizens was directed toward saving the sawmills. After two hours of hard fire fighting they managed to beat the flames and now the mills and lumber piles stand almost all alone in a great stretch of blackened ground, heaps of ashes and charred timbers.

Ewen has a system of water works but it is reported that the hose was in such an inaccessible place it could not be got out in time to be of much use.

Several persons were injured. One woman is reported missing. Hundreds of people are homeless and a great deal of suffering and hardship will probably follow in the destruction of their homes and property. Ewen is a town of 1,200 population. It was settled in 1889 as a lumbering place and the buildings built entirely of wood making them easy prey for the flames.[61]

In 1893 the town of Ewen had a loosely organized volunteer fire company. The previous fall they had ordered a fire bell along with other equipment, so that at the time of the fire they possessed 12 pairs of rubber boots and 12 coats. To help finance the equipment, they sponsored a dance held on Easter Monday evening. The DSS&A railroad donated a block of ground on which some time later an engine and hose house was constructed. It was located where the present town pump has been resurrected and is on the railroad right-of-way. Later, more equipment arrived consisting of 1,000 feet of hose and other accessories.

During the year 1896, fires were again considered dangerous in the western confines of the Upper Peninsula. The towns of Ontonagon and L'Anse were ravaged by fires, but both towns quickly bounced back. For example, the day after a fire in L'Anse, saloon keepers were doing business over packing crates in the town's ruined streets, according to the May l6th edition of the *Diamond Drill*.

During 1908, fires were reported on Isle Royale. *The Detroit News* related the following:

Isle Royale Cottages Burn; Boats Keep Off

CALUMET, MICH., Sept.12—The rain that had been expected did not come, but light showers fell early today and checked the forest fires somewhat.

The fire situation today in the eastern part of the peninsula is improved and the fires are reported dying out, but in southern Houghton, Baraga and Ontonagon counties the flames are gaining headway again. At Pelkie, which is in this latter district, a school house was destroyed early today, and other schools in the outlying districts are threatened, especially in the Otter River district.

Today's reports from Isle Royale in Lake Superior are discouraging. The summer cottages were destroyed and much standing timber has gone down. The fires are rapidly approaching Rock Harbor and Washington

> Harbor, summer resorts, and it is feared the big hotels and resort buildings at these places are doomed.
>
> The residents of the island, being isolated by water, have no means of fighting the fire, and it is feared that unless there is a soaking rain within 24 hours, the whole island will be devastated, and more than $1,000,000 damage will be done.
>
> A great cloud of smoke is rising from the island, so dense that lake vessels are unable to approach with safety. The inhabitants appear to be in jeopardy.[62]

Listed immediately below this article on Isle Royale was another issued from Lansing, advising state game and forestry wardens in the northern part of the state to abandon game and fish matters for the present and assist in fighting forest fires.

Warden Pierce instructed them to meet with supervisors and arrange for back plowing as well as to organize bucket brigades. Pierce advised that conditions in the northern counties were alarming, for streams were running dry and the whole of the land was parched for lack of rain.

During the year 1925 Gogebic County suffered severe fire losses when two fires destroyed 15,800 acres and 12,070 acres. Ontonagon County lost an additional 6,500 acres.

In 1930 Ontonagon County's fire losses covered some 3,550 acres, and again in 1931 over 11,000 acres were consumed by fires. During the same year, Keweenaw County reported 5,230 acres were destroyed and Baraga County lost considerable acreage as well.

During 1933 the Bergland fire swept Gogebic County, resulting in a loss of over 15,000 acres, while another fire swept the Pomeroy Lake area, resulting in yet another 14,000 acres being burned.

Once again fire struck Isle Royale during 1936, and at that time some 36,000 acres met their fiery fate. The CCC boys were sent in to assist in checking this enormous blaze.

During 1947 a total of 14 fires were reported in Region #1, including fires embracing Keweenaw, Houghton, Baraga, Ontonagon and Gogebic counties, including the Presque Isle River fire that destroyed over 2,000 acres; the Little Girl's Point blaze, taking some 1,700 acres; and the Lac LaBelle fire in Keweenaw County, resulting in a loss of over 3,000 acres.

These fires were summarized by the Marquette *Mining Journal*:

61 Fires, Still Burning In U.P.; Rain Hoped For

Fire Jumps River

Dorias J. Curry of Marquette, regional supervisor for the state department of conservation, appealed to hunters and residents to use extreme caution in the woods because of the high hazards. Curry related today how sparks from the 2,400-acre blaze north of Lac LaBelle, near Copper Harbor, in the Keweenaw, went across a river. The fire, worst in the Peninsula at present, broke in one sector and went across the Delaware River, which is a fair-sized stream.

New Fire Near Houghton

Fire fighters at Houghton reported that one blaze which burned over a 4,000-acre area at the tip of the Keweenaw peninsula has been brought under control, but said another fire was raging in the Winona district, just south of the city. A crew was organized last night to battle the newest conflagration. The Keweenaw fire, which destroyed acres of hemlock and the last big stand of pine in the region, was finally checked by a 20-mile bulldozer line.

A change of wind, which sent the flames back over the blackened area, also helped the 150 fire fighters.

The destroyed timber was owned by the Calumet and Hecla Consolidated Copper Co., Copper Range Co., and Ray Aldridge of Lake Linden, a timber operator.

Of the 61 fires reported in the Upper Peninsula today, one of the largest was burning in Gogebic County near Little Girl's Point. It covered 1,200 acres.

Twenty-nine fires were burning in the Lower Peninsula.[63]

Two years later, the Marquette Mining Journal chronicled the destruction of forest fires in the entire U.P.:

364 Forest Fires Burned 4,690 Acres In Peninsula: Estimated Damage $41,630

Three hundred and sixty-four forest fires this year burned 4,690 acres of land in the Upper Peninsula, the regional office of the state conservation department in Marquette reports.

The estimated damage caused by the fires was $41,630.67, and the cost of suppression was $41,616.38. The average number of acres a fire was 12.88. Although the forest fires' toll this year was about 66 acres less than in 1948, it is far below the seven-year peak destruction of 16,732 for 1947.

In 1943, there were 10,855 acres destroyed by 290 fires. The toll dropped to 6,057 acres, from 516 blazes, in 1944. In 1945 there were 2,291 acres burned and in 1946 there were 3,562 acres destroyed.

Smokers Caused Most Blazes

Again this year, smokers caused the most fires, l45. That included 32 blazes in District 3, which is comprised of Marquette and Delta counties and the west half of Alger County.

The second-largest cause of forest fires was brush burning, 78. Other causes: lightning, 10 fires; railroads, 22; campfires, 19; incendiary, 20; lumbering, 8; unknown causes, 13 and miscellaneous, 49.

The number of fires, acres burned and total damage by districts, follows:

District 1—58 fires, 1,512 acres burned and damage of $26,862.40. (District includes Gogebic, Ontonagon, Baraga, Houghton and Keweenaw counties)

District 2—123 fires, 1,525 acres burned and damage of $5,9770.70. (Iron, Dickinson and Menominee counties.)

District 3—96 fires, 572 acres burned and damage of $5,028.29.

District 4—87 fires, 1,081 acres burned and damage of $3,761.67.

The period of March 25 to June 15 was the period of high hazard in the 1949 season. Of the 4,600 acres burned, 4,042 acres were lost in that length of time. Thereafter, frequent well-spaced rains held hazard to a moderate to low level.

Three Big Fires

Three fires, which were out of control from four to 14 hours, accounted for the increased loss per fire in 1949. On April 21, a blaze which started from an incinerator on the Kingsford village limits, burned 570 acres on the west side of the Pine Mountain ski slide road.

On June 11, a fire near Rice Lake, in Houghton County, burned 990 acres in slash and second-growth timber. A skidding tractor or smoker were probably causes.

The following day, a blaze which blackened 360 acres of forest cover burned north of McMillan in Luce County. That blaze was started by a careless disposed of cigaret.

More Equipment Added

The program of building up the fire-fighting equipment in the Upper Peninsula inaugurated after the war progressed favorably during 1949.

Nine one-ton pickups were equipped with tanks and pumps for booster pumping along fire lines and for hose-line pumping from lakes and streams. Four four-wheel drive trucks were purchased and equipped with tanks and high-pressure pumps in department shops.

Assignment of these, and two received in 1948, were made to Norway, Wakefield, Newberry, Crystal Falls and Gwinn stations. These 15 units were equipped with FM two-way radio sets.

One heavy angledozer was added to the 16 previously in service, and sent to Crystal Falls. Two heavy equipment carriers were put into service at Gwinn and Newberry. Three new plow-drawing tractors are ready to replace three turned in this fall.

Six new heavy-duty fire plows were fabricated in Roscommon and Marquette shops in 1949, and 10 additional ones will be built in 1950. A new pickup trailer tanker is being readied for 1950 in the Soo station.

The value of fire protection equipment in the Peninsula is approximately a half million dollars, according to Dorias J. Curry, regional chief.

Curry also expressed his thanks to the persons "all along the line" who are taking time to be more careful with fires in the woods.[64]

This article, in addition to giving a good summary of the fires' effects in the U.P. during this period, shows how fires' causes have changed over the years, from basically nature's forces and slash left behind by careless logging practices to the imprudent disposal of cigarettes, campfires and miscellaneous incendiary causes.

U.P. Fires
Region #1 - 1891 To 1949

Another major evolution has occurred in the methods used to fight forest fires. We have gone from bucket brigades to the beginning of a motorized force maintained to primarily fight forest fires.

U.P. Fires: Regions #2 and #3—1863 to 1943

These two fire regions comprise the central section of the Upper Peninsula, which was hit by the following fires in this 80-year period:

1863

The entire village of Harvey (Marquette County) was destroyed, with the exception of the blast furnace and several log buildings that stood near the mouth of the Chocolay River. This fire was responsible for 100 residents being homeless. Farmers in the Cherry Creek area are believed to have started the blaze through careless land clearing.

A strong west wind came up which sent the fire scurrying toward the village at a fast pace completely out of control. The town's founding father, Charles Harvey, was in New York at the time his town was leveled. Upon his return he was shocked to learn that 18 buildings, including a sawmill, had been completely engulfed in flames and destroyed. Both Harvey and his son lost their homes and office. Immediately, the elder Harvey began to draw up plans for a new village, welcoming the opportunity for a fresh start.

1871

This was the year of the famous Peshtigo, Wisconsin fire that jumped the Menominee River and invaded Michigan. This event was covered in Section One.

1873

Michigamme experienced a fire just one year after its Michigamme Mine opened in 1872. A report found in the Marquette *Mining Journal* indicated that a forest fire had been burning for quite some time in the forested sections northwest of the mine until gradually it swept toward the village itself. A brisk wind fanned the flames, destroying everything in the town but a general store and a few dwellings. The town lacked a wide main street and in fact brush and stumps still lined the trail road leading into Michigamme, providing additional fuel for the onslaught of flames. The newspaper said that "the confusion, agony and terror cannot be described. Men rushed wildly to save their wives and children. Most of the inhabitants fled to Lake Michigamme, grabbing planks, logs and whatever else was available while wading out to safety. Some followed the bush to the south and were saved. The steam pumps at the mill on the lake were kept at work and that property was saved. Everything else was swept out of existence. Special trains were ordered to the relief of sufferers and the passenger train coming east ran the gauntlet through the fire, took up as many as it could carry and brought them to Champion, Clarksburg, Humboldt and Ishpeming. Food, utensils and clothes were contributed and sent by special train. Two charred bodies were found in the ruins, several are missing and one man is known to have drowned." [65]

1877

This year proved to be a very dry summer and a series of fires was touched off in Marquette County alone. With blazes erupting in a half dozen or so areas simultaneously, it was only natural the general populace was more or less on pins and needles.

A small fire had been smouldering for days south of Chocolay, back of Fraser's sawmill on the Cherry Creek. [Later, a fish hatchery was erected near this site] A sudden wind shift sent the fire scooting rapidly toward the Ewing farm, which was saved, but others succumbed to the flames. That same week in June found serious fires burning near Republic, Michigamme and L'Anse.

At Ishpeming, dark ominous smoke clouds filled the air as minor blazes broke out near New England, Salisbury, Deer Lake and Parsons.

Records indicate that several homes were lost at Palmer and at Sands. The Chicago & North Western railroad had 2,000 cords of wood stored in the path of these forest fires. When the men were called upon to assist in the removal of this hardwood fuel supply, they refused, for they were too worried about losing their own property and would not help. Thus the wood became a blazing inferno and was entirely consumed making one extremely hot, hot fire.

Ishpeming firemen had been called to the Salisbury location and they ran into some serious trouble there. While the volunteers feverishly worked to quell the flames, a quantity of hose burned and their fire engine nearly was destroyed.

Finally, through a great deal of hard work, the crew managed to save their fire equipment.

[Author's Note: Many of the small towns listed were called "locations." This was common nomenclature for this period. A location, in essence, was a mining town in which the homes were built by the company and rented to the workers. A company store was also included.]

Another interesting note from these fires of 1877 was the fact that the townsfolk of Salisbury moved their household belongings into an empty "beehive" kiln for safekeeping. So the huge brick oven, which was constructed to turn hardwood into charcoal through a burning process, was now used to protect the settlers' belonging from the fury of the flames.

During this period of high fire danger, both Ishpeming and Negaunee fire departments kept steam up in their fire engines in readiness of any emergency. Night and day, both communities literally kept the vigil. These two towns had been shrouded in smoke for several weeks. Fires were reported between Negaunee and Marquette and the immense Morgan blast furnace complex caught fire several times but the company's workers played water hoses upon the structure, ultimately saving it from destruction. Eventually the wind shifted, aiming the fires away from Marquette proper, toward the Chocolay River area.

At night, long wispy tongues of flame appeared to erupt from Mt. Mesnard north of Marquette as pines on top the mountain succumbed to the flames, affording the scene the look of an active volcano. The summer of 1877 proved to be one of extreme concern and worry for one and all living in the north country.

1889

Fire struck the small town of Bagley located in mid-Menominee County and caused the demise of two lumber camps, numerous barns, homesteads and a dam along the river. Bagley was considered to be a "boom-town" during the 1890s and boasted of a population numbering 225 citizens.

1890

During this year a fire leaped from pine ridge to pine ridge as it burned the forests lying to the north of the Dead River toward Lake Superior.

1894

U.P. Fires
Regions #2 & 3 - 1863 To 1943

Fires were particularly bad in the vicinity of Ishpeming, Iron Mountain, Norway, Salisbury, Sagola, Floodwood and Ewen. These fires reached their peak in early September, following prolonged drought, and like most big fires burned until extinguished by heavy rains.

1896

In October a fire started on Dead River north of Ishpeming and burned through to Lake Superior in the vicinity of Big Bay "denuding the mountains" and covering an estimated 100 square miles of the virgin wilderness. This fire burned unchecked for 10 days until the fall rains put it out.

1900

The year 1900 proved to be a disastrous one for the Menominee County town of Koss. On the morning of May 14th an approaching forest fire literally consumed this small village. Just a few homes, the Wis-Mich. railroad depot and the offices of the C.H. Worcester company remained virtually untouched.

The fires had started during the previous night and approximately 100 men were rounded up to dig ditches in an attempt to control the flight of the flames, but to little avail. All was lost—the sawmills, hotel, homes and most of the business places, as well as logs and lumber piled in the mill yards.

1906

Fire once again struck the same area on May 19, 1906. But this time it proved to be the village of Talbot that served as victim. Records claim it was more or less erased from the map. Ten houses, depot, store, warehouse, post office, hotel, blacksmith shop and a shingle mill were quickly consumed by the raging inferno fueled by some 22,000 cedar posts piled in the mill yard.

The Marquette *Mining Journal* reported that forest fires had swept a total of five Upper Peninsula counties:

> A stretch of territory over 250 miles in length is dotted with forest fires ranging in size from a few acres to several square miles. Villages and farms have been wiped out, timber lands destroyed and hundreds rendered homeless. It is impossible to estimate the amount of loss over the whole

area, but in just the immediate vicinity of Marquette the loss is considered over $100,000, involving only the destruction of personal property but not including devastation of timber lands or railroad property.

The town of Quinnesec, a mining camp three miles east of Iron Mountain, has been wiped off the map, and several other villages destroyed. Fierce fires were reported near Sidnaw, Munising Junction, Ewen, Thomaston and Trout Creek.

Photo courtesy Michigan DNR, Greg Lusk Collection

After a forest fire passes through, hot spots remain which often suddenly burst into flame.

April was unusually dry and the precipitation in the last months has been less than an inch. At least 25 farm houses in Chocolay, West Branch and Skandia townships were wiped out yesterday, leaving over 100 homeless. A strip of country 5 miles long and 2 miles wide in the vicinity of Magnum Station is a blackened wasteland. Forest fires raged between Marquette and Eagle Mills to the south, fanned by a 30 mile an hour wind, and that whole area of the Carp River watershed is burned over with many homes destroyed. The section house of the Marquette and South Eastern railway at Birch burned, but a work crew from the railroad, with locomotive and extra hose, prevented the flames from spreading to the Northern Lumber company's sawmill. This was made easier because underbrush all around the town had been cleared.

...The Chocolay valley containing some of the finest farms in the county had been swept as clean as if a tornado had visited it. Total farms destroyed probably would be well over 25 in the whole are of Chocolay, West Branch and Skandia townships. Although there were many narrow escapes, no casualties were reported.[66]

1913

A stand of jackpine a hundred feet tall was burned in a great swath nine miles long and three miles wide near the Yellow Dog and Salmon Trout rivers.

1923

Big Bay was the scene of a very serious forest fire that devastated sections 31 and 32 (T51N, R27W), which included the Sugar Loaf and Birch areas. Approximately 80 to 100 woodsmen were working in this area when the fire broke out. A group of 20 sawyers were cut off from their co-workers by the onrushing inferno and 5 of their men burned to death. Some of the men had been clearing railroad ties from the right-of-way in order to remove possible fire fuel from the forest fire, while others had started a backfire. Both initiatives were laudable. However, the 5 men were trapped in the course of events. This fire eventually consumed over 1,200 acres.

1924

Another fire along the Yellow Dog River destroyed 2,500 acres and ate up sugar maples and pines alike. Some loggers sought safety in the stream as fire raged all around them.

1933

A stubborn fire burned near Escanaba from August 5th to September 29th—a total of 24 days—before it was laid to rest. Over 600 men were called in to fight the blaze; 235 were CCC workers.

1936

Marquette County suffered fire losses again. This time over 1,500 acres were burned.

1943

Marquette suffers fire losses once again; 1,200 acres consumed.

The dates provided on the preceding pages afford an excellent overview of the constant threat of forest fires played out over the decades throughout the central Upper Peninsula. At times over a span of days, weeks, even months, conditions were ripe for forest fires to occur. As time passed, especially after the turn of the century, U.P. citizens fought bravely back and considered the fighting of forest fires as a very serious business.

But not every individual held to these worthy principles, as is indicated in C. Frederick Rydholm's *Superior Heartland*:

> Louis Kaufman, Marquette financier, who owned the famous Granot Loma Lodge located above Marquette, was in need of a farm, for he had recently purchased the renowned Bay Cliff herd of Jersey cattle. He built the farm on the side of a hill out of sight from Granot Loma. This venture was accordingly named Loma Farms.
>
> Peter Raish cut the timber and then there was the awesome job of pulling stumps. They used every method known at that time to get the job done. Eventually, a huge stump-puller was employed.
>
> They tell the story of how a fire broke out when the men were clearing the fields. The state was paying about 25¢ or 30¢ an hour for fire fighters at that time, and their progress left a lot to be desired as far as Mrs. Kaufman was concerned. She offered $1.00 an hour to get those fires put out. Well, fires started popping up all over their property and crews were coming in from all over the area to fight them. A conservation officer had to explain to Mrs. Kaufman why the fires were not getting put out when she was paying the men such extremely high wages. [67]

Rydholm's two-volume set of historical books held another interesting fire piece that dated back to the year 1939 and took place at White Deer Lake:

The Panorama Fire Tower, at the north end of the McCormick tract, was being manned by George Summers of Marquette. George lived in the log cabin a few hundred yards below the tower with his wife and baby. That fall or late summer, a fire broke out on the McCormick property. George located it from the tower and phoned the camp. Gordon McCormick mobilized his men. This was the first of several fires he was to fight, on or near his land, over the next four or five years. He really went after a fire tooth and nail—every second counted with him. There was a lot of fire-fighting equipment at camp. His family hadn't preserved a forest for over two generations only to have it go up in smoke. Gordon was appalled at men standing around talking while a fire raged, some pointing nonchalantly here and there, others waiting for something or someone before they could do anything.

He equipped his men with everything they needed to fight a fire, right down to a bag of sandwiches and a little "something for snake bite" (a north woods expression for alcohol) and they worked a fire with whatever means there was at hand—shovels, rakes, wet burlap, anything to contain the flames, The regular firefighters brought in by the state were amused by Gordon's excitement and enthusiasm. In just a few hours, the fire was under control.

A month or so later, George Summers delivered Gordon McCormick a check for 60¢ from the state of Michigan—the firefighter's wage of 30¢ an hour. Gordon, a millionaire, laughed heartily over this and said he would frame it.[68]

The next forest fire accounting, a very descriptive piece, comes from an 1889 issue of the Norway *Current*:

$20,000 IN ASHES

Terrible Conflagration at East Vulcan
25 Families Left Homeless
3,000 Cords of Wood Reduced to Ashes

Tuesday afternoon a telephone message was received at Norway that East Vulcan was on fire, and the fire engine was called for. As soon as practicable, the fire department was on its way, and considering the long distance and the weight of engine and horse carts, good time was made.

On arriving there the discovery was made that a fire had come in from the swamp to the east and south of the East Vulcan location and that already more than twenty dwelling houses had been burned, that the fire had climbed the hill to the mine and had already made a good start in the cordwood piles of the company, in which were an aggregate of more than 3,500 cords, and that it would be a struggle to preserve the machinery and buildings of the mine which were surrounded by the wood.

The steamer was placed at a tank near the pumping engine house, and in a very few minutes three streams were at work in as many different places. Teams were procured and for several hours cordwood was loaded from piles nearest the engine house, and hauled to a place of safety, in as lively a manner as willing workers could handle it, while the firemen kept everything (men included) as wet as possible. This was done to ensure every chance of saving the machinery, the loss of which would have closed the East Vulcan mine for six months and throw 250 men out of work.

Just about the time that things were the hottest and when a chain had been attached to the fire engine and horses stood ready to jerk it out of the furnace-like position in which it stood, if the fire continued the encircling process which it had kept up for four or five hours, thunder was heard and it began to sprinkle rain and finally to pour, and the shout which went up from hundreds of throats whose owners bared their heads to the storm, in exultation, was thrilling.

While the rain which followed did not put out the fire (there was hardly water enough in Michigan for that), it killed the smallest fires, and dampened everything so that the work from that time was comparatively easy.

About 3,000 cords of wood were consumed and when those woodpiles became one mass of living fire the sight was both grand and terrible.

In the meantime, those who had lived in the burned district, and who, in almost every instance, had lost all were being taken care of by their more fortunate neighbors, and when night closed no one was without shelter.

The fire laddies remained until midnight when all except chief Ahlich and the engineer and fireman returned to Norway, they remaining there with the engine as a matter of precaution. The boys worked like horses, and earned for themselves and their engine many words of praise, but every mother's son of them was a cripple next day.

Give them the water and they will put it where it will do the most good every time. An uncharitable individual at our elbow says, "they will do the same thing with beer."

A rather pleasant episode of the busy day was the appearance on the scene, when most needed, of that old fire veteran and former chief of our department, Sheriff Stiles. You ask, did he work? Well we rise to assent that he just did, and left for home when the train pulled out, without a dry stitch in his clothes.

Another pleasant incident, or rather a series of incidents, were the attempts of the boys to finish up the load of edibles brought from the Penn Co.'s store and spread in the Captain's office, and the pails of hot coffee furnished by Mr. and Mrs. John Lofy. They did nobly, but some remained. In view of the general shortage of that article, under which the writer has so long suffered, he was allowed a monopoly of the canned tongue. [69]

The writer of that long ago period clearly captured the spirit of the day, making his readers feel as though they were actually at East Vulcan watching those fire laddies in action.

The central U.P. fire regions held one more fascinating tale—an example of careless, or perhaps unscrupulous, newspaper reporting.

The 1906 Quinnesec fire was written up locally as well as in the Chicago, Milwaukee and Detroit papers. But some of the "big city" newspaper accounts were sensational and less than truthful, according to the next two scolding articles—first from the Iron Mountain *Press*, then *The Detroit News:*

FIRES RUN WILD

Thirty Odd Buildings Feed the Flames At Quinnesec

The forest fire which raced through the timber slashings of Dickinson and Delta counties, and portions of Menominee, Marquette and Iron counties last Friday and Saturday was a particularly fierce one and the damage is very heavy, but not nearly so large as portrayed by the wonderful liars sent out by the Chicago and Milwaukee papers to report the catastrophe. These reckless young men armed themselves with railway maps and, with cruel thoughtlessness, proceeded to wipe out of existence some dozens or more towns, together with the inhabitants thereof.

As near as the *Press* can learn, and we have made diligent and careful inquiry, not a single life was lost as a result of the fire.

The total property loss, reported in the Chicago and Milwaukee papers at from $1,000,000 to $10,000,000, will not exceed $200,000 and much of this represents timber values.

Quinnesec people were the heaviest losers, but at this point the destruction was not caused by forest fires, but was communicated to the buildings by a stump heap, which had been set on fire.

...To the north of Iron Mountain, along the St. Paul road, the losses are insignificant. Sagola had an exceedingly narrow escape, and but for a sudden change in the wind, from the south to the north, would have been wiped out of existence. The road from Sagola to Channing was rendered impassable for a time by falling trees. The railway bridge at Ford River was on fire several times, but was saved by the section men. At Channing the fire raced through the slashings in the vicinity, but no losses are reported. Fires were to be seen in all directions as far north as Floodwood and south to the Menominee River. We hear of settlers having close calls, and of having to work hard to save their homes. Alder & Gray, cordwood dealers, were reported to be heavy losers at Granite Bluff and near Sagola, but came through the fire safely and without loss. The St. Paul bridge over the North-Western road at Antoine was on fire and the southbound train was delayed several hours. The damage was trifling—a few ties and some cross timbers being burned. However, it served as an excuse for a dam-phool correspondent to wire his paper that "the village of Antoine, containing 700 people," had been totally destroyed, together with a mill and many business houses.

South on the St. Paul road the losses are small. At Cedarville (Cedar River) several cars loaded with timber were burned on the track. This fire warped the rails so badly that it was necessary to send a relief train from Iron Mountain to repair the damage. Reports of trains running through miles of fire are all bosh. The train due here at 2:30 p.m. Friday did not arrive until 1:00 a.m. Saturday, owing to the accident to the track.

On the North-Western to the west and north, chief damage was done at Saunders, where the long idle plant of the Hattenburg Veneer company, a boarding house and several inexpensive dwellings were burned. No lives were lost as reported. No damage was done at Iron River, Stambaugh or Spring Valley, beyond the destruction of a small quantity of timber owned by the Verona company, although there was much fire in the woods surrounding the towns.

South on the North-Western road, considerable damage was done at Talbot, where the mill, store and a dozen dwellings were destroyed. A number of other towns had narrow escapes, but the damage is not nearly so large as reported.

Niagara was reported wiped out. There was not even a fire in that town. Settlers in the vicinity are quite heavy losers, however.[70]

☒☒☒☒☒

"BURNED" TOWNS ARE STILL INTACT

Lured Stories Of U.P. Forest Fires Fail To "Make Good"

Hundreds Of Destitute People Are Conspicuous By Their Utter Absence!

QUINNESEC, MICH., May 23, 1906—(From a Staff Correspondent) Since my dispatch of 30 hours ago, written soon after my arrival in the northern country, I have either personally or by phone interviewed enough men to warrant me in saying that there has never been a spell of disaster in Michigan where newspaper writers of fakes have worked off on reputable newspapers such a volume of lies as has been printed about the upper peninsula fires of the past week. I will produce witnesses today to substantiate this statement and produce more in a few days.

Take Quinnesec first, for that is the largest town said to have been burned by forest fires, which after weeks at smouldering were last Friday fanned into hurricane fires. The Chicago *Tribune*, depending on resident correspondents, last Sunday printed, "Quinnesec destroyed, all residents homeless." This under the heading of "Forest Fires." Now for the facts. Quinnesec has a population of about 500. It is 48 miles from Escanaba. Mrs. Patrick McKenna, widow, aged 60, owned four frame stores on Main street which she rented.

One tenant set fire to a pile of rubbish in the alley Friday, the wind came up and about $75,000 worth of property in the center of the village burned. The fire jumped over the Catholic parsonage and burned the church of which Fr. Nosisch, of Iron Mountain, is pastor.

Supervisor Cundy, of Quinnesec Township, Fr. Nosisch, Village Clerk Pat Wilder and others say forest fires had no more to do with burning Quinnesec than a fire in Detroit.

No forest fire came within four miles of the village. 33 buildings were burned, and 16 families lost their homes. Iron Mountain and Norway, big towns of the county, will take care of these. Reports that three children burned to death in the village are not true. The steel trust has two big boarding houses in Quinnesec. Neither burned.

Quoting again from the Sunday Chicago *Tribune*: "Antoine, mining town, all but a few of the 700 people homeless." Tom Hanna, publisher of the Iron Mountain *Press,* says Antoine is a suburb of Iron Mountain and that all that was burned in Antoine was seven ties and two cross-trees. *Tribune* correspondent sent it in for Sunday that Powers was "wiped out." Powers is one of the Northwestern railway junction points and has about 300 people. I have been there today, There has been nothing destroyed in Powers. People there got much alarmed Friday, but the fire did not come within four miles.

The Chicago *Tribune* said Daggett on the Northwestern railway, between Quinnesec and Escanaba, was wiped out. Daggett wasn't touched. Also that Saunders was destroyed. Not so. Saunders is 16 miles north of Iron Mountain and Editor Hanna says nothing burned there but a mill that's been abandoned five years.

Cornell, "300 people are homeless" on the Escanaba railway, has, so Dan Wells and his cousin, Supt. Wells of the railway says, only about half a dozen families. Commissioner Dan Wells says the Escanaba Railway has about 250,000 acres along the line which is about 120 miles long. The lands extend 8 to 10 miles each side of the track, and there's hardly a square of it where the fire didn't appear.

Yet Commissioner Wells, after working with his agents for three days, says he can find but 14 or 15 homesteaders who were burned out in the entire 250,000 acres. The fakers have reported that "hundreds" in this district were burned out, but give no names.

The Northwestern Railway lost its station at Quinnesec, but little more. At Niagara, three miles from Quinnesec, is the pulp mill of Kimberly Clark, said to be the largest in Michigan. It employs about 700 hands. A representative of this mill reports that comparatively little of its supply of timber was injured by the fires.

They do not think any pulp mill will be inconvenienced by the fires.

Some of the fakers are now printing stories that upper peninsula business men, for reasons of their own, are trying to belittle their stories of the fires. Why business men should do so is not explained. One Chicago faker said it was so smoky in Escanaba Friday that he could hardly see to write his dispatch. Well, there's one saloon to about each 125 of Escanaba's population. Still, a great many people had narrow escapes from being burned to death last Friday.

John Fitzgibbon, Special Correspondent
The Detroit News [71]

U.P. FIRES: REGION #4 - 1877 to 1947

Department of Natural Resources Fire Region #4 takes in the eastern Upper Peninsula counties of Alger, Luce, Schoolcraft, Mackinac and Chippewa. The region suffered from the following fires in this 70-year period:

1877

The village of Onota in Alger County is destroyed by fire. [this fire will be covered in detail later in this chapter]

1882

A large fire destroyed an area along the Sturgeon River.

1884

Forest fires were raging from Wetmore to St. Ignace, and much damage was reportedly done.

1891

The spring of 1891 was extremely dry, causing scattered fires that spread wildly. Hall and Buell lost millions of feet of timber in Alger County near Au Sable. Towns were endangered. Wetmore narrowly escaped destruction. Rock River lost two barns and six houses.

1900

By this date, tinder dry slashings lay everywhere, ripe for the fires that raged with increasing frequency around the county. Some were ignited by human carelessness, many by lightning and some were started on purpose. Very few areas were spared the frightening experience of watching distant forest fires approaching with a steady swiftness that could possibly destroy both lives and property.

1902

Since the previous two years were very dry and the winters produced little or no snowfall, it was merely a matter of time before forest fires took their toll. A fire started near Seney and spread to Grand Marais and on to Munising, wiping out everything in its path.

1903

Pine slashings south of Wetmore in Alger County began to ignite. The heat became so intense that the railroad rails were said to have curled into hoops.

1905

A bad year throughout the entire eastern U.P. for fires.

1908

The *Alger Centennial* book reports: "The Miner's Beach area was burned so bare that the contours of the earth could be seen for long distances and jack rabbits could be seen running everywhere. The southwest side of 64 Norway pines (trees to big to kill) were only scarred, and they re-seeded the beach."

1910

Eight-Mile Corner in Alger County hit hard by fire.

1919

The Whorl Fire started on the banks of the Two-Hearted River (Luce County) and burned up to the outskirts of Newberry.

1920

A forest fire burned 300 to 400 acres in the Chapel Flat area in Alger County. It was believed this blaze was intentionally set.

1921, '22, '25

Eight Mile Corner hit again by fires. The latter one burned on the plains for three months, destroying Thayer Brothers' camp and then moving on to the Hovey Lake area.

1925

Hovey Lake Fire destroyed 16,640 Alger County acres. Schoolcraft County lost over 16,000 acres and Mackinac County fires consumed 5,280 acres.

1930

Driggs and Fox River Fires took some 40,000 acres of marsh and jackpines. The Camp 33 Fire of Schoolcraft County destroyed 4,994 acres and did $5,000 worth of damage.

1931

The Duck Creek Fire in Schoolcraft County encompassed 11,130 acres.

1936

The year of the Hanley Fire in Alger County. Also of the Green School Fire at Schoolcraft County, which was remembered for its severity and difficulty to control. This latter blaze destroyed almost 10,000 acres at a sum of $25,291. Furthermore, Luce County lost 2,400 acres and the Traunik Fire in Alger County wiped out 3,824 acres.

1947

Two fires burned in Chippewa County, one south of Sault Ste. Marie and another near Rudyard. Fires were reported near Rock and Manistique.

Another fire causing severe problems as one which was tough to handle was reported as a 1,000 acre blaze north of Newberry near the Tahquamenon River. It was in an inaccessible area and could only be reached by boat, making it hard to bring in crews and equipment to fight this blaze.

A third fire was reported near Hulbert in Chippewa County covering 600 acres.

A total of 27 fires plagued the district in this year.

The 1887 Onota fire, in Alger County, was started by the charcoal used to fire the Onota blast furnace. Charcoal kilns were scattered throughout this area, in groups of three to perhaps a dozen or more, which fed the fiery mouth of the furnace.

According to the following excerpt from a book titled *Alger County Centennial History—1885 to 1985,* a load of charcoal enroute to the furnace flared up in the delivery cart, setting a fire that spread quickly:

THE FIRE

> In the spring of 1877 fires raged in the woods around Onota. Everything was tinder dry, the sky continuously hazy. It was an uneasy time for residents with vivid memories. On May 31 a strong south wind was blowing smoke through the village. Suddenly, John Thiede rolled into town with his wagon on fire! Its load of charcoal had ignited while enroute to the furnace and the water holes normally used along the way had dried up. The teamster leaped down, unhitched his team and left the burning wagon. Fanned by the wind, the fire reached out over the dry terrain. In an instant the whole town was engulfed in flames. Residents fled the holocaust, plunged into the lake (Superior) for safety and then struggled along the shore seeking refuge at settlements around the bay. Within a few short hours Onota was wiped out except for the church and school. According to some reports, a saloon—possibly Dalbeck's—was also spared.
>
> Afterward most of the refugees were forced to rely upon county poor funds for resettlement. Many went to Marquette where Wm. L. Wetmore provided transportation to the east for those interested.
>
> Wetmore had purchased the Bay Furnace Company just two months before the fire and he was sent into bankruptcy. The furnace machinery

was purchased by John Jones and moved to Iron River. The loss of this industry, in addition to the furnace at Old Munising in the same year, left Grand Island Harbor a desolate place.

...With the closing of school in the spring, community life at Bay Furnace (Onota) ended.

Eventually, fire claimed most of the buildings at Onota. Louis Jacobson continued the practice of burning grass along the railroad to the clearings around his home. One fire got away and burned a log cabin, and in just a half hour, the last school.

Years later, in 1900, R.J. Clark & Company built a dam across the creek to run its logs out of Furnace Lake and into the bay. But it, too, gradually disappeared. In 1940 the Cleveland-Cliffs Iron Company donated 54.8 acres to the U.S. Forest Service for historical and recreational purposes, out of which a 10-acre plot was developed as a picnic site. And in 1947 the Munising Rotary Club, spearheaded by Harlow A. Wood, led an effort to preserve the furnace ruins by fencing them in and erecting a memorial plaque. (Now known as Bay Furnace Campground) [72]

Another interesting account was a report read to the Munising Women's Club by a Mrs. Ann Bissel on January 14, 1916. While it may not deal directly with forest fires, it nevertheless provides and understanding of the constant threat fire played in the daily lives of the populace:

...The one very unpleasant feature of that first year was the constant dread of fire and the many exciting battles with it. As the town had been cleared during the early winter, the brush piles back of the town had been left until spring to burn. ...after the largest part of the piles had burned the fire would smoulder...and we would be very comfortable thinking the danger about over, when up would come one of our south gales, and as everything was dry, in a little while there would be a roaring and crackling of fires all along, sometimes creeping up to the buildings, and then everyone would be out fighting it with pails and shovels, and as sand was more accessible at the time than water, the shovels were first aid.

Our fire department consisted of every man in town and the fire alarm was a huge tin horn. It was a hair-raising experience to be wakened in the night by the blowing of this horn, and between blasts the man would pound on the door and shout FIRE! It was very evident that the town would have to have more adequate fire protection than pails and shovels afforded, so Mr. Burtis agreed that if the village would lay pipe, he would do the pumping from his mill.

FIRE! FIRE! FIRE! Forest fires (some very near) and brush fires in the village of Munising were fearful happenings to residents and led the village council to create the fire department in 1898, even building a fire hall for it which stood on Lynn Street until 1938. The old hall had housed the teams which drew the fire wagons and sleighs. Bud Lambert, a long-time fireman said, "They were so well trained that at the sound of an alarm, they would be ready to move into their harnesses and gallop away."

The early fire fighters were summoned by the blare of a tin horn which was replaced by a bell and in later years by a siren.

Fire fighting was one good reason why streets were "rolled" during the winter before plowing came into the picture. While the "fire wagon" could get about fairly easily on the sand and macadam streets during the summer, the horse-drawn "fire sleighs" had to have clear paths through the snow to hustle to blazes in the winter. [73]

Moving a bit further to the eastern end of the peninsula, the Detroit *News Tribune* relates the following exciting rescue story from 1908:

DIES TRYING TO SAVE MEN PENNED IN LIGHTHOUSE

Malcolm McGregor, Mate of the *Scottish Hero*, Drowned In Lake Superior

KEEPERS OF THE POINT IROQUOIS BEACON WERE SURROUNDED BY FLAMES AS STEAMER SAILED AWAY THEY WERE STILL SIGNALING FOR HELP! LATER RESCUED.

MARQUETTE, MICH., Oct. 17—The steamer *Scottish Hero*, arriving here today, reported the death of Mate Malcolm McGregor, who lost his life in a brave but futile attempt to save two lighthouse keepers at Point Iroquois, in the eastern end of Lake Superior, from death by forest fires. The keepers sounded signals of distress as the *Hero* was passing Point Iroquois Thursday. The lighthouse is situated on a nigh narrow point of land extending out into the lake and heavily timbered. A raging wall of flame was sweeping up the point as the *Scottish Hero* hove to and it seemed that the imprisoned keepers must either perish in the flames or meet death in the icy waters of Lake Superior.

The seas were rolling high but McGregor and three sailors put off in an effort to save the men. Although they tried repeatedly, they were unable to land on account of the terrific waves which threatened to dash their little boat against the rock-bound promontory. They were finally forced to give up the attempt. In trying to board the steamer again, Mate McGregor fell into the water and was lost.

The *Scottish Hero* remained off the point all day Friday trying to recover McGregor's body but the attempt was unsuccessful. The distress signals were still sounding as the *Scottish Hero* steamed away. The crew learned with relief when they arrived here that a lighthouse tender from the Soo had saved the men and the station. [74]

There was one other small article in the same edition of this paper regarding Upper Peninsula fires. The article's brevity likely is because during the same period, the lower peninsula was aflame from Presque Isle County to Iosco County. This was the same week that the village of Metz was engulfed in flame and where women and children were literally cremated when a relief train ran into a wall of flame. Therefore, it is understandable that downstate fire news, more or less, crowded the severe U.P. fire situation off the front pages of the Detroit papers.

Still, a good description of its severity is rendered in the following article:

Over 50 Square Miles in the U.P. Burned Over

SAULT STE. MARIE, MICH. Oct. 7—Over 50 square miles of timbered land in this end of the peninsula have been burned over and tonight the woods for miles along the shore of Lake Superior and the St. Mary's River between here and DeTour are a mass of flames. No boats will move tonight on the upper lakes.

At 1:00 o'clock this afternoon darkness set in and boats were blowing fog signals as they crept along to find places to anchor. In a few places which were threatened the fires died down, but others sprung up, and the situation tonight is considered more grave than at any time since the fires started.

Kelden and Barbeau, small settlements south of the Soo, report fires in that locality beyond control. Hundreds of acres of valuable timber was licked up by the flames.

The fires are still unchecked around Gatesville and DeTour and Raber, but Bay Mills and Brimley and West Neebish are out of danger.[75]

The Upper Peninsula fires again made the front pages of the Detroit papers a few days later. The next two reports were featured in *The Detroit News*. The first explains that, while relief supplies were flooding into burned out Metz in the lower peninsula, fires continued to rage out of control in the eastern end of the Upper Peninsula. Large graphic headlines accompanied this piece:

TELL OF WALL OF FLAME 50 MILES LONG IN U.P.

Crews of Boats on the St. Mary's River Give Some Graphic Descriptions of Forest Fires

CHIPPEWA CO. IS FIRE-SWEPT

With relief supplies pouring into Posen and Metz faster than the relief committees in charge of the work can handle them, the people of the Presque Isle-Alpena fire district appear to be doing as well as could be expected. Many are living in crude shelters, however, and the prime effort is to get them housed before a cold wave hits them.

Attention is now drawn to reports of widespread and devastating fires in the upper peninsula, especially in the east end. Sugar Island, at the very door of the city of Sault Ste. Marie, appears to be ablaze from end to end. It is 12 miles long, and covered with hardwood. DeTour, on the southeastern tip of the peninsula, is fighting fires but is not in imminent danger.

In the back country of Chippewa County small towns report that settlers are coming in, but the name of no single settler who has been burned out is yet given. There are big forest fires all the way west, in spots, to within a few miles of the city of Marquette.

There is an unconfirmed report of the finding of three more dead bodies, those of men near Rogers City. If this is true the death list now numbers 45.

"There will be no rain for the burning districts of Michigan," states the Weather Forecaster, Mr. Thompson. "Lakes Superior and Michigan will probably have rain, Thursday, but I can give no hope that the fire-visited parts of the state will profit by it."[76]

☒☒☒☒☒

FOR FIFTY MILES THE LAKESHORE A WALL OF FLAME

SAULT STE. MARIE, MICH., Oct. 21—A representative of the *Evening News* just returned from Sugar Island says no lives have been lost there. If the wind remains where it is the residents will probably be able to save their buildings. He found the ruins of a house and barn several miles from the settlements, but indications were that they were vacated before the fire started.

On the mainland south of Whitefish Bay and west of St. Mary's River and the lake, the whole east tip of the upper peninsula is afire in large areas this morning, as it has been for 20 days past. Eckerman, on the South Shore rail line, just east of the Trout Lake Junction, where the St. Ignace line comes in from the south, is trying to fight back the flames. Other hamlets, mentioned in earlier dispatches to the *News*, are in the same fix this morning.

Near Donaldson, at least 40 square miles of territory is burned over. The fire is running rapidly and cannot be checked until rain comes.

Lumbermen have men fighting at every place possible, but it does no good.

As the result of the killing of timber by fire, the whole territory will have to be lumbered at once in order to utilize the wood before it falls to the ground and rots.

James Puller returned today from Sugar Island. He says that at 10 o'clock the northern end of the island was safe. McKinney's mill, reported burned last night, is still safe, the fire being at least a mile away. Puller said he could not see what conditions were in the lower end of the island.

Gatesville reports all the farm buildings of John Demski destroyed. Robert Kelly's farm of 160 acres was swept end to end. George Crochton lost all his farm buildings. The Mud Lake Lumber Co. lost several thousand acres of hardwood.

Gatesville is surrounded by flames. The inhabitants fought all night and saved the place after a desperate fight.

Messages say that last night the view from decks of vessels was one of grandeur. For 50 miles along the shore the flames were seen rising 50 to 100 feet and seemed to extend back from the lake for miles. Telephone messages from the southern part of the county at 10 o'clock say the fires are beyond control.[77]

Fire Control and Prevention

By the turn of the century, timber managers finally realized that their forest holdings were in dire need of fire protection, for they were losing far too many precious dollars to uncontrollable forest fires. In 1913 the Northern Forest and Protection Association was organized in Munising under the direction of Thomas B. Wyman. It was formed by large landholders who paid a percentage on their acreage for protection. Later, the State of Michigan took over fire control around the year 1915.

Even though many of the timber barons suffered extreme losses during the bad fire year of 1923, the forests owned by the Ford Motor Company suffered minor losses from forest fires. Why? Because Ford was the first company to practice serious conservation and cleanup methods, including gathering and burning branches and other logging debris. Ford also maintained its own fire towers and timber patrols.

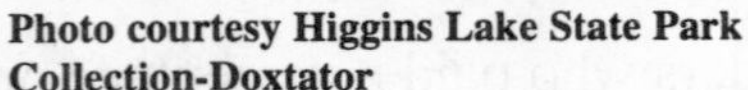

Photo courtesy Higgins Lake State Park Collection-Doxtator

Photo courtesy U.S. Forest Service, Kenton, MI

Michigan's first fire towers (left) had no enclosure. Watchmen were exposed to swarms of insects and the ravages of the weather. Later towers (right), like this Teepee Fire Tower near Kenton, vastly improved forest fire protection in Michigan.

Railroads Through Smoke & Fire

Early in this publication we covered the role played by the early sailing vessels, especially during the Great Fires of 1871. Now it is time to present a similar chapter regarding the railroads, which essentially played a dual role—one of villain and another offering both rescue and relief.

Lives were saved and lost through the intervention of relief trains. They, in many instances, proved to be the very lifeline for urban and city dweller alike when fire situations proved severe.

But in earlier times, locomotive engines were responsible for igniting many forest fires. In retrospect, they played both side of the tracks, although I strongly believe they did far more good than harm.

Railroads Through Smoke & Fire

One of the chief causes of Michigan forest fires, especially during the earlier years, proved to be the operation of the railroads. There was a period when it was estimated that as many as 55 percent of all reported forest fires occurred from locomotives or by hobos who regularly followed the tracks. Many of these blazes did little or no harm, for the railroad companies had men in their employ who did nothing but walk the rails, bridges and trestles as a routine precaution or a method of fire protection. Train crews and section hands were also well instructed in both spotting fires and assisting in their control.

Railroad operations, development and expansion took place in this state simultaneously with extensive land clearing and logging exploitation. Both industries were "King" in their time, providing not only jobs but a paternalistic environment, linking the fate of communities to their fortunes.

Actually, the two industries have been intimately connected or dependent on one another. Practically all of the railroads north of Lansing follow former logging roads or passed through areas formerly famous for large tracts of virgin timber. And, of course, timber and timber products comprised a large percentage of a typical train's cargo.

The huge amounts of slash left after forests were cleared soon became as dry as tinder. Such slashings also occurred along railroad rights-of-way as tracks forged further and further into the interior sections of both peninsulas. Ultimately these slashings, coupled with current logging operations and a lack of safety equipment manufactured for locomotives, resulted in many disastrous forest fires. To make matters worse, these early locomotives burned wood for fuel, which simply showered the rights-of-way with flying embers. As many locomotives were improved to using coal as fuel, fires did not occur as rapidly, but solving the problems still spanned many years.

The Michigan Department of Conservation (now the Department of Natural Resources) explained the history of locomotive fire safety equipment in a 1950 booklet:

> The use of spark arrestors was considered seriously early in the development of steam locomotives. First, screen or hoods were placed over the stack, then balloon and diamond stacks were invented. In 1883, the first attempt was made to arrest sparks in the front end or smokestack of the locomotive. This led to the development of the Master Mechanic and Mudge Slater spark arrestors which have since become standard equipment. While generally effective if properly installed and maintained, the front-end screen type spark arrestor requires frequent inspection and is not satisfactory with poor grades of coal. Its general use, however, has greatly reduced the number of fires started by locomotives. A later development is the Cyclone type of spark arrestor which does away with the use of screens and is more efficient. Its maintenance is more expensive, however, and it has not been used extensively.
>
> Sparks from the stack are not the only source of locomotive fires. Live coals, clinkers and hot ashes falling from ash-pans or deposited on the right-of-way, were early found to be equally responsible. Better designed ash-pans, frequent inspections and regulations prohibiting the dumping of ashes where they can start fires have done much to eliminate fires from this source. The use of oil for fuel, however, appears to be the solution of the locomotive fire problem.

Active interest of Michigan railroads in forest fire prevention and control dates from 1873, when they were made legally responsible for fires set by their locomotives. This resulted in frequent damage suits and paved the way for the adoption of safety measures. Not until 1903, however, were railroads required to use spark arrestors and clean up their rights-of-way, and not until a locomotive inspector was appointed in 1912 to work with the railroads was any serious attempt made to prevent railroad fires.

In general, the railroads have cooperated with the state locomotive inspectors and shown a commendable willingness to adopt measures suggested for the prevention and control of railroad fires. This has involved cleaning up rights-of-way, installation and maintenance of approved spark arrestors and ash-pan regulations as to where ashes may be dumped, posting of fire warnings in trains and stations, reporting fires discovered by train crews, patrolling behind trains on high fire danger days and cooperating with state and federal fire wardens in suppressing fires that occur along rights-of-way.[78]

The railroads played a multi-purpose role in respect to forest fires, for they walked both sides of the tracks. While they remained a chief cause of early forest fires, they also served as a prime source of rescue and relief. In many instances, trains provided the one and only means of escape for wilderness settlers and the populace of remote hamlets, villages and towns. Without the railroads, surely the final death tolls would have been much higher.

And, just as important, once the fiery conflagrations had done their dirty work, the railroads immediately sent relief trains to the stricken areas. In this manner food, clothing, supplies, animal feed, household utensils and a variety of other materials were ferried quickly into devastated fire sections.

We will see these dual roles dramatically played out during subsequent chapters relating the horrors that took place at Metz in 1908 and Au Sable-Oscoda in 1911. These two devastating firestorms occurred so close to one another that they awakened public interest regarding forest fire control.

"Remember Metz and Au Sable" became the watchword of that era, and signs bearing these words were ordered placed in all passenger coaches of the Detroit & Mackinac rail line, for they routinely passed through those two stricken areas.

Two 1906 *Detroit News* articles dramatically recount dramas depicting the relationship between railroads and rescue efforts:

RESCUE TRAINS RACE WITH FLAMES IN THE BLAZING FORESTS

In Five Sections of the U.P. Big Conflagrations Are Raging: Known Loss of Life is Small

6,000 SAID TO BE HOMELESS

Flee to the Railroads and Hundreds Are Picked Up: Searching Parties to Explore Further Inland: Whole Towns Destroyed

The forest fires raging in the upper peninsula of Michigan show signs of diminishing at one point. Menominee, one of five separate fire locations, says that reports are coming in that the wind has changed and the fires are dying out.

The area in which enormous fires are burning extends from Newberry, on the east, to a point just east of Bessemer, on the west; 230 miles from the shore of Lake Superior to that at Lake Michigan and reaches down into the northern counties of Wisconsin.

Six Michigan counties are involved: Delta, Menominee, Dickinson, Marquette, Iron and Luce.

...The Northwestern and the Escanaba & Lake Superior railroads have taken off all regular trains and are running trains into the fire district to bring out the people. The heat has so warped the rails in places that new ones have to be laid.

One Escanaba estimate is that 6,000 people have been rendered homeless. This fire looks like the biggest Michigan forest fire since 1871 and the one of 1881, both, however, in the "Thumb" district; more populous and more heavily timbered than the upper peninsula fire district is now.[79]

☒☒☒☒☒

ESCANABA, May 19th—A messenger returning from the burned district at 10 o'clock reports that the flames are still advancing in a southwesterly direction at great speed and the force of fire fighters is being assembled southwest of Woodlawn. They will attempt to check the advance by back-firing a large district.

It is learned that several camps of I. Stephenson Co., located at different points in the burned district, are completely burned out, and it is feared that many woodsmen have been burned to death.

A woodsman returning to the city this morning says that members of the crew became greatly excited when the fire advanced within a mile of their camp without being discovered, and in an attempt to escape in the darkness they became separated in the woods. The woodsman made his way to the railroad track where he was picked up by a relief train, but no trace of his companions had been found and that entire district is now fire swept!

George Hughes, a Northwestern engineer, arrived in the city at 10 o'clock this morning and reports that the entire district from Sands to Goose Lake is burned over and the homes of many settlers are destroyed. Hughes claims that the flames kept pace with his engine for a distance of 15 miles and the train was moving at the rate of 35 miles an hour.

Many homeless people brought into the city by relief trains are being cared for here, but great suffering is threatened unless prompt relief is given. Nearly all of the refugees have lost all of their possessions and must be supported by the public. The loss of I. Stephenson Co., alone from burned logs and standing timber, is estimated at $1,000,000 and unless the fire is checked the loss of that company will be greatly increased.

The families of many homesteaders throughout the burned section are missing and it is feared they have been lost. In some districts the flames advanced at the rate of 20 miles an hour, making the escape of the homesteaders living in small clearings in the center of the forest practically impossible. It is definitely known that the following villages were either completely destroyed or sustained heavy fire losses: Quinnesec, Spring Valley; Saunders, Niagara, Wisconsin; Talbot, Antoine; Cornell; Salva; Northland; Woodlawn; Ralph; Alfred and many, many other small hamlets. Hundreds of persons have been rendered homeless in this county alone.

The refugees are pouring into this city on foot, with teams and on relief trains. They have little with them, save the clothes on their backs. Some of them tell terrible tales of their experiences in escaping from the sweeping flames. One man declares that the flames were advancing in the vicinity of Cornell at the rate of 20 miles an hour, when he and all the residents of that place were taken on the relief train. Homesteaders, carrying packs containing a few personal effects, were found by train crews at all points along the right of way and were picked up and brought into the city or left at stations not threatened by fire.

A crew of a lumbering camp, together with 50 horses, fled before the fire for a distance of 12 miles and were reported safe at the Princeton mine at 8:30 last night.

Many of the relief trains were delayed because of the track being either warped or destroyed or bridges burned out. In places new rails were laid. Freight traffic on the Escanaba & Northern was abandoned early Friday afternoon, and the freight crews turned their attention to rescue work. W.R. Linsley of the peninsula division of the Northwestern road reported that several freight trains are believed to have been entirely consumed, being unable to proceed from the danger zone on account of impaired tracks.

Relief trains sent from Escanaba and other points not threatened by fire have brought in several loads of people who were cared for that night, and are being returned to the scenes of their homes today wherever such action is possible.

The companies sustaining large fire losses in this district are: Stephenson Co. of Wells; Escanaba Woodenware Co.; Pittsburgh & Lake Superior Iron Co.; Kellogg Switchboard & Supply Co.; Escanaba & Lake Superior Railroad; Chicago & Northwestern Railroad and many mill owners throughout the district.[80]

With the good transportation of today, it is hard for us to fathom people trapped in far off places deep in the wilderness, not being able to simply jump in their automobiles and head off down the nearest expressway to ultimate safety. But things were quite different in the late 1800s and early 1900s. To have lived in a totally isolated area, trapped on three, or possibly four, sides by a raging holocaust of a forest fire—it must have been horrifying! Those with a bit of forethought raced to rail lines in hopes that a rescue train had been dispatched to come to their assistance. Additionally, men living in the lumber camps also depended on the trains as their lifeline to civilization and safety during times of forest fire danger.

Apparently, people riding relief trains were often called upon to assist in clearing the tracks in order for the locomotive to keep moving along its appointed route, according to this interesting account from a Danish book by Holger Rosenstand:

> One time I was riding on a train in Michigan through uninterrupted woods. All at once, the train came from the green pines into a flaming, crackling sea of fire. The great heat from this fire was very noticeable. Then with a jerk the train stopped. A burning sawmill had fallen across the tracks and the train was quickly emptied of people. Everyone of those who had been sleeping, as well as the ones who had been awake, helped to clear the track. Under the guidance of the trainmen the burning timber was moved. The work progressed smoothly with each person putting forth energy in proportion to his eagerness to travel on. Never before had I seen such unity of purpose coupled with common sense. We worked as if we were professional firefighters without the usual banter which spices up an otherwise dreary work. The work was done with earnestness of purpose. The track was cleared, all aboard, and we traveled on. Soon after we had put the burning forest behind us, but some distance into the woods we met the fire again and were forced to make a long detour around the burning area.[81]

A 1991 article in the magazine of the Soo Line Historical and Technical Society tells of a small locomotive—the "Dinky"—which was specifically used for fire fighting. Owned by the Wisconsin Land & Lumber Company of Hermansville, it arrived at the company's hardwood flooring plant—where the famous IXL brand of flooring was made—on May 22, 1883.

Photo courtesy Larry Easton, *The Soo* magazine and IXL Museum

The engine fondly known as "The Dinky" used by the Wisconsin Land and Lumber Company in fighting forest fires.

Purchased from the Wm. K. Porter Company of Pittsburgh, the engine was a Pioneer No. 1, weighed some 31,000 pounds with a fuel box located in the cab. The Dinky carried 180 pounds of steam, 10" x 16" cylinders and had 36" diameter drivers. It possessed a rigid wheelbase of 5'3", with a total wheelbase, including the rear pony wheels of 13'4".

Easton's article provides another dimension to the work of trains in protecting our resources—and their cargo—from forest fires:

Fire Fighting

(Harold Earle recalls some of his experiences with the "Dinky" in his memoirs:)

"It was in September, either 1909 or 1910 [Author's Note: Probably was 1906, as our other previously reported newspapers indicate] that we had forest fires all over the Peninsula, mostly small fires, but hundreds of them threatening to destroy logs and other forest products piled along the railroads of our own Hermansville & Western and the Soo Line. Between keeping the mill supplied and operating and fighting fires, we were all working extra long hours. We had rigged up a couple of large wooden water tanks on a flat car with a steam pump mounted on one of the tanks, connected to the engine's steam dome with a rubber steam hose.

"In the evening, the foreman, Bye Kent, summoned a crew consisting of Eddie Hartnett, engineer, the Soo Line conductor, pilot, and a brakeman whose name I do not recall. I invited myself to go along. First we filled the water tanks and then started a run of four miles on the H & W, which was being used for the last season and had been little used or maintained for the previous several years. Young trees had grown up so close to the rusty rails that the branches brushed the sides of the cab of the little old saddle tank Porter locomotive that was locally known as the 'Dinky' because of its small size. The engine had only an oil wick headlight which was out of order. The coal box was in the rear of the cab, as a saddle tank locomotive has no tender. The only light we had was supplied by a railroad oil lantern. We pulled the flat car behind us and the wheels squealed around the curves, and we alternately speeded down-grade and almost stalled on the up-grades.

"One cannot imagine a darker night, except for the places lighted by small creeping fires, which only made it seem darker as we passed beyond them. At one point we burst into a farm brilliantly lighted by numerous old stumps, each of which was a flaming torch. We could see the farmer with wife and children helping to extinguish the fires nearest the hay stack, barn and house, with water carried in pails. It was a scene I could never forget. The folks seemed to be doing all right. The clearing was small and quickly our train plunged down into a black tunnel of trees toward our objective, a big log landing a short distance beyond, toward which the fire was creeping.

"When we stopped, the crew was outside getting out the water hose. When they called for steam from the boiler, Eddie was busy draining the lubricator and preparing to refill with engine cylinder oil. So I crawled out the fireman's front window to the running board beside the boiler. I could see nothing, but bumped into the rubber steam hose, felt along it to the pipe connection and along down the hot pipe to the valve. Not wanting my face above the uncertain connection of steam hose to pipe, and having located the valve which I could reach from inside the cab, luckily for my caution, I crawled back inside the cab, reached out and started slowly opening the valve. There was a sort of hiss, then a sharp shrill whistle, followed by a blast of steam.

"Having no idea as to what happened and having no desire to be a hero, I thought a tube in the boiler had let go and the rest of the boiler might be going some place. I just wanted out and quick! I jumped to the deck of the cab and the second jump took me to the ground, where I landed against a gravel bank on all fours, to the great amusement of the engineer and crew. The connection was repaired and we emptied the water tanks to good effect and returned to town

"There was a fire reported beyond the Farnham siding on the Soo Line, about seven miles east of Hermansville. The tanks were filled again and we proceeded to the depot for dispatcher's orders. Meanwhile, Bye awakened the store manager and got three cans of beans, three packages of crackers, three cans of sardines and three pounds of cheese for the five of us.

"The Soo Line express No. 7 was due at Hermansville at 11 p.m. and was late, as it was almost that hour. No. 7 had already left Gladstone, the last telegraph station before Hermansville. But in those days of 'iron men and wooden cars,' chances were taken in emergencies, and this was an emergency. This time the engine was backing and pushing the tank car, which the men with hand lanterns were riding, while I was just watching from the fireman's side and seeing absolutely nothing except an occasional gray streak, which I judged to be one of the old-time road crossing signs, 'LOOK OUT FOR THE CARS.' I would then ring the bell (until the bell cord broke) and Eddie would sound four blasts of the whistle as required by law, although we were well beyond the crossing by that time.

"After we had proceeded what was thought to be the proper mileage, but being completely lost, realizing that No. 7 was hurtling toward us making up lost time, we were pretty nervous. Bye said to me, 'Look for a house!' Inasmuch as I could not see a thing ten feet away, that sounded silly to me. But Bye knew that there was a log cabin nearly a quarter of a mile from the track at Farnham siding. Fortunately, the occupants of the house followed the old custom of leaving a small kerosene lamp burning on the window sill. Not having a hand lantern or light of any kind near me, as the others had, I was surprisingly able to pick out a tiny spark of light in the distance.

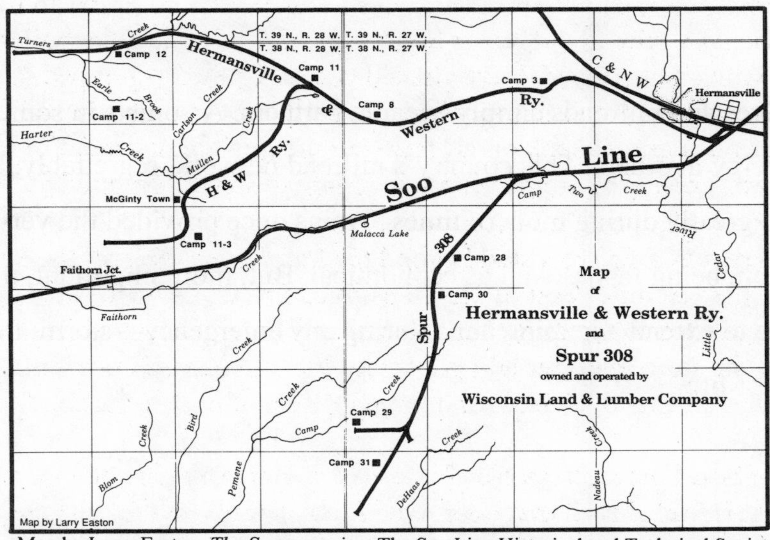

Map by Larry Easton, *The Soo* magazine, The Soo Line Historical and Technical Society

Map of Hermansville & Western Railroad—and Spur 308—owned and operated by Wisconsin Land and Lumber Company.

"We stopped and discovered that we were alongside the siding sought. We had passed the first switch into it because the switch light had gone out. We stopped and backed up to the switch and quickly got into the clear. We had just time to grab the three of everything for lunch and some water pails to sit upon, all of which took hardly a minute, when the headlight of No. 7 flashed around the curve and was upon us and our conductor gave the 'highball' signal with his lantern, answered by two whistle blasts from No. 7. I often wondered what the Soo Line engineer thought when he discovered us—probably a mental picture that engineer carried for a long time, too.

"It was 2 a.m. when we got home after finishing up our fire fighting and got back to Hermansville, as weary a crew as one would be likely to find. I think the Soo Line dispatcher must have heaved a sigh of relief when No. 7 reported in and out of Hermansville. Of course he did not know that someone had goofed and let the switch light burn out at Farnham siding and about the trouble we had finding the siding." [82]

Forest fires and railroads simply became partners. Arsonists in some cases; angels of mercy in others. This country's railroad network, regrettably, has diminished so greatly during modern times. Trains once provided the very best of transportation, being fast as well as economical. But, more important, they were always there to extend a helping hand during any emergency—storm, flood, tornado or forest fire.

Section 4

The Metz Fire Of 1908

Metz—The Village Vanishes

Lest we forget, a Michigan State Historical Marker is located at the site of present-day Metz where once their original school was located. This commemorative sign reads as follows:

-The Metz Fire-

On October 15, 1908, raging fires swept the pine forests of Presque Isle County. When the flames approached the village of Metz, a train jammed with women and children left for Posen, five miles away. At Nowicki's Siding, two miles out of town, huge piles of blazing wood lined the track, leaving an open car full of refugees in the center of the flames. Sixteen were killed and dozens of others badly burned. Throughout this part of the state hundreds were left homeless, as many homes and farms were devastated. Supplies soon poured in so that shelters could be erected, before the onset of the northern winter.

BE CAREFUL WITH FIRE...

REMEMBER METZ AND AU SABLE!

The D&M Railroad over a period of years after the tragic fires at Metz and AuSable hung a sign with the wording listed above, as a reminder to keep the memory of these catastrophic events alive...A laudable, "Lest We Never Forget" gesture.

Metz —The Village Vanishes

Headlines screamed: **God Punished Us!**

Not necessarily so. In reality, climatic conditions proved to be at their worst since the scores of devastating fires swept across the Thumb of Michigan during the fall of 1881. 1908 proved to be extremely dry and hot, but due to a wet spring, forest undergrowth flourished dramatically. In late August and early September, several killing frosts turned ferns, weeds and brakes into powdery kindling eagerly awaiting an opportunity to feed and fuel a pending disastrous fire.

The drought was widespread. The Fernie, British Columbia conflagration burned over 64,000 acres, resulting in the loss of nine lives. Chisholm, Minnesota was destroyed when encroaching flames ate up 20,000 acres. Isle Royale, located far off Michigan's Keweenaw Peninsula, was not immune to adverse weather conditions. Uncontrollable fires swept this Lake Superior island home to native Michigan moose, threatening their natural browse as well as their very existence.

Weather-wise, the stage was properly set for disaster at the small turn-of-the-century village of Metz, according to the *1909 Eleventh Biennial Report of the State Game, Fish and Forestry Booklet*:

> The cause of the Metz fire and other related forest fires in this area of the state in 1908 was traceable directly to climatic conditions. The deficiency in rainfall for the months of July, August, September and October

> in that year was shown to be greater, in the records of Michigan Agricultural College, than for the same months of any year since 1864, when the meteorological station at the college was established. Weather conditions covering the period from April to November were most unusual and favorable for destructive forest fires. The warm humid weather with frequent warm rains, covering a long period during the early season, produced a heavy growth of brakes, ferns, fireweed and other forest ground vegetation. This condition was followed by continued dry hot weather, beginning in the month of June and ending the last part of the month of October.
>
> In the Upper Penusula and northern part of the Lower Peninsula, the frosts during the months of August and September killed much of the forest ground vegetation, which the hot dry weather soon converted into tinder of the most inflammable nature. Severe killing frosts occurred in the Upper Peninsula on October 2 and in the northern counties of the Lower Peninsula on October 3. These frosts added dead hardwood leaves to the dry ground growth, and the hot dry weather following, with hot southerly winds, produced a condition for fires not before occurring in Michigan. On October 14, 1908 the very air seemed to be charged with inflammable gases, and fire would travel at great speed.[83]

Most of the men in Metz were farmers, lumbermen or both. Many worked in the woods during the winter, while farming during the rest of the year. At the sawmill near the railroad tracks were piled stacks of logs, railroad ties, cedar posts and poles as well as hemlock bark for tannery use; all waiting for shipment by rail to market sources. Space was limited, so additional wood products were stacked on cutover land directly across the road from the village.

The township of Metz had been founded in 1878 and drew its strength from a sturdy stock of Polish and German immigrants. By 1900 more than 600 families resided in and around the village of Metz. In addition to scores of neat

Photo courtesy Jesse Besser Museum

General view of the village of Metz after the great forest fire of 1908. The foundation of the Detroit & Mackinac Railway is in the foreground.

---

homes, this railroad shipping center also proudly sported a hotel, three general stores, a boarding house, a sawmill, livery stables, a blacksmith shop, plus a post office and train station.

The Detroit & Mackinac Railway was the town's focal point, for it not only brought business to town, but offered easy accommodations to both Cheboygan and Alpena as well. Two trains traveling in both directions stopped daily. The village was the hub of surrounding farm and lumbering areas.

Like many a Michigan frontier town, Metz gained a rowdy reputation. The saloons, which were only open to men, hosted lively discussions of crop prices and lumber markets, the telling of off-color tales and jokes, banter over individual hunting prowess and snickering over the many, wily, winsome ways of the ladies. Fights were commonplace, trouble-makers were evident.

Regardless, in no plausible or conceivable manner were the great fires of 1908 directed by the Almighty God as punishment for the proverbial barflies of the Metz saloons.

Pure and simple, it was the dry spell that proved to be the crux of the devastation that suddenly erupted October 15, 1908.

While no one can report with certainty exactly what caused the fire, Dr. Wm. W. Arscott, coroner for Presque Isle County, declared that the blaze originated from an out-of-control brush fire near Millersburg where workers were clearing land. Strong winds evidently upgraded this smoldering of debris into a full-fledged inferno cutting a swath some 30 miles long by three miles wide on a course that ended only when the flames reached the shores of Lake Huron. Then it is assumed that a sudden wind shift turned this conflagration westward, traveling toward the ill-fated village of Metz.

While on the surface this theory more or less points out a logical starting point for that terrible disaster, other sources reported the fire was mainly due to flying sparks passed off from a D&M passenger train.

Actually, we have no way of determining exactly what occurred that fateful afternoon. But actual accounts taken from *The Detroit News* remain as a legacy; a graphic description of just what took place that fateful day as flames warped metal track rails like jackstraws appeared in that paper, from a correspondent reporting directly from the scene:

News Correspondent Returns From The Scene And Reports...

MILLERSBURG, Oct. 16—The *Detroit News* correspondent has been on the scene of the Metz fire and has just returned (1 p.m). 15 men, women and children burned to death in the awful fate of the victims of the worst fire that this section ever knew.

These people were all on a train which tried to take them out of a town, Metz, most of which last night was a raging volcano. The train was in charge of Conductor Kinville, Engineer Foster and Brakeman Wm. Barrett and Fireman Art Lee. The train was made up at Metz late in the afternoon when the fate of the town was evident, and there was no other avenue of escape. The train was composed of eight or nine wooden cars, and one steel gondola. Into this open car were crowded 30 or 40 men, women and children with a mass of household effects. All went well for a mile or so out of Metz towards Posen and safety.

Then at Nowicki's siding the rails spread and the engine went into the road-bed and stopped. On either side of the track were piled immense quantities of cedar ties, posts and poles, hemlock bark and other inflammable forest products.

John Nowicki's house stood just back from the track. All these were a mass of flames close up to the track for 29 rods on either side.

The flames swept over the doomed train, setting it on fire, igniting the household goods in the car with the people. Many jumped and tried to make their way to safety, and most of these succeeded, although fearfully burned.

Three mothers and nine small children stayed in the steel car whose sides were red hot and they were cremated. Their remains were identified only by objects on their bodies which fire could not destroy.

Art Lee, the fireman, sought safety in the water tank on the engine, and was literally boiled to death. Wm. Barrett, the brakeman, died on the engine.

The charred remains of John Nowicki, Jr., were found on the road crossing the track just ahead of the engine. All the bodies were found except that of Mrs. John Nowicki, Jr. Conductor Kinville and Engineer Foster crawled down the track on to Posen and escaped, so badly burned that his recovery is doubtful. The others all escaped, some back to Metz, others into the open fields, but all badly burned. [84]

Rumors ran rampant from one small town to the next. Telegram reports dribbled in to railroad offices in Bay City, where officials nervously awaited the final confirmation and tabulation of the dead and dying. Newspaper accounts over the following days graphically brought tales of the death and destruction to the general population throughout all of Michigan. Each dawning day brought additional horror stories to examine until the flames were finally finished. A sampling follows:

Train Stopped In A "Hell Of Flame"

POSEN, Oct. 16—Arthur White, of Metz, one of the survivors of the fire, tells the *News* correspondent the following story of the disaster. "All went well until we reached a point about a mile out of Metz. Then we ran into a regular hell of flames and smoke, which swept over the open car, setting our clothes on fire and singeing our hair. All of a sudden the engine went off the track and we stopped right in the midst of a mass of flames which surrounded us. My brother and his little boy were next to me. He said we must get out of this. I lifted the lad over the side of the car and dropped him and got out myself. I couldn't find my brother, but I picked up the boy and struggled through the flames and smoke to an open field."[85]

☒☒☒☒☒

"300 On Train"
So Reports The R.R.—Many Missing

ALPENA, Mich., Oct.16—There must be a large number of people missing. At the Tawas headquarters of the line it is stated that there must have been about 300 people on the burned relief train.

Just before a south-bound train for Alpena pulled out of Posen this morning, George Boston, a Bay City traveling man, and three companions reached Posen in safety from the scene of the wreck. They had made their way through the smoke and flames with the air so thick that it was impossible to see 10 feet. Although all were considerably burned, they refused to come on to Alpena on the train, fearing a repetition of the dreadful experience which they had just been through. They are now at Posen, where it is thought there are also a number of others from the wrecked train.

☒☒☒☒☒

Trainmen Jump In Water Tank

BAY CITY, Mich., Oct.16—The latest information (10:30 a.m.) from the forest fire district along the Detroit & Mackinac Railway is to the effect that a relief train sent from Alpena last night to aid the people at Metz, 25 miles north of that place, was destroyed by flames and 16 people burned to death. The disaster remains to be confirmed.

According to a message received by D&M officers here, the train left Alpena, reached Metz, took the people and household goods on board, and started north toward Cheboygan. When the train reached Hawks Station it found fire on both sides of the track and was unable to proceed. It then started back, intending to go to Alpena with the sufferers. After passing Metz the train ran off the track near Pulaski, the fire having burned the ties and spread the rails.

The forests on both sides of the track were ablaze, and the train soon caught fire. There was no escape for the passengers, and they were burned to death.

The engineer and fireman took refuge in the water tank of the locomotive, but were soon forced to flee, and were also caught by the flames and burned to death. The Detroit & Mackinac officers are endeavoring to confirm this story.[86]

⊠⊠⊠⊠⊠

Alpena, Fighting To Save Itself, Awaits Return Of Rescue Train

ALPENA, Mich., Oct.16—Seventeen persons are known to be dead, and scores of others may have been lost in the forest fire which has swept across the D&M railway at Metz, Presque Isle County.

The dead are mostly women and children, though two trainmen are known to have perished. They burned up in a steel gondola car when the relief train of which it was a part left the rails and was trapped in what must have been a sea of flames. Some survivors have reached Posen, a station of the line about 30 miles from here. Posen appears to have marked the southern edge of this fire belt; Millersburg, the northern. A special train with coffins and a corps of doctors has been sent from here.

Section 4, Chapter 1
Metz —The Village Vanishes

It is now known positively that Fireman Arthur Lee and Brakeman William Barrett of the wrecked train perished in the flames while they were making an effort to escape.

Engineer William Foster and Conductor John Kinville were with the other men when the dash for liberty was made, and the latter succeeded in breaking through the fire district into the open, but their comrades were overcome by smoke and fell exhausted to the railroad track. Their dead bodies have been recovered.

Engineer Foster is terribly burned, is blind, and may not live. Station Agent J.E. Annis of Metz is in the same condition. It cannot be definitely learned how many perished in the fire which destroyed the relief train.

A telephone message from Posen states that 16 dead bodies have already been taken from the wreck, all of which are charred almost beyond recognition. A second relief train has been sent to the scene with food and medical assistance.

It is feared now that many lives were lost at Metz when the town burned, as all avenues of escape were cut off before midnight. Communication with Posen is cut off and details cannot be obtained until the relief train returns to the city.

Mr. and Mrs. Nowicki, an aged couple who lived in the village of that name, roasted alive in their little house near the railroad tracks.

The train which burned had been sent from Hawks Station to take out the people whose lives were threatened by the encroaching forest fire and the train was derailed by the spreading of the rails, due to heat.

What scenes of horror must have followed when the terror-stricken refugees found themselves helpless amid the fire from which they had been fleeing are not yet known from the lips of any survivor. Conductor Kinville and Engineer Foster managed to crawl into Posen early this morning on their hands and knees, both badly burned. Kinville is reported blind from his burns. No story has been obtained from them yet, owing to lack of wires. Only the bare report that they are alive and in the village has come out.

From Millersburg, about noon, came the first positive confirmation of the fate of at least a part of the train's passengers. It was but a brief statement. It said that 17 burned skulls had been found in the ruins of a gondola car, which made up part of the train, and that the body of Fireman Arthur Lee had been found in the water tank of the engine, where he had sought refuge and had perished. The report also said that a Mrs. Cicero, of Metz, and three of her children were among the dead. That is all which the anxious newspaper men and railroad officials were able to get over the wire from the village of Millersburg up to noon.

Wires are down in many places through the county and it may be several hours before anything additional can be learned from Millersburg. It is thought possible that there may have been only women and children and helpless persons placed aboard the relief train which met such a horrible fate and that some at least of the strong men of the hamlet may have stayed behind to fight for their homes.

The operating department of the Detroit & Mackinac Railroad at East Tawas has been unable thus far to secure any information except the tidings from Millersburg. The road has not yet received any statement from either the conductor or engineer who are at Posen. Neither have they been able to learn the fate of any of the little villages north of Millersburg on the line of the road.

The people were driven into the church this afternoon at Cathro, the only building left in the settlement. The minister and his family were driven out in their night clothes last night. More reports of farm buildings burned reach here hourly. No relief is in sight and a brisk wind is blowing. Tonight may add more fatalities to the list.

Alpena Fighting Flames

At Alpena the entire fire department and hundreds of volunteers are engaged in fighting the flames which are burning in the brush inside the city limits. The tannery and bark piles of Moench & Sons, worth many thousands of dollars, have been repeatedly threatened. Several fires were started in the downtown district, but were extinguished before they did any serious damage. Three large barns of Mr. L. J. Sylvester, in Green Township, were burned Thursday afternoon.

A huge pile of sawdust within the city limits at Cheboygan caught fire Thursday afternoon, endangering the whole city. The forest fires around the city are said to be the worst of the year. Several barns have been burned and many farm homes are threatened with destruction.

From West Branch, Caro, Mackinaw City, Gladwin, Standish, Traverse City and Lansing come reports of forest fires in the country around the cities.

Fires have also broken out in the Upper Peninsula. Foster City, which was once before menaced, is again reported in danger. A special train is sent to that place from Escanaba by the Chicago & Northwestern Railroad officials Thursday night to aid the fire fighters in the town. Flames are also devouring the timber around Menominee and the authorities at Ross reported Thursday night that the place would be wiped out unless help was received at once. An engine was sent from Menominee.[87]

Photo courtesy Jesse Besser Museum

Detroit & Mackinac Railway officials in the fatal steel gondola car in which 13 people perished.

These are the first reports of the Metz tragedy as they filtered in. The shock of them horrified the citizenry of Michigan. As the days passed, more details came forth, such as the following account from a Pontiac survivor of the rescue train disaster:

"We Lived In A Sea Of Flames!"

Frank Becker Tells His Experience in Getting Out of the Doomed Town Last Thursday Afternoon

PONTIAC, Mich., Oct. 17—Frank Becker, a traveling salesman for the Mascot Cigar Co., of this city, was one of the passengers on the ill-fated relief train that was wrecked between Metz and Posen. He arrived home this morning.

Photo courtesy Jesse Besser Museum

Heat from the fire of 1908 twisted the tracks of the Detroit & Mackinac Railway.

"No words can describe that awful night," he declared." I do not believe that any human beings ever went through a more terrifying experience and lived. It was only by sheer luck that I myself escaped.

"I was in Metz, which is one of the places that I make on my trips. All day Thursday the people were in a state of nervous apprehension over the forest fires which seemed to be on all sides. When the people from the surrounding country began to come fleeing in, abandoning their homes to the mercy of the flames, it seemed time to get out. The station agent sent for a relief train, and when it arrived about 5:30, we all hurried on board. There were about 40 or 45 people on board, I think.

Into the Roaring Flames

"When we had gone about a mile and a half from Metz we saw what seemed to be a veritable furnace ahead of us. The woods, which came close to the track, were a roaring mass of flames. It didn't seem possible

Photo courtesy Jesse Besser Museum

Heat from the fire not only twisted the tracks, it also melted and warped the train's steel wheels.

that we could get through, and the engineer stopped the train. But the flames were closing in back of us and there was no hope of going back. So he concluded to run for it. We covered up as best we could and breathed only when it was absolutely necessary.

"On we went through the roaring, crackling flames, which in some places were leaping clear across the track. The heat was awful. The steel car in which we were riding became almost unendurably hot. Just as it seemed that we couldn't endure it any longer, we came out into a clearing place.

"We went on, with the flames on both sides of the track, but not so close as to be dangerous. Then, when we were about half way to Posen, we saw another stretch of red flame leaping high against the sky squarely in front of us. The engineer stopped again. But on every side, no matter where you looked, there was the same angry red glare. The flames were creeping closer and closer, and there seemed no place to escape. We were in a sea of flames. He started the engine again and we dashed straight at the flames. I had my head covered up, but I could hear the crackling and roaring and feel the awful heat, when all at once there was a jar and we stopped. The engine had jumped the track. It was everyone for himself. We were right in the midst of a roaring mass of flames. The smoke was so thick that you couldn't see three feet in front of you. I wouldn't have given much for my chances of life that minute.

Heard Babies Wailing

"As I leaped from the car I could hear the wailing of little babies and the screams of women and children. My God! Those sounds are still ringing in my ears. Every time I dropped off to sleep last night I was awakened by those same shrill agonizing shrieks. But there was nothing that we could do. It was everyone for himself, and I wouldn't have given a plugged nickel for my own chances of life at that moment.

"Blindly staggering and groping my way through the choking smoke I ran a little way back down the track. The others had scattered in all directions.

"I saw a dark place in the inferno of flames, and kicking over a blazing fence, I made for it. It proved to be a small plowed field. I lay face downward in the plowed ground and thanked God for the relief from that choking, blinding smoke. I lay there for hours, scarcely daring to look up. I could hear others shouting around us, but I didn't know how many there were. Along about 3 o'clock in the morning the fire began to subside and the smoke to clear a little. I looked around and found that there were nearly 30 in the field. We were the only ones who escaped.

"We who had escaped went back to the train, which was a smoking mass of twisted iron. Many of the women and children lay charred, blackened corpses in the steel car. Some of them were the wives and children of men in our party, and the grief of these men was something awful. We found the fireman in the tender of the engine, literally scalded to death. The coal in the tender had caught fire, boiling him alive. We walked on down the track and two miles down we found the engineer, burned to death. I don't know his name, but he was a brave man.

"I lost everything I had but the clothes on my back, but I think I am the luckiest man in the United States. I escaped with scarcely a burn."[88]

When the fire came into the village that long past Thursday of October 15th, many families were scattered—some had been out of town on business, while others departed on the ill-fated rescue train. Children, fortunately, had been dismissed from school. Now Metz stood directly in the path of the wind-driven, out-of-control fires.

St. Peter's German Lutheran church was the first structure ablaze. Next, the piles of hardwood ignited. These stood a mere 70 feet west from one of the town's stores, which also quickly burst into flames. One by one, homes and businesses were consumed by fire—the sawmill, saloons, train station,

Nowicki's Hotel, livery stables, Centala Brothers, Hardie Brothers and Konieczny Stores.

In less than three hours time, Metz had vanished.

One of the last men to leave the doomed community was the assistant D&M station agent, George Cicero. The employee kept the telegraph wires open while alerting a train that was ready to flee from nearby LaRoque. He kept them informed of developments until the flames were nearly touching the depot.

Cicero was tagged a hero by *The Detroit News*, in a story with headlines full of pathos:

FIRE HERO STAYS: LOVED ONES PERISH

George Cicero, The Last Man Out Of Metz, Reaches Posen, To Learn Wife And Two Children Are Lost

Assistant Station Agent in Town Which Was Vortex of the Forest Fire, Drove With Son Through Woods After Town was Gone

ALPENA, Mich., Oct. 17—The last man out of roaring, seething, doomed Metz was George Cicero, Assistant Station Agent and Baggagemaster at the little station. "I can send no more, this building is all afire." This was the last message that came out of Metz. Cicero sent it and then, with one of his three children, a little boy, fled through the burning forests to Posen.

His heart was high with hope, for had he not placed his wife and two other little ones on the train? They would be at Posen when he arrived, he kept telling the boy as they plunged along. When he reached Posen they told him: "The train was burned. Your wife and children were burned up."

George Cicero is the heroic, pitiable figure that arises above the dead level of grief and wretchedness which has its scene here today and in the refugee camp at Posen.

Cicero—wan, haggard, but still full of nerve—told his story to the *News* correspondent here this noon, and while he talked he had one arm around the shoulders of the boy he had saved. They are all that is left of the family. This is what he said:

"Thinking that my wife and children would get safely away I waited to see if nothing could be done to save the depot. Fire was then consuming dwellings on the outskirts of the village, and soon after the train had gone I realized that my task was hopeless. As building after building went down before the flames I was at a loss for some moments what action to take. I saw flames leap from one building to another, and soon they were on the depot. It was my only chance to make a dash for safety, and taking my young son, the only one I have left, into the buggy with me, I lashed my horse through seven miles of burning forest towards Posen. As we drove at a breakneck speed I was encouraged at the thought that my wife and children would be awaiting me at Posen and one cannot imagine the terrible shock I received when upon reaching the station found that the train had been wrecked and my wife and little ones had perished in the flames."

The bodies of Mrs. Cicero and the children were brought to this city last night, and will be buried Monday in the same casket, a tiny box which would hold the body of a two-year-old babe. Their bodies, as was the case of all in the gondola, were burned to a crisp, and were identified only by the number in each family and by certain pieces of jewelry they wore.

All survivors of the disaster have practically the same terrible story to tell of the suffering woman and children, and it seems strange to many here, making all due allowance, that the men did not assist them from the death trap instead of fleeing to the woods.

The fact cannot be suppressed that it is being said that had the men given five minutes of their time to the women and children all or most of them would have been saved from a horrible death. The survivors state that they had no time to assist the women, and were scarcely able to reach a place of safety themselves, after acting as quickly as they did.[89]

These 1908 newspaper accountings certainly were insensitive, to say the least. How dreadful for survivors to read of loved ones being "cremated," "burned to a crisp," "boiled alive," their "ashes fit in a 2-quart jar."

Another tragic element of the previous article is the pointing of fingers at the men riding the disastrous rescue train.

The Detroit News printed many eyewitness reports of tragedies, heroic deeds, almost unbelievable escapes and ever-increasing tales of death and destruction:

Boy Refugee With Sister's Remains In Handkerchief

MILLERSBURG, Mich., Oct. 19—One young woman who narrowly escaped being caught in the trap set by the forest fires relates an interesting story. She is Miss Cassie Nowland, of this place, and at the time the flames broke out afresh near Metz, she was teaching school, a quarter of a mile from Metz. She had 26 pupils, little ones, in her charge. Her story follows:

"At recess, 2:30 p.m., it began to get smoky, but no fires were in sight. The doors blew open and I saw a small fire in the field. In 20 minutes the woods all around were in flames. Still I did not realize the danger. About four o'clock Mrs. Grambau came into the school house exhausted. I dismissed school and we sang the closing song. Grambau told the children to hurry home, but they could only get to the neighbors. We started home only a quarter of a mile and could hardly face the wind. Soon we heard of the burning of Metz. Sparks were now flying through the air and the men were working hard to save the place.

"About 6 p.m. the houses of two neighbors burned and the heat and smoke were so intense that all of us women had to go into the cellar. Refugees from the fires began to come in. They had escaped by lying in the plowed fields. At 7 p.m. two men came in from the wreck of the relief train. They had a terrible time getting through the woods. All through the night people kept coming. At 2 a.m. a boy by the name of Dost brought the charred remains of his little sister in a handkerchief. His father and mother were with us. It was awful, their grief. Then one of their little girls, carrying a baby, got there. Her skirts were burned off and her hands and face badly burned. We made coffee for the people all night—there must have been a hundred of them. It was a terrible experience and I never, never want to go through another like it."[90]

☒☒☒☒☒

Finds Wife And Children Among Dead In The Road

ROGERS CITY, Mich., Oct. 19—After a three-day fight with the flames Rogers City is at last free from the danger. Not a house or store in town was injured and the brewery which was reported lost is untouched.

To east and west, however, the flames did untold damage. On the west side the fire burned along the lake shore beyond the life saving station, 16 miles from here. East conditions are as bad.

The most awful tragedy in the section happened Thursday night when the flames swept suddenly upon the lumber camp of Herman Erke.

Mrs. Erke and four of her children were in the camp, together with three lumbermen, John Saup, Leo Busch and John Grosinsky. Erke was in Rogers City.

The story of the flight from camp toward the shore of the lake is told graphically by John Grosinsky, the sole survivor...

"It was about 8 o'clock, Thursday night," said Grosinsky, as his head and hands were swathed in bandages. The skin of his face a horrible brown and one eye nearly closed. "I was preparing for bed. Suddenly the smoke grew thicker and in a few minutes I could see the red glare through the trees. The fire made a terrible noise as it rushed on our camp. We grabbed the children and rushed for Lake Huron, about a mile away. We ran as fast as we could go, but the fire beat us. The smoke choked us. We just managed to keep the trail. I had one of the kids in my arms. I don't know which one, perhaps it was the baby. I don't know. All of a sudden there was an awful puff of fire. I could see the others fall on their faces, but I kept on. I dropped the baby somewhere I guess. All I remember is that I ran into a little clearing and fell down and stayed there till they found me."

The children ranged in age from 2 to 12 years. Of the family of seven, only two survived—Herman Erke and his eldest daughter, who is away at school. The Erke victims were buried Sunday afternoon in an inland cemetery five miles from town.[91]

☒☒☒☒☒

Victims Buried Without Even Sheet To Cover Them

ALPENA, Mich., Oct. 19—At Metz today was enacted a pathetic scene as in the churchyard the bodies of Mrs. Edward Hardies and her three children and Robert Wagner, victims of the terrible forest fires, were laid at rest. Two graves were dug close together and two rough wooden boxes sufficed for all that remained of the four people.

Mrs. Hardies and her children were placed in the same improvised coffin, which contained only a few charred bones when the cover was nailed on it. Their remains were not uncovered at the grave. The large party of mourners who accompanied the funeral cortege to the grave bared their heads as the service was read, and just before the internment was made, Miss Rose Wagner, sister of the dead boy, insisted that the box containing his body be opened that she might have a last look at the unfortunate young man. It was then that the pathetic side of the scene developed.

The girl was the only relative of the dead boy who was able to attend the funeral. The parents, Mr. and Mrs. Fred Wagner, are confined to their home in a seriously burned condition. When the box was opened a terrible spectacle was presented. The rough box contained the body of the dead boy just as he had been picked up in the field near his home after the fire swept through, killing him and nearly resulting in the death of his parents.

There was not a stitch of clothing on the body except a pair of shoes partially burned away. His hands were over his face just as he had placed them as protection against the terrific heat. His flesh was burned terribly and as the mourners viewed the remains they were forced to tears. That this unfortunate boy was not properly cared for before burial was not the fault of his people. They had not even a sheet in which to wrap the body, so completely was their property destroyed.

This condition did not exist at the Wagner home alone, but in almost every home in Metz Township. There are not a dozen sheets in the township. The graves of the dead are located at the rear of the German Lutheran church—now destroyed.[92]

Further information surfaced after publication of the preceding article. The Rev. Ernest Thieme, the Lutheran pastor of the Metz parish, reported the terrible, horrifying scene that greeted him at the Wagner home: "Barns and granary were gone but the house was standing. In the house I viewed what I could hardly bear, it was so terrible. The elder Wagner sat on a chair, with his head all bandaged. That part of his face which showed appeared to be charred. His sunken eyes appeared feverish and looked like stars. He held his burned hands straight out from his body. An old lady's dress hung from his shoulders and covered his nakedness. His legs were also covered with bandages.

"Next to him, on his left, in a corner lay his wife in an even worse condition. Her face was also badly burned and her nostrils burned away. She had deep burns on her whole body. One hand was almost entirely destroyed by the fire and on the other one the fingers were badly burned. Her back was covered with burns and her burned soles were cut from her feet. At that very moment their son was lying dead on the roadway and I felt it would be an act of mercy if the Lord removed them from this vale of sorrow."[93]

Still later reports indicated that both of these terribly burned fire victims lived, although Mrs. Wagner eventually lost both feet and her right hand.

Refugee From Fire Nearly Drowns Trying To Escape Flames

CHEBOYGAN—Ernest Robbins was brought here from Mackinaw City where he was let off a passing boat. Robbins was working in the woods 20 miles south of here, when he found himself surrounded by fire and only one way out. That was by Lake Huron, in front of him. He knew where an old flat-bottomed boat was lying on the beach, and made his way through smoke and fire to reach it, burning off most of his hair and badly burning his eyes. A heavy wind took him out into the lake and he was soon out of sight of land and the blazing woods. Tossed around all night on Lake Huron, his boat was sighted this morning by a passing freighter, and Robbins was taken aboard.[94]

As may be expected, a miracle or two occurred during the Metz disaster. One such incident was described in a later edition of *The Detroit News:*

Father's Refusal To Leave Home Saved His Children

Persistent refusal to yield to the pleadings of his children to place them aboard the rescue train, leaving the burning Village of Metz, saved the family of John Zimmerman who with his five children arrived Monday afternoon at the home of his brother, Henry, #12 Plum Street. With them came the two little daughters of Mrs. Edward Hardies, rescued by the merest accident from the steel gondola car in which their mother lost her life.

...The two Hardies children, Theresa and Louise, were in the ill-fated gondola car with their mother when the car left the track and the awful holocaust began. They escaped by clinging to the coat of a man who was jumping from the car. Stunned by the fall, little Louise was lying on the ground, while Theresa, a year older, groped her way to a clearing, where she was afterwards found by her cousin.

Stumbling along in the blinding smoke and heat beside the train, Edward Hardies felt something that yielded beneath his foot. He stooped and snatched up the body of little Louise and succeeded in getting her also to a place of safety. His return was cut off and his wife and other children perished.[95]

Metz—An Ascent From Ashes

The numerous period newspaper articles presented here have afforded the reader the feeling of actually living through this era, experiencing the pathos of that unfortunate time and place when a holocaust ravaged this small, quiet village on that fateful day in mid- October, causing Metz to vanish from the face of the earth.

Almost immediately relief began to pour in to aid the hapless fire victims. The restoration and rebuilding of the town was underway. People from all over Michigan contributed money for the homeless, the destitute and the injured. But I am sorry to say greed, too, played a small role during this unfortunate happenstance. Human nature is like that, isn't it?

Metz—An Ascent From Ashes

Photo courtesy Jesse Besser Museum

A street scene in Metz, before the fire of 1908.

When the Village of Metz vanished into oblivion, all that remained were ashes, charred ruins and smoking rubble. The only building still standing was St. Dominic's Catholic church, which actually was positioned just out of town to the southwest. Additionally, the stone steps from the German-Lutheran church were visible, marking where St. Peter's once proudly stood. By and large, the village liberty pole survived the fire as well, although the halliards were burned off. The cocky weathervane at the top of the pole remained in working order pointing out wind direction for whoever had a need to know.

By now, the victims of the great fire were recorded at perhaps 26 to 27 lives lost (later figures recorded 29 people died). A total of 83 families were burned out and perhaps 1,500 people proved to be either homeless or in dire need of food, supplies or money. The situation was grim. While survivors searched the nearby woods and farmland for corpses, many townsmen felt that unknown fatalities may have also occurred in deeper forests at isolated logging camps.

The Metz fire was not simply a localized conflagration. We already have learned that the blaze may have started near Millersburg and traveled toward Lake Huron, only to double back again, aimed in a westerly direction. During the course of days, fire also threatened the towns of South Rogers, Nagel's Corner, Hagensville, Hammond's Bay, Cathro and Liske. The Detroit News reported fire conditions across the state:

Incident Of The Fires

> WEST BRANCH, Mich., Oct. 17—The forest fires have assumed most alarming proportions. The city is hemmed in on three sides. The Michigan Central railroad has taken all cars possible out of the branches and is sending an engine and cars to bring out the household goods of all people in danger. Train crews are stationed at different points along the line instructed to be ready at a moment's notice. West of the city is a piece of timber containing hundreds of acres of hardwood which is burning fiercely. Two small towns on the branch railroad running out of the place are out of provisions and are not able to have trains bring in their supplies. Four men have gone blind from the effects of the smoke.[96]

☒☒☒☒☒

PETOSKEY, Mich., Oct. 17—A summer resort near Conway is threatened with destruction, forest fires creeping upon all sides. A pall of smoke hangs over Bayview, the big Methodist resort, but fires are not near enough to cause anxiety. At Pellston fires are held in check in wood and refuse piles. Engines and apparatus have been sent from Charlevois, Harbor Springs and Petoskey. East of Brutus, the fires are sweeping towards Riggsville.[97]

☒☒☒☒☒

CHEBOYGAN, Mich., Oct.17—This city is in no danger. The heaviest loss is in the standing timber of M.D. Olds, on the Huron shore south of the city. An immense tract of hardwood burned over, destroying the new camps being built. The men escaped with only their clothes, and one horse, being driven out last night at midnight, and compelled to run to the lake shore.

Lakeside resort has been burned, the groves and cottages. County farmers are saving their homes, but all the stuff in the woods has burned. The Indian Reservation south of Mullet Lake has burned over and the Indians are homeless.[98]

☒☒☒☒☒

HARRISVILLE, Mich., Oct. 20—A message was received this morning from Deputy Warden Fred Beede, of Harrisville, seat of Alcona County, asking for help. Beede declares that the situation is so critical that a shift in the wind will mean the destruction of the town.

"Fire surrounds us on three sides," says the deputy. "So far the wind has blown continually off the lake. That is all that has saved us. If it ever shifts, the town is doomed. The people here have been up day and night for a week, and they are completely worn out. Unless they have assistance soon, they will have to give up the fight and abandon the town. If men were sent up here to help us they could save human lives and property every day." [99]

☒☒☒☒☒

BLACK RIVER, Mich., Oct. 21—The fire situation in Alcona Township is alarming. B.D. Nicholson has lost his barn and his entire crops together with all his farm machinery. Clarence Scriber's farm house was destroyed and the family barely escaped with their lives. While the people extended temporary help, something will have to be done to tide them over during the coming winter.

Black River, a station on the D&M, has been saved by the most heroic measures, and is still surrounded with fire. Unless rain comes soon it is in great danger of being wiped out. Everyone is a fire fighter, and for the last week it has been constant fighting to keep the flames from invading the village. Thousands of dollars worth of forest products are piled along the tracks.[100]

☒☒☒☒☒

SAULT STE. MARIE, Mich., Oct. 17—Nine towns in Chippewa County were saved by heroic effort, and each had a population of from one to five hundred. They are Rudyard, Soo Junction, Trout Lake, Brimley, Bay Mills, West Neebish, Detour, Raber and Gatesville. In response to an appeal from Point Iroquois, the government tug *Aspen* left to go to the assistance of the lighthouse crew who had been fighting the flames for hours. The last message stated that the lighthouse might be destroyed, as the woods were like a roaring furnace.

Settlers near Whitefish Pointe are seeking the shore of Lake Superior as the flames approach their homes.[101]

As the days passed and reports of havoc wrought by the many fires statewide came in, it was apparent help would be needed—lots of help. And the sooner the better.

Photo courtesy Jesse Besser Museum

Survivors of the Metz Fire receiving supplies brought in by the Detroit & Mackinac Railway.

Almost immediately, friends and relatives provided temporary shelter to the scores of misplaced persons. The Detroit & Mackinac Railway quickly followed suit by clearing tracks of debris so that Red Cross relief trains could be scheduled.

So many supplies were needed, especially at Metz. Temporary shelters had to hastily be erected. People needed food, for here once again, only a two-day supply was in evidence. Horses, cows and other livestock as well simply had to have hay and grain. Lumber, building supplies and tools were scarce. Clothing was desperately required. Farm implements, furniture, stove and basic kitchen utensils rounded out the list still further.

Fortunately, relief came from all over Michigan. Contributions were gathered at Alpena and the D&M railroad delivered the goods to Metz. The National Guard was ordered in to help distribute relief supplies and to keep order.

However, a few individuals took advantage of the situation. Sad to say, reports came from Posen that some burned out farmers returned several times for additional goods.

In yet one other instance, a schoolhouse saved from the flames because it was located well away from Metz was not thrown open to serve as a shelter for those unfortunate burned out victims who had little more to warm them than the clothes on their backs. Reasons given were that the people in charge felt the school would lose its operating money if the building were used for any other purpose than holding classes for the students. These individuals should have thrown caution to the wind and opened those school doors, offered what food was available, clothing and bedding, providing temporary shelter at least for a day or two when matters were at their absolute worst.

Within a week Metz was, like a Phoenix, rising from its ashen grave. Temporary buildings were quickly framed and covered with rough siding, forming shelters for the homeless. Business places sprung up as well—first a post office was erected, then a depot, a freight shed and general store. Two-family shacks were designed to see some families through the coming winter. Undoubtedly they were crowded, but they served a need. People were thankful.

Reportedly, the only adverse whisper in the village during these days of reconstruction was, "beer!" With the reputation the town had attained, none of the men wanted to openly request a bit of the spirits. But once again human nature took over and before long any working man wanting a drink could find one to satisfy his thirst.

One other problem that confronted these brave Michigan people in their need of reconstruction was that so many fire claims were presented that several of the insurance companies, including the Presque Isle County Mutual Insurance Company, went broke—belly-up, absolutely stripped of funds. As a result, many of these turn-of-the-century settlers were forced to literally start life anew—from scratch.

The Detroit News reported how Michigan citizens rallied around people and entire communities in need:

Big Camp Of Fire Refugees Near Metz Calls For Help

Relief in Form of Food and Clothing Being Gathered in Alpena and Other Cities

ALPENA, Mich., Oct. 17—Relief from all sides is pouring in for the refugees from the burned villages of Metz, Bolton and South Rogers. They are camped in the open fields near Posen.

The churches of this city have united in sending out their members to canvass the town in quest of clothing and provisions for the suffers. Relief headquarters have been established in the Temple Theater, where the goods will be taken for distribution.

The relief committee is busy ascertaining who the deserving are, and clothing will be handed out to those who lost their all in the forest fires. The D&M railroad officials are doing everything in their power to relieve the suffering. They are transporting provisions and clothing, and taking a keen interest in the welfare of the destitute people.[102]

☒☒☒☒☒

ALPENA, Mich., Oct. 19—The north wind brought chilly weather, which is particularly trying to the Metz refugees. They are sadly in need of warm underclothing, shoes and stockings, bedding and stoves. The food supply is sufficient for a few days, but no longer. Lumber has been sent, but more is needed. Tools are scarce. Cooking pots are few. Hay and grain for the remaining horses and cattle must be procured. In the immediate vicinity of Metz there are 81 families without homes, nearly all penniless and in want. They average five persons to a family. There are others in Posen, a few in Rogers City and several others at various places along the D&M line.[103]

☒☒☒☒☒

Michigan Rises To The Succor Of The Fire Sufferers
Detroit Will Give $15,000

What is for convenience called the Metz district fire—the Presque Isle, Montmorency and Alpena county blaze—has burned itself out, advancing from the west to Lake Huron. Rogers City and Alpena are safe.

In the Metz district the known dead number 26, but estimates run as high as 50. The number of persons burned out and practically destitute in the refugee camps at Posen, Metz, LaRoque, Onaway and other towns appears to be about 3,500 to date. Gov. Warner is at Metz. Flint, Saginaw, Battle Creek, Bay City, Port Huron and many other cities out in the state report relief plans. The relief movement is well under way. Public meetings have been held in Detroit and other cities and already carloads of provisions, clothing, stoves and other supplies are on the way north. Detroit plans to contribute $15,000 in cash and supplies.

The Red Cross in Detroit is taking up offerings of clothing and cash.[104]

☒☒☒☒☒

Hungry Hundreds Flock In To Meet The Relief Train

News Correspondents Describe Pitiful Scenes When the First Car Reached Scene of Big Fire

Oct. 20—Relief trains are rapidly delivering clothing, food, lumber, fodder, furniture, bedding and cooking utensils, as well as cash, to those of the families of the north, who have been made destitute by the forest fires.

Thus far the relief appears to have gotten well going only in the district immediately contiguous to Metz. This includes Posen and LaRoque, the little stations on each side of Metz. Meantime, refugees continue to flock in from the back country of Presque Isle, Alpena, Ogemaw and Montmorency counties, and reports indicate that the supplies are not arriving fast enough. The hamlets of the back country have not yet been reached.

...Detroit, Grand Rapids and every other city and town in the state, seemingly, is getting supplies together, and carloads have already gone forward.

Relief from the cold, which has caused so much discomfort to the homeless victims of the fire-swept district, is promised by the weather forecasters, and is already in sight.[105]

☒☒☒☒☒

How They Stormed The First Car Of Supplies

METZ, Mich., via Alpena, Oct. 20—The carload of merchandise contributed by Bay City brought the first outside relief to the fire district and also gave what was most needed, clothing. When the car arrived at Metz yesterday it was fairly torn open by the D&M officials, while a crowd of ragged, hopeless-appearing victims, moving like wraiths in the early morning mist and shivering in their insufficient clothing, crushed eagerly about the car door. Clothing was first handed to the women and there was not an article that was not needed and not nearly enough to supply all. The women fared better than the men.

Just as Supt. Luce's special was about to pull out he noticed a man without a coat, vest or hat. Without a word, the railroad superintendent handed the shivering man his own coat, hat and vest. Word that a new car had come spread rapidly and soon trains began arriving. Hour after hour the increasing stream kept up. Many women wept as clothing and food was handed out. Parcels of food were opened and eagerly eaten. By noon the cars from Bay City and Alpena were exhausted.

While it is a fact that the railroad executives answered the calls of the needy perhaps quicker than most other agencies, the Red Cross quickly followed their humanitarian efforts. This organization was responsible for quickly erecting a number of 12 x 12-foot shacks to temporarily house refugees. They also instructed Father Kaplanowski of St. Dominic's Parish to distribute food and materials to the people of Metz.

Governor Fred Warner visited the reconstruction scene. Upon his return to Lansing, he set up the State Fire Relief Commission, which became responsible for handling future distribution of goods and monies. At a much later date, this commission reported that some 4,615 members of 930 families had received relief throughout the vast fire district.[106]

Incomplete reports placed the area burned in 1908 at 2,369,067 acres, the damage at $2,570,446, and the cost of fire fighting at $61,287.

One other interesting historical fact that surfaced during research is that the D&M railroad officials demanded an inquest be held in order to determine any responsibility for the deaths. The results of this coroner's jury were reported on October 23, 1908 and the railroad was totally exonerated—no way, could they be held accountable for the loss of life or resulting devastation. It was declared "An Act of God!"

"God Punished Us," Say People Who Bore Bad Reputation

ALPENA, Mich, Oct. 21—(From a Detroit News correspondent) "God Punished us," the people of Metz are saying today. "We have been wicked and He sent the fire for a punishment."

For some time Metz has had the reputation of being a "tough" town. Posen was once considered worse than Metz, but of late years it has calmed down, while its neighboring town, with three saloons and a hotel bar and a bottle of whiskey in many a house, has fallen heir to its bad reputation.

"Life was safe enough in Metz," said one man who is familiar with the place. "It was a bad town, nevertheless, and all on account of liquor. There was little immorality, but the men would get drunk and pound each other and rap visitors over the head with beer bottles if they refused to buy. Nobody wanted to stay there overnight."

There has been no liquor in Metz since Thursday, and as a consequence the people have worked hard to arrange comfortable quarters for themselves. Some are grumbling because there is no beer, but a good many will probably pass up strong drink for a considerable period in view of their belief in the judgment of a wrathful Deity.

A rumor circulated among the refugees yesterday morning that Metz is haunted and that the ghosts of the dead women and children burned in the gondola were heard howling among the ruins. The wind was quite high and rushed through the bare trees with a whistling noise not unlike the gibbering that spooks are supposed to engage in when they desire to express their feelings. The superstition is not hampering the rebuilding of the town.[107]

Was Metz an immoral town? Did the ghosts of the dead women and children really haunt the barren countryside? Or was Metz exactly like almost every other Michigan village during that era; one perhaps filled with likable and unlikable people—some good, some bad, some religious, some not? Let's let the ashes of the past lie as they may, but let's never forget the horror of Metz or the terrible holocaust that reduced this once bustling village to naught but ashes.

Devastation Beyond Metz

As horrible as the Metz disaster proved to be, Metz was not the entire story. Fire swept other northeastern counties of Michigan as well. Alpena was in and out of danger as was Presque Isle County including Rogers City and Hammond Bay at the mouth of the Ocqueoc River.

Hundreds of townspeople spent night and day working almost around the clock to keep the fiery reaper from their doorsteps. In this chapter we will learn of fire danger that threatened other villages, towns and farming and logging areas above and beyond Metz itself.

After the tragedy with the Metz rescue train, many people were afraid to board similar disaster trains to safety. Can you blame them?

Devastation Beyond Metz

Although this great disaster in Presque Isle County was named after the town and township of Metz, which bore the brunt of it, it also raged over a vast area covering a great deal of northeastern Michigan, and in the end, was stopped only at the shore of mighty Lake Huron. Estimates at a later date, figured these fires destroyed about 2.5 million acres, making it one of the largest forest fires in the modern history of Michigan.

A fine booklet titled *The Metz Fire of 1908*, written by the late Herbert Nagel and published by the Presque Isle County Historical Society, offers additional insight into what took place in surrounding communities while the village of Metz held the news spotlight:

Devastation And Danger In Other Sections Of The County

It was Metz Township that bore the brunt of the conflagration, sustaining the greatest loss of life, property loss, and other casualties, yet the townships of Belknap and Pulawski were also hard hit. Over thirty farmsteads were completely destroyed in these townships.

The gale winds that drove the fires in the southwestern part of Presque Isle County through the tinder-filled forests in a five-mile-wide swath in the direction of Metz, also swept fire into Case and Allis townships and made an assault on the village of Millersburg that fateful October 15.

Citizens of Rogers City, too, battled to save their village as the fires blazing through the county reached the forests around the village.

Devastation Beyond Metz

The forest acreage that burned so swiftly through the various sections of the county amounted to hundreds of square miles, most of them uninhabited except for logging camp personnel. There were many camps in every part of the county, at the mercy of the fire. Typical was the Meredith Camp, located about five miles southwest of Metz, on the north branch of the Thunder Bay River. The Meredith family saved themselves in the river, but their camp was destroyed.

Incidents At South Rogers

South Rogers, like many other way stations along the D&M Railroad, was a small cluster of business places and homes. It was located a few miles west of Metz and there you could get the stage to Rogers City, which still had no railroad. The stage also carried the mail to and from Rogers City and the railroad. Forest products and farm produce were loaded at South Rogers for shipment.

The village was platted and high hopes were held for its continued growth, but, as with Metz, those hopes were shattered that same October day as the little settlement was swept away by the flames.

Shortly thereafter, a D&M engine and crew approached the area while patrolling the track in the wake of the Metz fire. Crewmen saw four small children crouching in the ditch beside the track, one only about six months old, as they sought protection from the flames and smoke. The men took them aboard the engine, then learned that the mother of the little refugees had returned to their home, which was still standing, to save something. They found her overcome by smoke, lying in a field. They took them all to a safe area and so saved one family.

Bordering South Rogers to the north was a farm whose owner had a large wind-driven grist mill. He decided that morning of October 15 that he would grind grain. The strong steady wind that was blowing made it an ideal day for the job. The story told around the countryside over the years was that he continued grinding away, in spite of the great danger his buildings and those of his neighbors were in. His buildings caught fire and house, barns and windmill were lost. He believed one must grind when the wind is favorable, so stuck to his task to the last.

A Dignified Retreat

Another odd little event took place at the Prell School, a little one-room country school about two miles northwest of the village of Metz, as the crow flies, and a mile north of South Rogers.

Hattie Nagel, now Hattie White, of Rogers City, was a pupil at this school and was in attendance on October 15, 1908. In 1979 she related her recollections of that day:

"School was in session until early afternoon. At that time, a man hurriedly entered the school and advised our teacher to dismiss the children. He said a terrible forest fire was swiftly coming this way. He cautioned the children who lived in the direction of Metz or South Rogers not to return to their homes, but to go in the opposite direction to the St. Michael Church area, and their families would follow.

"After he left, our teacher did not immediately dismiss the school. She asked us to pick up our songbook called the 'Knapsack.' The song she chose for us to sing was 'Row, Row, Row Your Boat, Gently Down the Stream.' She then dismissed us in her usual orderly manner, fire or no fire!

"I lived about a mile north of school and when I arrived home my father had horses and wagon ready. My mother had given birth to a baby girl a few days before and my father had made a bed of hay in the wagon box and covered it with a blanket. He carried my mother and baby to this bed. Then, with me and my brother on board, we set out for my aunt's home near Nagel's Corner.

"My father returned home to try and save our buildings and the neighbors'. We did not see him again for days. Our home was saved, although the fire crossed the road only a quarter-mile away, into our woods, only hours after we left."

John Lewis

John Lewis was a resident of the town of Hammond Bay, a logging town near the mouth of the Ocqueoc River in Presque Isle County. He operated a saw and shingle mill there.

A busy place in the 1890s—and a rowdy one, with three saloons—the village had no reason for being after the timber was gone and by 1908 most of the residents had moved away.

It was home to John Lewis at the time of the big fire, however, and on October 15 he was driving his rig, with a fast pair of horses, to the town of Metz. This is his story, as told to the Millersburg newspaper, the *Presque Isle County News:*

"I had business at Metz and reached town about six o'clock in the evening. Everything was on fire, the flames raging through the hardwoods and slashings with a vehemence and force I never imagined possible.

"I was only able to penetrate to the outskirts. One house lay in ruins and another close by was blazing. I had picked up a farmer who lived south of Metz who was trying to get home to see what had become of his family. I left him here, trying to get through on foot, frantic with anxiety.

"Seeing there was no use remaining, I turned back. The big Lutheran church was in ruins. I now hoped to get to Hagensville, north of Metz. On the first mile I saw only two houses still standing. I met a farmer and he told me of the many farmsteads that were destroyed, along with crops, forest products, etc.

"On going a little farther, I soon saw I would not be able to get to Hagensville, as both sides of the road were encased in flames, so I turned back and by a different road, through Belknap township, finally arrived in Moltke at the town hall.

"Never in my life, and I went through the famous fire of 1881 in the Thumb of Michigan, did I see such flames. They raced through meadow and timber with equal ease. The tremendous wind simply lifted them along, leaving a black and smoking ruin sending out now and then a handful of sparks. Fences and telegraph poles burned as if soaked in oil."

At Moltke Mr. Lewis was told that Millersburg had burned to the ground. However, he decided to go there anyway and finally managed to get through by a grist mill owned by a man named August Luft. It was situated on the Ocqueoc River near what is now M-68, and the Crow Dam, an abandoned sawmill and logging settlement nearby, at which every building was destroyed but one. He drove though a blackened ruin, reaching Millersburg at one o'clock in the morning, his eyes in very bad condition from smoke.

Such was his story, as related in the Millersburg *News*. Nothing was reported, in the paper, about the condition of his horses. They had carried him from the burning town of Metz, through the back roads of the townships of Belknap, Moltke, Ocqueoc and Case on a seven-hour trip through this eerie night. He must have breathed a sigh of relief as he approached Millersburg and saw that the town was still standing. Though the rumors that he had heard proved to be untrue, it was true that Millersburg had fought for her life that day and it was very much in doubt at times whether she would survive.

A Place Of Refuge

The southeast corner of Belknap Township, north of South Rogers and Metz, was in very grave danger. There were many farms there, as well as the hamlet of Hagensville, all in the path of the oncoming fire.

Except for many of the men, who remained to protect their buildings, if possible, most of the people fled. The women, children and old folks, with a few belongings, walked or traveled by horse and wagon to a location in Belknap known locally as "Nagel's Corner." There stood St. Michael's Lutheran Church, to which most of them belonged. In addition there were a parochial school, parsonage, Nagel's Store and outbuildings, a sawmill, town hall and several farm homes and barns. About sixty people spent the night of October 15 there.

The woods of a nearby farmer to the south were set afire in a backfire operation to reduce the impact of the inferno coming from the southwest, and so protect the church and surrounding countryside. All farms in the county had large woodlands that were usually connected with others, thus giving fire a continuous pathway.

The backfiring helped as the nearest tinder had been burned in a smaller fire. The main fire snaked its way swiftly along to the south of the area, having been cheated of some of its prey. It went in the direction of Hagensville, then on to Rogers and Pulawski townships, and thence to Lake Huron.

A resident who was a small girl at the time, living about a mile north of the church, said what she remembered most about the night were the terrible smoke, the red sky, and, most of all, the ringing and ringing of the church bells.

The next day it was learned that most of the homes the people had fled had been saved. The men who remained at home had spent the night wetting down roofs, putting out small fires caused by burning debris flying through the air, and watching their own wooded acres being laid waste before their eyes. There were others who, even by their greatest efforts, could not save their homes, and so were added to the many homeless ones. However, no lives were lost in the South Rogers or Hagensville areas.

Rogers City

In 1908, the village of Rogers City had a population of about seven hundred. Nestled on the shore of Lake Huron, it was closely confined on three sides by the forest, predominantly evergreens. The shipping of forest products from the surrounding area and the manufacture of products made of wood were the main industries. Wood was everywhere. Rogers City seemed a certain setup for destruction if the raging forest fire of October 15 came near.

The *Presque Isle County Advance* reported that the first awareness of the peril Metz was in came with the news that a train was being assembled to rescue Metz settlers. The townspeople at Rogers City realized that they, too, must exert great effort if they were to be spared.

They made good use of the hours before the storm reached them. They hauled hundreds of barrels of water and stationed them along the forest roads that circled the town, with pails at each one. In some places, they backfired the woods, if they felt it would help.

The fire, moving relentlessly with the wind through Pulawski Township and the Hagensville area of Belknap Township, was soon upon them. About a mile east of town, the woods, with thick underbrush, grew close to the shore of Lake Huron. Nothing could be done to stop the fire there, but the men succeeded in confining it along the path the wind drove it. There was considerable damage to the area west of the village, as well. The flames swept up the shore for sixteen miles, all the way to the Hammond Life Saving Station. To the south, the fire burned wide swaths of forest, but, by some strange quirk, left strips of woods green and untouched.

Saturday, October 17, was the day the fate of the town hung in the balance, and the women and children were frantic with fear and anxiety. Lake Huron was the only means of escape, if the fire could not be held back. Fishing tugs were being kept ready, but they could carry only a limited number of passengers. It was at this critical time that the Str. *C.H. Starke* arrived on the scene. She belonged to Paul H. Hoeft, prominent citizen and main employer in the town. He ordered her captain to remain in port until the emergency was past.

Many people dug holes in their backyards and buried their most necessary household goods and valuables. Others with teams of horses stood by to move people and goods up along the shore to safety.

None of these plans had to be resorted to. On Sunday, October 18, the danger passed. Rogers City was fortunate, indeed. Not one building was destroyed.

There was one casualty. The story has been told and retold of a young lady who had just bought a new hat. To have it burn was more than she could bear. She buried it by the lake. When the danger to the town had passed, she dug up her hat. But, alas, the water had ruined it! It was never reported whether the townspeople bought her a new hat, but her tale of woe, so long remembered, must have brought a smile to many and helped relieve the terrible tensions of those four trying days.

Millersburg

Millersburg was the second largest town in Presque Isle County, claiming about one thousand inhabitants. The coming of the railroad and the vast amount of timber in the area were what gave it birth. In the township of Case, it was built where the railroad and the Ocqueoc River intersected. There were sawmills all around.

Since the burg was the second largest town in the county and centrally located, its citizens had hopes that it might become the county seat. The local newspapers, the *Presque Isle County News*, and the Rogers City paper, the *Presque Isle County Advance*, had a running battle on this issue. There was good farm land around Millersburg and a confident can-do population. Like the residents of all the little towns, they wanted their village to grow. The adjoining town of Providence also had ambitions and there was rivalry between the two.

However, in the afternoon of that Thursday, October 15, when the onrushing fires from the south began threatening Millersburg and Providence from every side, all rivalry was forgotten and every available man fought to save the mills that were in greatest danger. If the fires that broke out in the mills from flying embers became uncontrollable, it would be impossible to save the towns.

Fire first became extremely dangerous at a shingle mill on the northwestern edge of Millersburg known as the Thompson Mill. Before the situation was under control there, the firefighters had to divert their attention to the big Hamilton Mill on the southern outskirts. The fire was raging through the woods south of town, sending showers of sparks and embers into the sawdust piles, lumber and other products of the mill. The town fire engine was brought into use and for four hours the men fought to save the mill and keep the fire south of the Ocqueoc River. If they failed to control the fire here, it would be impossible to save the town. A quarter mile east of town, the Williams Mill was surrounded by fifty men who worked many hours before it was out of danger. So, by great effort, the mills were saved and Millersburg was spared.

A Fiery Ride

The fires that threatened Millersburg did not stop there, but flashed north into Ocqueoc Township in the direction of Lake Huron. The abandoned settlement of Crow Dam on the Ocqueoc River was consumed and the farmsteads and dwellings in Ocqueoc Township were endangered. Most of them survived, but great areas of forest were devastated.

Miles to the west of Millersburg, in Allis Township, the fires were also raging. McKay's Mill was located there, a band mill considered to be the best and most modern in northeastern Michigan. In charge was Dick Plume, who had ten men working for him, cutting logs.

On October 14, the strong wind drove the fire in the direction of the mill, seemingly from all directions. The men worked hard and managed to keep it under control until evening, when it got a good start in dry hemlock logs and could not be contained. Soon it was into the huge lumber piles, a large amount of cedar, and the mill itself. More than a million and a half board feet of lumber were destroyed.

With horses and wagons ready, Plume, his wife and children, and the ten men fled, their way in the night lighted by the great fires around them. During their flight they drove through eighty rods of road where the heat was so intense they felt it was a miracle they escaped.

On Friday morning Plume and his wife drove into Millersburg seeking medical aid. His face was badly burned and his eyes were swollen shut. He was treated by Dr. N.C. Monroe, the town doctor, who told him he would not lose his eyesight.

Incidents such as this, taking place in widely scattered sections of the county, give an idea of the vastness of the area ablaze and the ferocity of the fire.

Clergyman Related What He Witnessed

During the month of October an Episcopalian clergyman, Bishop Williams, of Detroit, wrote of his experiences during the few hectic days he was stranded in the Metz area. We now present excerpts from his writings:

Section 4, Chapter 3
Devastation Beyond Metz

"This is the first chance I have had to sit down and write since I left Alpena last Wednesday morning. It seems months ago and yet it is but four days. I do not know whether I can recount the story of those days....After conducting services at East Tawas, I sat up until 1:30 a.m. Thursday morning, then took the train and went to bed for four hours. At 5:30 we changed cars at Alpena and went up to the ill-fated village of Metz. The air was dense and bitter with smoke. Fires could be seen here and there along the line and a steady southwest wind was blowing, but nobody seemed alarmed. I left Metz around 7:30 a.m., a careless, confident village. At 4:30 p.m. it was a desolate waste of sand and ashes.

"I drove on to Hagensville, four miles back of Metz. All through the evening the smoke got denser and the fires kept creeping up from southwest of town, the breeze blowing stronger and stronger from that direction. Men were out in the woods trying to save their logging camps, tan bark, etc. By afternoon it was considered that the few houses of the little hamlet of Hagensville were in danger and the men were all called out of the woods to defend their homes. Buckley and I gave up the service, but later had a baptism. People who had come to church had run back home to try to save their buildings.

"Mr. Buckley and I then tried to get back to Metz and take a train for Onaway, which was due at 5:34. We tried the direct way first, he in the stage, I in a private conveyance. The stage, which went ahead, soon found the road impassable, it being overswept by fires and a bridge on fire. People were fleeing from their homes with such few belongings as they could pick up. The stage stopped in Hagensville and Mr. Buckley stayed there, as the stage driver said it was no use to try to get through.

"My driver decided to try it and so we set out on another road. We soon began to meet people who had left their imperiled homes and were seeking safety. Old women and little children, trudging for miles through the pall of grime. Still we went on. The smoke was terrible. I had to spread my handkerchief on my face and breathe through it. Still we went on, until finally we came face to face with a wall of flame near the road and had to turn back. We were within a short distance of Metz.

"On returning to Hagensville, we found the houses filling with refugees and the men watching the fires. As evening came on, two homes of members of our church were in imminent peril. The mothers and children were taken out of them to the house where I was staying. Mr. Buckley and I took our bags to the little church nearby and then went to see what we could do. We went into the smoke as far as we could and found we could see Merediths' house and the Taylors'. We stayed there for two or three hours, watching for sparks and stamping them out. The smoke was suffocating; our eyes felt like two burnt holes in our heads.

"At least the danger seemed past and Mr. Buckley and I went back to the little church where we stretched ourselves, with all our clothes, on the hard floor, with our bags as pillows. We got what sleep we could, but were up every little while, watching the fires which glowed around the little hamlet on every side.

"In the morning we went back to the Merediths' for breakfast, and soon the rumors of the catastrophe at Nowicki's Siding began to come in. Mr. Meredith had heard the night before that Metz was gone and Mrs. Meredith was very anxious about her daughter. Her four little children were with her in Metz. Later Friday morning the news came that this daughter and children had all perished. Of course the poor wild woman was frantic. Mr. Buckley and I did what we could for the family. When the old father went to find out for himself the truth of this report Friday afternoon, we determined to get out.

"We found that no one could spare a horse, and anyhow the bridges were down. However, with a young man to help, we shouldered our bags and walked for miles through the ashes, cinders and smoke to where Metz once stood. On the way we met old Mr. Meredith, howling like a madman, "My dear ones is ashes! My dear ones is ashes!" We sent him back with a neighbor and went on.

"At Posen, I got an upbound train to Cheboygan. We passed through fifty or sixty miles of country with a forest fire every mile or two. I heard from the waiter in the dining car, who is a member of St. Matthew's, Detroit, that there were some newspaper rumors about me, and that made me all the more anxious to get word to you. I had been trying every means to get a wire through, but all lines were down. I could send nothing until I got here Friday night. I got on the Michigan Central lines. I know how anxious you would be and I did hear rumors that the newspapers had reported me dead. However, I could not have gotten a message to you sooner than 2 a.m. Friday night. Saturday morning I was beset by telegrams from newspapers.

"...So here I am, safe, but my heart goes out to the poor, imperiled and stricken people I have been with. Their life, anyway, is so barren and ravaged, and now many have lost their little all and are penniless in this frightful country, all blueberry waste and ashes. I go to Chicago tonight and hope to arrive Tuesday at 10:30 p.m. God bless and keep you and bring us safely together again."[108]

Another man of the clergy, Pastor Ernest Thieme, lived through the tragedy. Thieme was the spiritual leader of the St. Peter's Church at Metz and at St. John's at Hagensville during these trying times:

It was not until Saturday morning that I was able to make an effort to see how my parishioners had fared. I walked a long way before I came to a farmhouse that had been spared. It now housed ten families. Most of the rumors of tragic events that I had heard at Metz were here confirmed. They said four of my parishioners had tried to save the church, while at the same time their own homes were going up in flames. One of them injured his lungs, breathing the hot air.

Sunday I buried, at one funeral service, ten of the members of our church who died in the fire. It was a strange worship service, which I conducted with a loudly sobbing congregation alongside a church in ashes, conducted over open graves. I never experienced such despair in my whole life. At first, I could not even begin. I leaned against a lonely standing fence post and wept, perhaps the first time since I was a child. But with the announcement of the comforting word of God of Psalm 46, "God is our refuge and strength, a very present help in trouble," my own heart gained strength.

That very day the Detroit & Mackinac Railway sent word to me that on the following day, Monday, I was to help them distribute food and clothing among the suffering people. I was on the job early, long before the train arrived. Then the unfortunate, needy, hungry people came from all directions. All were lightly clothed, like people on a warm summer day. This was the way they had fled in the face of the fire. Now, they had a bitterly cold night behind them, and little food for several days. There were those who had fled barefooted. Children had rags wrapped around their feet.

When the train arrived, the Catholic priest looked after the Polish needy and I after the German. This distribution continued all week, until the most immediate needs were met. We were so grateful that our hands were filled so we could help. We estimated the number of poor and homeless at about 1,500. Money is being raised throughout the state to build shelters for the people and their animals. Of the eighty-three families of Metz Township that burned out, twenty-nine were members of our congregation.[109]

☒☒☒☒☒

-1979-

More than seventy years have gone by since the tragic time of the Metz fire. A Michigan historic site marker telling about it now stands on the Metz Town Hall grounds. Here, before the fire, stood the schoolhouse. St. Dominic's Church, on Centala Road, two miles from Metz, which was spared by the fire, has since been dismantled, and a new church has been built in the village. The Lutheran Church, which burned with the rest of the town, was rebuilt, but the old Metz never returned.

Nowicki's Siding is just a name held in memory because of what took place there. Nothing remains at this once busy loading point where the Detroit & Mackinac Railway crosses the Hagensville Road.

No one passing the site of the formerly bustling town of South Rogers, on the corner of Metz Highway and South Rogers Road, would guess that a small village once stood there. Never big, it did have business enough for two saloons in its heyday. Now, though the name lingers on, it is a town without inhabitants.

Hagensville, too, is gone, Now the name is used to designate the intersection of Highways 638 and 441, as well as the surrounding area.

LaRoque, which is adjacent to Hawks, is still a destination point on the Detroit & Mackinac Railway, but the depot is gone, together with all buildings in the area. Only the side tracks remain.[110]

☒☒☒☒☒

Holocaust

by George Angus Belding

Men gazed at the sky one summer dawn—
Their faces were furrowed, haggard and drawn.
Upon the dry land for sweltering days
Lay a smoky blanket of yellowing haze.
Slashings were tinder from lack of the rains
And a hot fetid gale swept in from the plains.
The sun climbed aloft through reddening scud—
'Twas colored like ashes stained redly with blood.
The wind brought gray flakes that swirled in the air—
Gray ashes that mottled men's faces and hair.

Then came a sound as of surf upon stone—
On wings of the wind came its ominous tone
'Ere a living red wall, a flaming line,
Galloped down swiftly upon the tall pine,
As the dragon of fire drove out of the south
And reached for the timber with ravenous mouth.

In panic in front of that red racing death
Fled the things of the forest with panting breath—
The badgers, the weasels, the wildcats and bears—

The squirrel and the woodchuck, the foxes and hares.
On pinions of fear flew the forest fowls—
The hawks and the bluejays, the redruffs and owls.
Other things, too, were attempting to flee—
The frogs and the snakes—the wild honeybee.

Then strong men grew pale at the awesome sight
Of billowing flames at the treetops height.
The tall pines writhed as captives at stake
And resinous clouds enveloped the brake,
Serpentine tongues swept the tamaracks,
Exploding the trunks in thunderous cracks—
Toppling to earth with a roaring crash—
The beech and the spruce—maple and ash.
Torture and death were abroad in the land
And the flames left naught but the blackened land.
Destruction and death were wedded that day
Of that awful year that's so far away.
But one who has watched a proud forest die
Remembers its passing with many a sigh![111]

Section 5

Au Sable-Oscoda Fire of 1911

Sibling Rivalry—Twin Cities Burn
Au Sable - Oscoda 1911

Twin fires destroyed twin cities on the same day back on July 11, 1911. It is likely that a spark from a passing engine ignited weeds along the railroad tracks and the fire spread toward Oscoda, while a forest fire approached its twin across the river, Au Sable.

Anyone who has ever visited Au Sable River country knows that there are times when fires are actually good for the land. Take for example the blueberry (wild huckleberry) crop. To actually produce top quality fruit, periodic fires are needed. Far back in history, early Amerindian people burned blueberry marshes for this specific purpose.

The Michigan Department of Natural Resources also prescribes controlled burns to improve the habitat of the Kirtland's Warbler, often called "The Bird of Fire."

Sibling Rivalry—Twin Cities Burn
Au Sable - Oscoda 1911

Located on the sunrise side of the state, the twin towns of Au Sable and Oscoda, like siblings vying to outdo one another, both grew at a rapid pace prior to the disastrous fire that literally wiped one of the sisters off the face of the map on July 11, 1911.

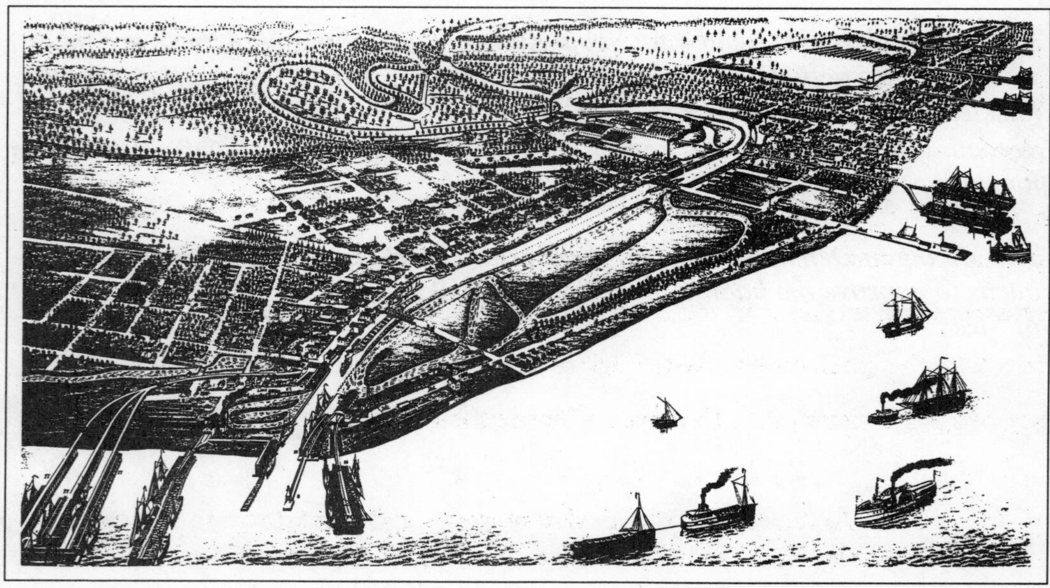

Map courtesy of the Iosco Historical Museum

Early map of the twin cities of Oscoda (right) and Au Sable, before the devastating fire of 1911.

Of the two communities, Au Sable was the larger of the twins. She was located at the mouth of the mighty Au Sable River with a population of some 10,000 residents. Prior to the "big burn," Au Sable contained six sawmills, a sash and blind factory, three stores, three hotels, three churches and a bank.

Additionally, the Au Sable River Boom Company was in the business of sorting and corralling logs floated down the river by the various lumber companies.

Other establishments included The Brady and Buhl Saloon, Cowie and Murphy Fish Dealers, a billiard hall owned by John Dempsey, a saloon with John Egan as proprietor, the Hawkins House Hotel, the Lee House, a customs collector named John W. Glennie who also served as banker, Holmes & Company Fish Dealers and the McDonald & McCormick Saloon and Billiard Hall.

One of the town's main interests was the Loud family mill, a huge, sprawling complex. A new canning factory was being built just before the fire took place.

During the month of October 1908—the time of the Metz fires—an Episcopalian clergyman, Bishop Williams, of Detroit, made his annual visit to the churches and missions in the counties of Presque Isle, Alpena and Cheboygan. In a letter he mailed to his wife back in Detroit, Bishop Williams presciently described these sister cities three years before their demise:

> I left Alpena early Wednesday morning and went down to Oscoda and Au Sable, where I spent the day. The two names stand for a shriveled, wizened, little town, formerly of ten thousand, now about two thousand, consisting of flimsy houses built of kindling wood on heaps of sawdust and sand. This is the style of most of the villages in this part of Michigan.
>
> The atmosphere was very dense with smoke. It parched your throat and bit into your eyes. If ever the fire should catch in that town, it would be burned up in five minutes, like Metz. No insurance company will take a risk here, yet the people seemed careless and confident.[112]

Historians speculate the conflagration of 1911 delivered the fatal punch to the fast-waning lumbering era in northeast lower Michigan. Many industries simply did not or could not afford to rebuild. Oscoda received far less damage from the fire than her sister city, Au Sable, but neither town rebuilt to its former stature after the fires.

Photo courtesy Neil Thornton

The devastation along Main Street after the Oscoda fire.

Au Sable never recovered. Her tombstone could read: "Settled in 1850. Incorporated as a village October 15, 1872. Moved to city status in 1889. Burned July 11, 1911. Died officially in 1920. Buried in 1929."

Like many villages, towns and cities at the turn of the century, the twin ports of Au Sable and Oscoda were constructed mainly of wood—wood cut from their forests and planed at their local mill sites—during what was still the "hey-day" of Michigan's lumbering industry. There were no cement sidewalks—wood chips and sawdust basically made up the bulk of roads and walkways. They served the purpose well, keeping mud down on rainy days and providing traction for horses' hooves during icy winter months. No one looked ahead and pictured these sawdust trails as prime fodder for run-away flames licking up dry tinder like a two-headed devil-dragon—one aimed for Oscoda, the other toward Au Sable.

How did this fire, considered by many to be the last spectacular blaze of that century, start? Which town was responsible, if either was? Actually, we don't know for sure, but we do know that this particular summer season was extremely dry and hot. Newspaper accounts and weather statistics indicate that the week of the fire, the Oscoda-Au Sable area was parched earth with numerous fires reported—in Alpena, Waters, Alger, Turner, Boyne City, parts of Cheboygan and Presque Isle counties, and other small forest fires in as many as ten northern Michigan counties. For days, a forest fire was known to have been slowly advancing toward Au Sable, hovering just outside the city limits, but the local populace paid little heed to the blaze, figuring they personally had little to fear and were not in immediate danger.

But they were wrong. The winds picked up speed on the morning of July 11th, at a reported rate of some 50 miles per hour, which caused a fanning effect bursting this comparatively small forest fire into a disastrous inferno. At the very same time the town began to burn, a passing train deposited sparks along the right-of-way one mile west of Oscoda, igniting the dry, tinder-like grass and weeds.

The sweeping winds carried the flames, which quickly gained momentum until, within mere moments, the fire raced across the Au Sable River valley, leaving three-fourths of the town of Oscoda smoldering in its wake. At this point, the twin fires joined forces and destroyed both towns.

People fled for their lives as tongues of flame virtually licked at their heels; docks were set afire hampering the efforts of relief vessels; trains pulled out of town through walls of searing flame. As in most other tragic fires covered in *Michigan On Fire*, there was little opportunity or time to salvage personal possessions. Life itself was far more precious.

The ultimate death toll was never officially determined, but it is believed to have been that some five to twelve individuals lost their lives during the double firestorm. For many individuals, Lake Huron's sheltering sand dunes offered the only surviving lifeline. Others were rescued by boats until the very docks the fire victims were standing on caught fire. The railroad trains managed to remove many people to safer surroundings, such as Tawas City to the south and Alpena to the north. But generally speaking, the majority of the population from these two affected towns were forced to wade out into the waters of Lake Huron or the Au Sable River, where blazing sparks and bits of burning wood and embers rained down on them.

It took weeks to bring some family members back together, for several may have been picked up by boat while others fled by train. The rescue barge was advised that a similar fire had wiped out the Tawases to the south, so once that vessel put out to sea, it headed toward the far distant port of Port Huron. Events took place with such swiftness there simply was little time to make detailed escape plans. The situation became a matter of survival. Within a scant two hours, just 20 houses were left standing in Oscoda, while only 4 buildings remained in the main section of Au Sable. The twins were mortally wounded and one would die!

Still, quirks of fate played a dramatic role. A recent accounting by a survivor, Mrs. Zelda Garza, tells how she and her blueberries were saved. She was 12 years old at the time, and she and others had been picking the berries and packing them for shipment. They had to be carefully sorted, then placed in quart boxes and packed into crates. The next step was to ship them downstate by boat from the local docks. On the day of the fire, her family happened to have a large supply crated and ready for transportation when the wall of flames entered the sister cities, forcing the townsfolk to drop whatever they were doing to flee for their very lives.

Photo courtesy Neil Thornton

How Au Sable looked after the great fire of 1911 that destroyed two cities within a few short hours.

"The fire moved very fast and I recall how church steeples would fall and spread the fire," she told the Detroit *Free Press*. "We threw a few things on the wagon and headed for the sand dunes. We had no time to take food, but some man came through the crowd with a cow and a tin cup and each child received a cup of milk.

"When it was safe we returned to our home spot. Nothing was left except those crates of berries. The tops were scorched, but the bottom crates were fine."[113]

A small unsolved mystery came about while survivors searched the rubble that once had been the stately "Swanson" home. Previous to the fire, a photograph in a metal frame had occupied a place of importance on the grand piano in the living room of this home. After the fire, the charred remains of the piano were in the ruins but the photograph was recovered barely scorched, even though the frame itself had melted. All else in the house had been destroyed, with the exception of this one surviving photo and a hand-painted cream jar that also showed no signs of having been in that dreadful fire.

The people who died in the fire did so by trying to rescue their valuables. Houses seemed to explode or burst wildly into flame, rather than simply catch fire and slowly smolder. Many people were trapped by this fire phenomenon.

A few trinkets and other possessions were saved by burying them deep in sandy soil. Silver vases and precious china survived destruction in many instances. Two china plates fused with bits of metal, are displayed today at the Iosco County Museum at Tawas City, along with historical photos, both before and after the consumptive firestorm had passed.

As with the death and destruction at Metz, some blamed the townsfolk and their assorted sinful ways for the utter hell that broke loose on the eleventh day of July. Rev. Bird, the pastor of a local Methodist church, told a *Detroit News* reporter, that the "curse of God" destroyed the twin cities known as Au Sable and Oscoda. He said the two towns had been running wide-open, that wickedness reigned supreme, and that their terrible punishment was merited.

Rev. Bird provided many examples of the sins committed within the boundaries of the sister communities—Sunday afternoon cock fights where wagers were made on the Sabbath and "Blind pigs" that sold spirits on Sundays. His faithful followers should have been attending church services regularly instead of partaking in such sinful events, he said.

As time passed, many of his parishioners claimed that he made these controversial remarks while he was somewhat addled by the excitement of the havoc. In turn, the minister adopted a decisive "The Lord calls and the devil drives" theme of blame, rather than acknowledging the fire as a natural disaster.

As with all grave calamities, some people profited from others' misfortune. Perhaps an item that may have been considered a bit late and a dollar short was an advertisement for fire insurance found in the Bay City paper three days after the fire disaster. On the front page, Ribbie & Murphy of Bay City dared to offer low-cost fire insurance billed as "the best protection on earth!"[114]

The Au Sable-Oscoda fire destroyed about $2 million worth of property. Railroads suffered huge losses, as did the lumber barons. The Loud Mill was never rebuilt. Along with the loss of their mills, the Loud family lost thousands of acres of lumber and their fine mansion. The family itself moved first to Bay City, then later they took their lumber business to Oregon. The total economic base of the sister cities had been completely wiped out.

Photo courtesy Neil Thornton

Photo showing the remains of the once prosperous Loud Company mill. All that remains is the smokestack and the office vault where money and records were kept.

Again we turn to The Detroit News for contemporary accountings of the fires:

Three Bodies Found, Scores Missing In Fire-Swept Towns

First Authentic Story from Oscoda and Au Sable Tells of Loss of Life and Million Dollar Damage

Father Of 10 Children Burned To Death On Doorstep

Remains of Two Others Picked Up on Street: Many Who Sought Safety in Boats Believed Met Doom

BAY CITY, Mich., July 13—The towns of Au Sable and Oscoda have been effaced from the surface of the earth. Where they once stood there is nothing.

Because of the confusion attending the rounding up of the refugees and the compiling of lists of the residents, there is no way of telling how many people lost their lives.

Three bodies have been found. Scores are missing and all or part of them may have perished.

The destruction is as complete as was that of Sodom and Gomorra. It is more complete than that of Pompeii and Herculaneum, for they were simply buried and were dug up by later generations.

Destruction more absolute than that of the twin cities of the Au Sable can not be imagined.

Where stood handsome homes, churches, stores and mills, as well as in the humble sections of the city, there is nothing but ashes, bits of twisted iron and an occasional stone foundation.

But Little Left

To enumerate the losses would be an impossiblility. To tell what is left is easy. In Au Sable, one school house is standing. It is known as the "lower school" and is located in the midst of several acres of the bare sand, through which there was nothing for the fire to fan. This school house was a place of refuge for several score of people during the night and this morning. To the east of the school and at the southern point of the town are two dwellings, which were out of the path of the flames. The Detroit & Mackinac Railroad buildings are gone.[115]

Tells Story Of Burning Of Oscoda

Tales of Horror as Fire Swept Town Related by Refugees

First To Reach Detroit: The Captain Swore, Then Cried as Ropes of Steamer Burned

Boat Aflame as it Left Scores in "Hell of Fire," Says Survivor

Many Left On Dock

The first refugees from the fire to arrive in Detroit were Mr. and Mrs. George W. Paquette, with them four children and Mrs. Paquette's sister, Maud Marin. They were driven from their home at Oscoda by the flames and boarded the steamer *Niko* just as the fire, which had reached the dock, burned the rope which held the vessel to the wharf. Their little home in Oscoda was destroyed before they could save any of their effects, and the only things they were able to carry away with them were but a few personal items.[116]

☒☒☒☒☒

Summary Of The Fire Situation In Michigan

With three people known dead, scores missing who may have perished, two towns wiped off the map and nearly a dozen others reported either destroyed or greatly damaged, Michigan is facing the worst forest fire situation the state has ever seen.

Northwest winds, said to be the worst possible for a situation of this kind, were blowing down over the burned and burning districts of the northern portion of the lower peninsula, spreading fires in almost every direction.

There is no rain in sight. Weather men say that a long and hot spell is all the state can expect for several days. Without rain there is certain to be a much larger loss of property than at present and the figures with reports in from all districts, now would undoubtedly reach well towards $3,000,000,000. In nearly every portion of the area affected, families and men from lumber camps are reported missing or cut off from the outside world. Trains are held up by walls of flame and ruined bridges.

Mayor Crowley, of the devastated city of Oscoda, has wired asking that the state troops be dispatched to assist in patrolling the fire zone and bringing order out of the chaos which now exists. Gov. Osborn stands ready to order out every man of the Michigan National Guard if the situation warrants the move.

Towns And Counties Affected By The Fire:

Au Sable:	Wiped out.
Oscoda:	Wiped out.
Millersburg:	Nearly wiped out.
Onaway:	Their settled portion destroyed.
Metz:	Wiped out for second time in three years.
Posen:	Wiped out for second time in three years.
LaRoque:	Wiped out.
Tower:	Reported entirely destroyed.
Alpena:	Loss $500,000
Cheboygan:	Once threatened, but now safe.
Trowbridge:	Threatened with destruction—part saved.
Alger:	In grave danger.
Lewiston:	Threatened for a time—fire under control.
Lake City:	Threatened with destruction.
Ball Siding:	In grave danger.
Antrim County:	Fires in many places.
Oscoda County:	Fire swept.
Iosco County:	Fires sweeping over Michelson—partially burned.[117]

☒☒☒☒☒

Bay City Troops Start For Au Sable

BAY CITY, Mich., July 12—Capt. Beckwith, with 31 men of his local military company, leaves on a special train early this evening for the fire swept district. They will take 150 state tents and all the state blankets on hand.[118]

☒☒☒☒☒

Women And Children Sleep On Decks Of Rescuing Steamer

Are Brought Into Port Huron From Oscoda Today: 400 Left Crying On Docks

Survivor Tells of Terrible Scenes as Boat Ablaze at Each End is Forced to Put Out Into Lake

PORT HURON, Mich., July 12—Two hundred and eighty-five victims from Oscoda arrived in Port Huron this morning on board the lumber barge *Niko*, in charge of Capt. Ralph D. Myers of Tonawanda. The *Niko* left the dock at Oscoda a half hour after arriving. Both bow and stern were on fire when she cut loose. Most of those who were on the *Niko* were women and children. Husbands were left behind fighting the flames.
The people on the *Niko* report that there was no other means of getting out of town and that many were seeking the beach with the intention of standing in the water in order to get relief.[119]

☒☒☒☒☒

Word Of Missing Kin Is Sought By Many Detroiters

Relatives Appeal To *The News* to Aid In Search

Scores of Detroiters who have relatives living in the fire zone appealed to *The News* today to find their missing loved ones.

S.A. Marshall, of the McGraw Building, has a mother and sister living in Wilbur, Michigan, 10 miles north of Au Sable. No word has been received from Wilbur regarding the fire.

Mrs. Matilda Cutter, 907 Fort Street, Bay City, mother of Mrs. Mary Fulton of Grosse Pointe, was at Riverview farm one-half mile from Oscoda.

Edward Metcalf Fisher of Westminister Avenue, reports that Mrs. Charles Snyder and her daughter living in Oscoda, Mich. have not been heard from.

Miss Anna Hanson, 115 Howard Street, has not heard from her parents, Mr. and Mrs. Arne Hanson of Oscoda.

Rex House is unable to hear from his uncle, C.B. Oakes, who, with his wife and three children, lives in Mio, Oscoda County.

Mrs. J. McHalor, 1074 Connolly Avenue, Detroit, fears that her people have been lost in the fire that swept Oscoda. Her father, J. Scalar, was in the lumber business in that city. It is known that his mill was destroyed, but it is not known whether he with his family escaped harm.[120]

There were many, many names on this given list—relatives anxiously searched the newspapers for word of their loved ones. A listing of refugees that safely arrived from the fire district was printed alongside the first column. This listing, of course, gave names of the survivors brought to Port Huron by the lumber barge *Niko*.

Fire disasters prove to be no different than wars, floods or hurricanes. In all cases, those left behind simply cannot notify family members immediately, so they must wait, leaving loved ones elsewhere to worry and wonder. At any rate, simply rereading these historic accountings of the Au Sable-Oscoda fire provides and understanding of just how tenuous our lifeline actually can be.

The Aftermath

12 To 72 Hours Later

Here we learn of two cities nearly destroyed. Will they both be rebuilt or will one or both die—simply, perhaps, fade into oblivion?

We also learn of the fire situation in the immediate area, for other fires threatened additional towns, villages and wilderness outposts.

Relief efforts indicate plans for rebuilding and making the fire victims as comfortable as possible. But many folks could find no work, and moved their families downstate to be able to make a living. These were sad days for Oscoda and Au Sable.

The Aftermath - 12 to 72 Hours Later

Photo courtesy Neil Thornton

Street scene showing soldiers guarding the burned remains of the bank after the Oscoda Fire.

A few interesting sidenotes offer a backward glance to events and mores that dominated the lives of the populace of the sibling sister cities known as Oscoda and Au Sable. In 1911 *The Detroit News* was already enjoying its 38th successful year in the newspaper business, while the relative newcomer, The Detroit *Times*, had only been publishing some 16 years. (The *Times,* of course, has long been absent from Detroit newsstands).

Also in this era, Ty Cobb ruled the baseball world; railroads were the "King" industry; logging was the number one business in the state's northern counties, newspapers sold for 1¢ per day or delivered weekly for 7¢. The telegraph wires were the lifelines of the news. If they were down or disabled, townsfolk statewide waited, worried and wondered.

While the headlines of the July 12 *News* screamed, "Michigan Fires Still Rage," a sense of normalcy was returning, for once again a comic strip occupied its usual prominent front page location. In this particular issue, a brand new presentation called "Mutt and Jeff," by Bud Fisher, took over this spot. In fact, throughout this issue many new comics were making their debut, including "Silk Hat Harry," "Sinbad the Tailor," "Sherlocko the Monk," "Buck Nix," "Joys and Gloom," "Hall Room Boys," "Us Boys," "Family Upstairs" and "Desperate Desmond."

Advertisements, too, were common on the front pages of the newspapers of the day. The July 12 edition of *The Detroit News* contained front page ads for:

- Chamberlain's Tablets—"to regulate the liver and bowels and invigorate the stomach."
- Klassem's Pile Remedy—"50¢ will relieve your distress. Free samples at Gray & Worcester's or sent by mail."
- Hotel Hofman—"Rates $1.00 and $1.30. With bath, $1.50 and up. Luncheon 35¢. Dinner 50¢."

But, of course, this edition also contained news articles about the fires of the day before and the relief efforts getting underway:

Detroit To Aid Fire Refugees

Mayor Thompson Acts Promptly For Relief Of Sufferers

$2,000 Appropriation

Remainder Of Old Fund To Be Used At Once

May Call The Council

Special Meeting To Take Active Measures

Gov. Osborn Says State Will Help

SAULT STE. MARIE, Mich., July 12—Gov. Osborn declared this morning that he had already asked for an inquiry into the fires at Oscoda and Au Sable. He expressed deep sympathy at the news of the catastrophe and stated that the state stood ready to assist the refugees in any way possible. He said that tents and blankets will be distributed among the homeless and that if financial assistance is needed state officials will circulate the petitions to raise such money as is needed.

With a nucleus of $2,000, the remainder of the appropriation made by the city of Detroit for the sufferers in the forest fires of 1908, Detroit will move to give first aid to the bereft citizens of Au Sable and Oscoda.

Without waiting to receive information as to the needs of the burned over district, Mayor Thompson called J.L. Hudson, who was chairman of the old relief committee, who conferred at noon today and a tentative plan was arrived at. All of the members of the old committee who are in town will be in conference with the mayor at his office at 2 o'clock. The men who are sure to be there are Mr. Hudson, Wm. Livingston and Charles H. Sawyer, former secretary of the Board of Commerce.

It is planned that one of the three named will be dispatched into the fire country today, taking with him the $2,000 from the old appropriation. He will be empowered to spend the money for first aid, in the way of clothing and food for the fire victims.

As soon as information can be given as to what is needed, the members of the committee remaining in Detroit will take steps to raise more money.[121]

☒☒☒☒☒

Wind Again Springs Up But Promising Rain
Alpena Gets Fractional Fall Of Moisture
And East Tawas Sees Cause For Hope

While Waiting For Ruins To Cool
Homeless Plan Rebuilding Of City
Oscoda And Au Sable To Rise As One From Debris:
No Further Word Comes From The
Burned And Threatened Towns

EAST TAWAS, Mich., July 14—A heavy thunder shower at 9 o'clock thoroughly dampened this dry and dusty territory and removed all danger of forest fires.

The telegraph operator at Au Sable wires that the rain there was heavy also, extinguishing the smoldering ruins of the twin towns. It is believed that the rain in general is all over the upper part of the lower peninsula.[122]

☒☒☒☒☒

EAST TAWAS, Mich., July 14—"A bad fire is burning now at Kunze crossing, six miles from here," declared Superintendent of Car Service, G.A. Pinkerton of the D & M Railway at 11 o'clock today.

At noon the wind had risen to 20 miles an hour and there were thunder clouds speckling the sky. The prevailing direction of the wind is east, shifting slightly to the south at times.

The Fire Situation In Michigan

Millersburg:	Half destroyed, succeeds in repelling the flames which encircle the town, but is in danger yet.
Sigma Village:	Kalkaska County is surrounded by flames.
Berryville:	Otsego County is wiped out.
Onaway & Tower:	Fate hangs in the balance.
LaGrand:	Reported surrounded by fire.
Kerston:	Hillman division of the D & M—loses 6 houses.
Antrim County:	Nine lumber camps are burned.[123]

☒☒☒☒☒

Waiting For Ruins To Cool, People Plan A New Town

AU SABLE, Mich., July 14—J.H. McGillvray, secretary of the executive committee, said this morning: "Oscoda and Au Sable will be rebuilt as one town and placed under one government. The loss of life and property loss of residents are the only things to regret. The city will be built up clean, with modern construction and material. All the uncouth, unsightly shacks and ruins are gone. We have nearly 100 houses, unharmed. We have two modern school buildings. Every industry the towns had before the fire, it will have again!"

Will Rebuild Mill

Edward Loud of the H.M. Loud's Sons Lumber Co., declared the firm will rebuild. Herbert Markham, secretary of the Oscoda & Au Sable Canning Co., states that his firm will replace the mammoth plant, which had just been completed a few days before the disaster, with one of twice the capacity. The Iosco Turpentine and Chemical Plant, in course of construction when the fire broke out, is not harmed and will be carried to completion at the earliest possible time. S.S. Noble, resident manager of the company, says that 29 extra men will be placed on his payroll Tuesday.

The big fishing interests, Hull & Sons, Langlota & Herrick and Capt. Oscar Hurkett, will resume if the operators can get credit for material. Huckleberries that will bring in the market approximately $30,000 are safe on the unburned swamp grounds, adjacent to the city. The big water power project, with its electrical energy, will bring in more industries.

Better Than Before

I predict and earnestly believe the towns that were, will be a better town in two years than before the catastrophe. So far as heroes of the occasion are concerned, every man, woman and child did their best under the circumstances. So far as known, there is nothing to criticize adversely in the actions of anyone.

The homeless people are the gamest bunch of losers ever developed by misfortune. Christian Yockey, Charles Hennigan, James Hull, Edward Hub, Joseph Turcotte and many others were burned severely while fighting the flames. Despite their injuries, they are still working on the job directing the work of relief.

Hull & Sons fought the fire in their lumber yard at the risk of the lives of father and sons, and would have saved their lumber yard but for the sudden change in the direction of the wind. They lost everything—about $100,000 with no collectable insurance on account of the removal of a part of their mill plant just three days before the fire. Gurgotte lost his new home and foundry and machine shop worth in all $12,000.

The home of Congressman Loud, destroyed in the Oscoda Au Sable fire, contained an invaluable collection of war relics and curios, a friend of Mr. Loud in Detroit recalled today. All was lost in the flames.

Mr. Loud was on a dispatch boat at the battle of Manila Bay and many of his relics were mementos of that conflict. Others he gathered while with President Taft, Rep. Nicholas Longworth, Alice Roosevelt and others on their trip to the Philippines.[124]

[AUTHORS NOTE: This article stated that the Loud mill would be rebuilt, yet my research indicated it was not, with the Louds moving to Oregon]

☒☒☒☒☒

Clothing And Shoes Needed By Sufferers

Bay City Mayor Makes Second Appeal To Detroit Citizens

Refugees Have Sufficient Food is Latest Advice

Head of Local Relief Committee Says
$3,000 in Cash From City is Enough

Members of the citizens relief committee met again in the office of Mayor Thompson today and discussed plans for granting further aid to the northern Michigan fire sufferers. Charles R. Sawyer, who was delegated to go to the victims, reported to the committee, which adjourned its meeting to meet again tomorrow.

This morning the committee sent two carloads of lumber and consignments of food, cooking utensils and grain for cattle to the afflicted districts. More will be dispatched this afternoon.

Mayor Thompson is holding the private subscription and it is possible that all may be returned, it being thought that the $5,186 appropriated by the city will be enough.

In one or two instances it is believed unscrupulous persons have been granted assistance at the mayor's office, and at the session held this noon, it was decided not to give any more money to applicants. They will be referred to Secretary Williams of the associated charities, who will investigate their stories and if found to be reliable, they will be given orders calling for assistance.

At noon today Mayor Thompson received a telephone call from Mayor Woodruff of Bay City, requesting further assistance from Detroit for fire sufferers. The Bay City executive said that no food was needed but he requested clothing outfits and shoes for 200 children, 300 women and 200 men.

The Pere Marquette Railroad has come forward with an offer to the mayor to transport free of charge to the fire district all clothing and supplies for the sufferers. The railroad also furnished transportation yesterday to Oscoda for two misses of 18 years, Misses Germaine Berube and Maude Tubbs, who escaped from the fire with only the clothing which they wore at that time.[125]

☒☒☒☒☒

East Tawas Mayor To Assist In Relief By Governor's Warrant

EAST TAWAS, Mich., July 14—The following message has been received by Mayor James Laberge:

"Lansing, Mich., July 14—Your request to issue call for assistance has been complied with. I am reposing trust and confidence in your integrity and ability. I do hereby appoint you a member of the fire relief commission.

Singed: Chase S. Osborn
Governor"

Gov. Osborn today appointed Homer E. Buck of Bay City as a member of the fire relief commission.[126]

☒☒☒☒☒

31 Detroiters In Fire District Not Yet Reported Safe

Many Women and Children Are On Vacation Among Numbers

Thirty-one Detroiters are still in the north Michigan fire zone, and fears are felt about their safety. Only a few of those reported to be in danger have been heard from. Mr. and Mrs. George Joslyn and Miss Augusta Joslyn have returned home from Oscoda, where they were visiting. Miss Margaret Foley, 784 Second Avenue, is reported safe at East Tawas and Earnest Kurtz, secretary to Mayor Thompson, has also been heard from. Dr. Marshall Dow, 2041 Woodward Avenue, returned to the city yesterday, while Mrs. John Bollman, 27 Wendell Street; Mrs. Walter Smith and child, Livernois Avenue and Mrs. Harry Meister also have returned.[127]

The Bay City Tribune reported on another consequence of the fires. Perhaps it wasn't a life or death matter, but, apparently, an important consideration to some: "A serious situation in East Tawas. There is no tobacco in town. East Tawasians, generous to a fault, gave to everyone who asked for a 'chaw' or a smoke and there isn't a grain of tobacco in East Tawas. A rush order has been sent to Bay City to be filled in the morning. By tomorrow the East Tawasians will again be able to bask in the light of 'My Lady Nicotine's eyes.'"[128]

The city of Au Sable had been a town for over three quarters of a century. The savage moment that rendered her a hell of flames that horrifying day of July 11, 1911 dealt Au Sable a death knell, for indeed the devastation was so complete that little was left but a mass of ashes; the town never fully recovered. By the year 1929 its history ceased. Where once stood twin sister cities, rivaling one another, competing for favors, struggling to outdo each other, now one lay dead and dying while the stronger of the two survived. Like Siamese twins, often the weaker infant must succumb. Oscoda suffered far less total destruction than Au Sable and today remains a viable settlement catering to locals and tourists alike.

On July 11, 1991, on the 80th Anniversary of the Great Fire of 1911, a historical marker was officially dedicated at the Oscoda Township Park beach commemorating this tragic event. It was on that day and exact hour (2 o'clock in the afternoon) that an errant forest fire, coupled with burning embers from a passing train that ignited the right-of-way, destroyed nearly all of Au Sable and downtown Oscoda. At least two survivors of that great fire were present at the dedication—Josephine (Bissonette) Allen and Rosetta (Reinbold) Grenier.

One survivor who was to address the gathering was Hamilton McNichol, who, along with his family, played a major role in the rebuilding of Oscoda. Unfortunately, Mr. McNichol died just one week before the dedication ceremony.

According to the local historical society members, observance of this event is not merely a look back at a tragedy, but a glimpse into the courage and resourcefulness put forth by the people of these twin cities both before, during and after the Great Fire of 1911.

Neil Thornton's Version Of The Fire Of 1911

Historian Neil Thornton was kind enough to allow us to reprint material from his excellent book, Along the Historic Riviere aux Sables. This gives us yet another viewpoint of what happened to the twin cities.

(Many of the historical photographs used in this section come from Mr. Thornton's collection.)

Neil Thornton's Version Of The Fire Of 1911

Newspaper writer and researcher Neil Thornton wrote a set of historical feature articles in the 1970s and '80s for the Tawas *Herald* and later for the Iosco County *News Herald* and Oscoda *Press*. Also during his career he privately published several books. One of these books—*Along the Historic Riviere aux Sables*, contained a chapter on the Great Fire of 1911.

Thornton gathered much of his historical data from his personal library, the Michigan Pioneer Collections and old newspaper files. The results of his research into the total devastation that easily could be called "Day of Judgment" are presented here:

The Fire Of 1911

The summer of 1911 was hot and dry—the front page cartoon of a Michigan daily newspaper showed a citizen knocking on the gates of hell pleading, "I'm looking for a cool spot." The devil answered, "Come in quickly and close the door."

Chicago, Illinois, had no sense of humor on the subject: Heat was held responsible there for 201 deaths in the five days prior to July 6. In Michigan, highs recorded by Port Huron from July 2 through July 11 were 99, 101, 82, 100, 77, 85, 74, 93, 92 and 94.

Here in Iosco County, The Tawas *Herald* reported on July 7 that "Saturday, Sunday and part of Monday were among the warmest days known here in a long time, the mercury ranging from 94 to 100 in the shade. A heavy thunder shower Monday afternoon did much to relieve the condition and cooler weather has since prevailed."

In spite of the thunder shower, brush fires continued to break out in the plains region of Iosco County and some of the fires were set intentionally to improve the following season's huckleberry crop. Old smoldering stumps caused smoke in the western sky. There had been brush fires for several days—but nothing important. The turpentine factory west of Oscoda, which utilized old pine stumps in its process, was threatened on Sunday, but was soon forgotten.

The *Herald* reported on July 7 that H.J. Markham, secretary of the new Oscoda Canning Company, "was in the city Tuesday to arrange with the buyers to take the entire huckleberry crop marketed here."

Markham never had a chance to purchase the country's huckleberry crop. The *Herald's* headlines on July 14, 1911, read: "Oscoda and Au Sable wiped out by fire; Flames devastate the twin cities and leave only a few scattered buildings standing; was a terrible holocaust!"

The old Tanner Lumber Company mill, site of the canning factory, was one of an estimated 600 buildings—commercial, industrial and residential—which were destroyed by fire on July 11, 1911.

Seventy-six years later, the scars of that fire have vanished, except in the memories of the dwindling few white-thatched persons who recall the most famous conflagration in Northeastern Michigan history. Oscoda and Au Sable's "modern" history starts with that fire, as anything combustible dealing with the twin cities' past burned on July 11, 1911.

Never reputed to be as prosperous as Saginaw or Muskegon, Au Sable and Oscoda had their day. When the lumber industry was at its peak, from the 1870s through the early 1890s, the towns were already looking backward rather than forward to their glory.

Harnessing of the Au Sable River for hydroelectric power was just beginning and Cooke Dam, the first of six installations on the river, was to open a new era in the history of Northeastern Michigan when it began generating electricity on February 9, 1912.

But this important event was still in the future on that hot July day of 1911. It was Tuesday and another day of work for mill hands. The steamer

Niko, of Tonawanda, New York, had arrived to take on a load of lumber. The barge and her captain were to play an important role in a few hours.

A hot wind off the plains west of Oscoda fanned and fired a house near the Catholic cemetery. Some said later that the blaze was caused by sparks from a steam locomotive, but no matter; the flames advanced eastward, driving cattle and other farm animals before it towards the towns. It picked up momentum on Loud Island, when it raced through the cedar yards. At this point, the fire was still neglected and unnoticed by most of the townsfolk.

The fire divided at Piety Hill where the river held it back; to the north, it swept across the river to Smith Island and to the south it crossed by the bayou fronting on Loud's "Little Mill."

The work of the fire had enveloped the AuSable and Northwestern Railway freight office, where a large keg of gasoline burst, spreading flames in all directions.

Finally realizing the danger, sawmills in the towns were shut down and the men began to fight the fire...but it was too late. Most of the men quickly ran home to look after families and possessions.

The resulting holocaust destroyed sawmills, docks, residences, store buildings and everything in the path of the raging flames before burning itself out on the Lake Huron shore.

Quoting from the July 14 report in The *Herald*:

"Forest fires in the vicinity of the D&M station, a mile from the towns, were driven by the strong southwest winds into the cedar yard of the Loud Company. The dry cedar bark and slabs made a fierce flame, which was carried across the river into the Village of Oscoda, where it consumed the entire business part of the town and all but 30 of the dwellings.

"What few homes were saved was by the most heroic work of the people and volunteer fire department, coupled with a sudden change of the wind to the north.

"The escape of the people was, in nearly all cases, very narrow and the heroic acts would fill columns of newspaper space if recorded. About 280 people from Oscoda escaped on the steam barge *Niko*, a lumber carrier which had just arrived for a cargo of lumber. These people were landed at Port Huron, where they were cared for.

"Others took refuge in the lake where they stood submerged to their necks for hours and some took to the plains and clearings in the vicinity. Considering everything, the loss of life is very small."

The fire did not even lose momentum as it reached the river, but crossed and raced into Oscoda's business district near the present day Bruce Myles Insurance agency.

By some accounts the off shore wind ranged between 40 and 60 miles per hour. Through this time, the City of Au Sable had been spared. The fire had crossed to the Oscoda side of the river at the bridge and had been quenched on the Au Sable side. The town appeared to be safe.

Many had fled the fire in Oscoda by crossing the river. Now, at 7 o'clock in the evening as the fire appeared to be dying down, fresh winds out of the north forced the fire to cross the river and sweep into Au Sable, firing the big Loud mill and from there to the balance of the city.

The town was leveled in a matter of minutes. Flames were to shoot 60 feet in the air; buildings appeared to explode and crumble, rather than burn.

Even though alerted by the experience of seeing Oscoda burn, many had made no preparation, and fled before pursuing flames as all their possessions were destroyed.

The fire burned so rapidly and fiercely that few realized the actual danger until they were forced to flee for their lives. Practically without food, clothing or shelter, the night was spent on the beach, on the sand plains or anywhere that safety could be felt.

Wednesday, July 12, found hundreds homeless. East Tawas and Tawas City housed 600 survivors. Although the Tawases were almost stripped bare of food, they managed to ship 1,300 loaves of bread and three barrels of ham to Oscoda-Au Sable. Many people camped on the sand at the mouth of the river; between 70 and 100 slept in an Au Sable fish house; hundreds camped around the town in any shelter they could find.

All that remained of Au Sable was the schoolhouse (surrounded by several acres of sand), two other buildings and the Detroit & Mackinac Railway buildings which were one mile west of town.

In Oscoda, four complete blocks were saved on Piety Hill (about 20 buildings), two pack houses and another house on the north end of town.

The most commonly given estimate of cash losses was two million dollars, at least half of which was suffered by the Louds. Their stores, expensive homes, tramway, docks, freight cars, railroad engines, sawmills, a planing mill, shingle mill, bolt mill, lumber yards, cedar yard, pump houses and huge piles of lumber at the docks were lost.

Will McGillivary, Oscoda editor, estimated 600 buildings in all were destroyed. *The Detroit News* reported the aggregate insurance at $75,000.

While the Louds lost heaviest in total money, one cannot lose more than everything, as most people did. Five lost their lives—Jacques Lavoie, boxmaker, who died of burns; Francois Clairmount, aged musician, who was found under his house; William Batts, handyman at the Hotel Elliott; Samuel Rosenthal, merchant, was found dead alongside a trunk he was trying to save; an unidentified peddler, who was found pinned under a fallen viaduct.

Aid was given to the survivors almost instantaneously. Port Huron opened its heart and pocket books to the *Niko* survivors. They arrived at Port Huron penniless and in "wash clothes." A committee was formed which hustled them to hotels and lunchrooms for a meal and then to the Masonic Temple for lodging.

(Charles A. Jahraus, Tawas City attorney, was in Au Sable and made his escape on the *Niko*. He said that "Capt. Myers showed great heroism in holding his boat at the dock until fire cut off all possible chances of more people reaching the boat and the boat was on fire." A committee of passengers decided that Port Huron was the most available point to land as they had been informed that the Tawases were entirely destroyed by fire that afternoon.)

Detroit sent an estimated $5,000 worth of relief goods. Ironically, this figure included three carloads of lumber. The State of Minnesota sent a check for $2,500. Carloads of shoes, clothing, bedding, blankets and tents were sent from Alpena and other Michigan communities.

Section 5, Chapter 3
Neil Thornton's Version Of The Fire Of 1911

A dense pall of smoke had settled over Iosco County and older citizens of the Tawases still recall the eerie half light as the sun filtered through the suffocating smoke. Relief trains were sent from the Tawases and several hundred persons were brought here. A train was made up which left Tawas City at 11:30 a.m. with food provided by the people of the Tawases for the relief of those who still remained in the burned out towns.

More provisions were sent from those towns Wednesday morning and later trains arrived from Bay City, Alpena and other points with relief.

High winds that day caused many fires throughout Northeastern Michigan. Damage to a tannery at Alpena amounted to $350,000, along with destruction of a number of homes; Onaway, Millersburg and Tower also suffered severe losses, while Cheboygan was threatened by a fire which started in a great sawdust pile there.

The *Herald* reported as follows on July 14, 1911: "The launch, *Reliance*, will take an excursion to Au Sable on Sunday. Fare for the round trip, 50 cents. Accommodations for 30 people. The first 30 people making applications will be accommodated. Inquire of A.J. Berube or Albert Nash, East Tawas."

The twin towns at the mouth of the Au Sable River were soon overrun by hundreds of sightseers, who picked through the wreckage of burned out homes to find blobs of glass and other souvenirs of the intense flames, or marveled at the immense piles of scrap iron remaining from burned out mills.

The tragedy of the fire was the breaking off of long friendships among neighbors of two communities; entire families, left destitute in a matter of minutes, suddenly had to leave to find housing and employment. Some moved to nearby towns to live with relatives, while others moved to Detroit and other industrial centers of the state.

Au Sable lay completely barren for years and the city government finally reverted back to township status, but Oscoda was quickly rebuilt. The scars from that long-ago fire are now all but forgotten as both Oscoda and Au Sable are modern, progressive communities.[129]

And so ends our story on the demise of the sister cities of Au Sable and Oscoda. May such a terrible disaster never again occur—God willing!

CONCLUSION

The History Of Forest Fire Fighting In Michigan

Gregory M. Lusk, Assistant Regional Forest Management Supervisor for the Marquette regional office of the Michigan Department of Natural Resources' Forest Management Division, has promoted knowledge of the history of Michigan forest fires through lectures and slide presentations.

One of Lusk's slide shows includes the following summary of the state's forest fire fighting efforts:

> "Remember Metz and Au Sable" became a fire prevention slogan that helped materially to keep public interest alive and to secure support for more adequate protection efforts.
>
> The menace of forest fires was first officially recognized in Michigan in 1817, with laws providing penalties for "Willful or negligent setting of fires on the property of another or allowing fire to escape to the injury of another." Additional laws allowed burning to be done under permit only, recognized public responsibility for fire suppression (1837) and made railroads responsible for their locomotives.
>
> In 1899 the Legislature established the Forestry Commission and marked the beginning of state reforestation and fire suppression efforts.

Organizational difficulties plagued the early state fire organization. Unification in 1920 of the state protection effort under one head led to better coordination and a growing sense of state responsibility. Progress also was made in development of the state's fire detection system. Lookout towers were being built at strategic points, and many miles of telephone lines were constructed.

Each lookout was equipped with a detailed map of the area covered, an alidade for determining direction from the tower, and a telephone or radio for reporting detected fires.

The federal government first came into the picture when some 83,157 acres of public land were set aside for national forest purposes in lower Michigan. In February 1909, the Upper Peninsula and Michigan National Forest in the Lower Peninsula were created and placed under the jurisdiction of the recently formed USDA Forest Service. Protection of federal and adjacent lands was undertaken in 1911.

Photo courtesy MI DNR, Greg Lusk Collection

An early fire fighter's water back pump.

The first communications efforts centered on telephones and maintenance of many miles of lines. In 1934, the department realized that radio might be the solution to its communication problem. By 1940, approximately 120 battery operated sets were installed in fire towers. The earliest use of aircraft-to-ground communications was started in 1934.

The first state-owned equipment consisted of 18 long-handled shovels purchased to equip fire fighters in 1912. This purchase was questioned by the Auditor General; it was six months before the bill was paid. Horse-drawn plows, hired from farmers, were used when available. With the development of the back pump in about 1920, the use of water on the fireline became general and led to the use of power pumpers and tankers, particularly for mop-up work on peat and slash fires.

The state purchased its first tractor in 1917 for use in fireline construction on the Higgins Lake State Forest. Not until some years later was power equipment provided for fire suppression.

The use of the automobile dates from 1915. The Public Domain Commission, organized to take action on major forest fires, equipped two or more fire wardens with a Model T Ford.

In 1928, the Conservation Commission authorized the purchase of 12 trucks for fire control work, mainly for hauling firefighters, tools and supplies.

Horse-drawn plows early demonstrated their usefulness for fireline construction but were handicapped by lack of power for tough going.

The use of tractors overcame the power difficulty, but made heavier and sturdier plows necessary.

This made a transportation problem. The answer in Michigan was the development of a rubber-tired sulky plow, with a trailer hitch, that could be hauled to fires on its own wheels at road speeds by a car or truck. Various plows were tried out.

Photo courtesy MI DNR, Greg Lusk Collection

Loading a tractor on a flatbed truck for transportation to a fire scene.

Eventually the plow was designed to be attached directly to a tractor with a hydraulic lift. This proved to be the backbone of the state fire-fighting fleet. It was easy to handle and was extremely mobile.

Photo courtesy MI DNR, Greg Lusk Collection

Workers putting down a field well on site of nearby forest fire.

The use of water in fighting forest fires has always been limited by its availability. This resulted in the development of the backpump and its wide use on fires, particularly those in light fuels. Water supply in the 1920s was handled by hauling it in 10-gallon milk cans.

About 1930, it was discovered that in many places groundwater was available near the surface and could be readily available by means of shallow driven wells. The first were hand pumped, but soon small gas engine pumps began to be used. In 1933, Gilbert Stewart of the Forest Fire Experiment Station, developed a portable well sinking kit.

Use of heavy pumping equipment was found to be invaluable for mop-up work in heavy fuels, particularly in peat or slash.

For running fires, tankers with power pumps were developed and used in the early 1930s. This quickly led to equipping pickups and fire trucks with tanks, power takeoff pumps and booster reels.

Photo courtesy MI DNR, Greg Lusk Collection

Example of an early department sand trencher in action.

The effectiveness of thrown dirt in knocking down fires and the mineral soil fireline suggested the possibility of combining these features in a line-building machine. A unit was developed at the Forest Fire Experiment Station around a bulldozer.

In 1929, the Department of Conservation established its famous Forest Fire Experiment Station. Initially, the station readied a far-flung program of research in fire effects, fire behavior and equipment development. It soon specialized in heavy equipment, set the pattern for the equipment centers that would come after World War II, and today is unrivaled as a source for state and rural equipment development, serving both Michigan and a consortium of northeastern states.

Photo courtesy MI DNR, Greg Lusk Collection

Firefighters spraying a blaze.

The station has contributed materially to the standardization and development of forest fire equipment and is largely responsible for the progress that has been made in Michigan in this direction.

From 1910 until 1925, the average annual acreage burned was 500,000 acres in Michigan. From 1935 until 1950, it averaged 24,000 acres per year. A continued reduction in that figure until the present has been realized. The average annual acreage burned from 1984 to 1988 in state protection areas was under 7,000 acres. Over 10,000 wildland fires are handled yearly in Michigan by fire departments, federal and state protection organizations. This reduction has been accomplished through improvements in organization, equipment, training, prevention and cooperation.

POSTSCRIPT

Michigan Fire History Postscript

By Robert H. Ziel
Fire Management Specialist
Michigan Department of Natural Resources
Marquette, Michigan

The stories told here have probably inspired concerns about wildfires. The same concern you feel today motivated our state to action early in this century. Dramatic advances in firefighting equipment and tactics have brought about a steep decline in both the number and size of forest fires in Michigan.

With airplanes, tractor-mounted fireplows, and wildland fire engines we can find the fires earlier, respond quickly, and attack fires aggressively. The network of fire departments across the state provides local firefighters for virtually all parts of the state. Though the situation appears to be well in hand, the fire ground is shifting beneath our feet.

On May 5th, 1980, the Mack Lake fire took the life of one firefighter, destroyed 44 homes and buildings, consumed two million dollars worth of timber and burned over 20,000 acres in its first 6 hours. On May 6th, 1986, 22 fires burned over 8,000 acres in Marquette County and forced the evacuation of nearly 9,000 people. And on May 8, 1990, the Stephan Bridge Road fire destroyed 76 homes, 125 other structures, 37 vehicles, and $700,000 worth of timber while scorching 5,976 acres in less than 5 hours. These catastrophic fires still threaten human lives and property with some regularity, especially in the pine forests of northern Michigan. Lest anyone think that only large fires in pine areas are dangerous, on Halloween day in 1990, a person burning leaves in Cass County lost control of her fire. In a very short time, four homes were lost and a fifth one damaged.

Residential development in the "flammable forest" has risen dramatically in the last 20 years. These homes, camps, and cottages are more difficult to protect for several reasons. The owner and builder, in an effort to keep a natural setting, nestle structures into clumps of trees and shrubs. Desired building materials often include shake roofs, wood siding, and large windows. Long, narrow, winding driveways are created to further enhance the desired sense of seclusion. These buildings are frequently heated with wood. And whether through desire for natural appearance, limited maintenance opportunity or neglect; owners leave grasses, leaves, and pine needles to accumulate around the base of these structures. These factors make homes more vulnerable to approaching fires by placing fuels close to structures and restricting access by fire trucks.

The fact that more people and their possessions have moved into rural and forest settings also makes our job more difficult, due the ways fires are started.

People cause more than 90 percent of our fires. Among those, approximately one-third are caused by residents in their own back yards. Each spring, the ritual of yard cleanup usually includes burning of leaves, grass and twigs. People frequently burn trash in backyard incinerators.

Often, precautions taken are woefully inadequate. Many times we investigate debris-burning fires only to find that the owner abandoned the burning leaf pile and returned later to a wildfire spreading out of control. Some burn without enough help or proper tools. And very few folks have the knowledge to recognize how weather conditions threaten their control.

The fire service community is trying to prevent these problems by requiring anyone who wants to burn out in the open to obtain a burning permit. That is our opportunity to evaluate their burning materials, the expected weather conditions and their safety precautions before approving the request. These permits are usually obtained locally from either the Michigan Department of Natural Resources, US Forest Service, or community fire department.

Once a wildfire starts, damage is sure to occur. At each fire, firefighters must make decisions to minimize that damage. Where once that would have meant attacking the fire immediately, now the first thought is about human safety. Are people threatened by the advancing fire? Do they need to be evacuated to safety? Just think of the time required to go from house to house warning people about the approaching danger. Some of the most disturbing stories are told by police officers and firefighters who find themselves arguing with people who do not want to leave with the flames only minutes away. These are only the first acts of bravery at the fire scene.

Protecting the homes in the path of wildfires becomes the second priority because of the high values at stake. Despite inadequate resources, rural fire departments are charged with protecting structures over larger areas each year. Unlike urban locations, rural settings don't have regularly spaced fire hydrants to provide large volumes of water. Imagine trying to stand your ground with a 30-year-old fire truck in the front yard of a home as a wildfire approaches.

Despite all this, public expectations remain high. People demand the same response, skill and effectiveness that they came to expect from city fire departments.

Only after protecting life and property can firefighters focus their attention on attacking the fire to stop its spread and to protect the natural resources. In some cases there aren't enough trucks, tractors, and operators left to do the job. We cannot forget the overpowering force of raging wildfires. When these fires are born of explosive fuels such as jack pine and hot, windy weather, few tools are available that can make a difference. In those cases, firefighters are left with trying to contain the flames from the rear and sides while hoping for changes in fuels and weather.

Wildfire in rural Michigan is a reality that people living there must be aware of. The forests and grasslands that we take for granted were born of fire. We cannot, though, take for granted protection from this problem. Beginning in early school years, children are taught fire prevention and fire protection. In much the same manner as homeowners keep flammables away from the furnace, steps can be taken to protect our homes from threatening wildfires.

Examine this picture and compare it with your home. What things can you do? What changes can be made to make it "fire safe?" Since 1944, Smokey's message hasn't changed: "Remember...Only you can prevent forest fires!" And with more homes in the forest each year, Smokey's message—calling people to take an active part in protecting our homes from wildfire—is as important as ever. Won't you please give him a hand?

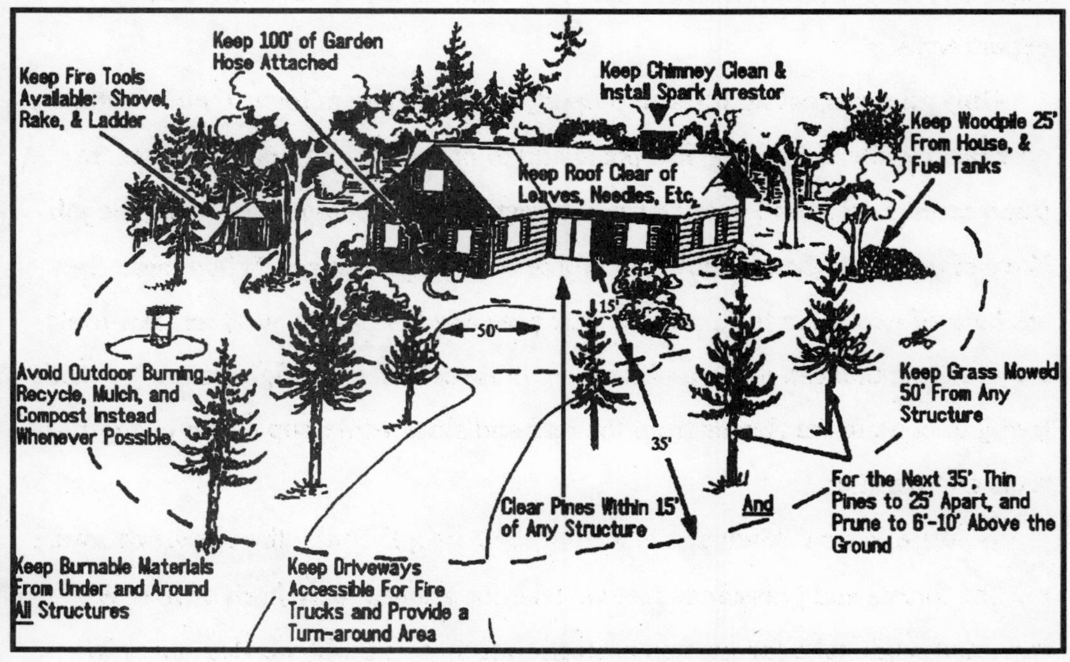

Footnotes

Section 1, Chapter 1

[1] *Forest Fires and Forest Fire Control in Michigan*, by Mitchell and Robson. Michigan Dept. of Conservation / U.S. Dept. of Agriculture—Forest Service, 1950.

[2] *History of the Great Fires in Chicago and the West*, by Rev. E.J. Goodspeed, 1871.

[3] *The U.S. Commission of Agriculture Report on Forestry*; 1872.

[4] *Climatic Conditions Preceding Historically Great Fires in the North Central Region*, by Haines and Sando. Published by the North Central Forest Experiment Station, St. Paul, Minnesota, 1969.

Section 1, Chapter 2

[5] "A Boy's Memory of the Big Fire," by Kirk Shepard. From *Menominee County Book for Schools*, by Ethel Schuyler, 1941.

[6] "Birch Creek, First Farming Settlement," contributed by the Menominee Historical Society.

[7] "Lilacs Mark the Graves of Fire Victims," by Penny Mullins. Menominee *Herald-Leader,* May 12, 1990.

[8] "Delta Woman, Survivor of Peshtigo Fire, Recalls Blaze on Anniversary," by Jean Worth. Marquette *Daily Mining Journal*, Oct. 12, 1960.

[9] *Menominee Revisited*, written in the late 1800s by Josephine Ingalls Sawyer. Published by Mid-Peninsula Library Cooperative of Iron Mountain, MI, 1982.

Footnotes

Section 1, Chapter 3

[10] Article by editor Orlando H. Godwin, Manistee *Standard*, Apr. 6, 1872.

[11] "Sunday October 9, 1871: A day of anxiety and distress," written in 1948 by Mrs. Ben Wolters (Anna Speet), Holland *Sentinel*, Oct. 9, 1980.

[12] "Holland Was, But Is No More. CATASTROPHE—Days of Terror, Distress and Suffering," from a joint issue of *De Grondwet, De Wachter*, and *De Hollander* on Oct. 12, 1871 (translated in 1984 by Mary Wagenaur, Holland Historical Trust Collection of the Joint Archives of Holland, Hope College. Ref. #T88-30F). The next four pages of this article list all the destroyed business places and streets of homes.

[13] "Tells How and Where The 'Big Fire' Started," by Albert Kamferbeek. From a newspaper clipping supplied by the Holland Historical Trust Collection of the Joint Archives of Holland. Source and date unknown.

[14] *The Holland Fire of October 8, 1871*, by Donald L. vanReken. Self-published, 1982.

Section 1, Chapter 4

[15] *Steaming Through Smoke and Fire,* by James Donahue. Published by The Historical Society of Michigan, 1990. This fine book should be read in its entirety, for from cover to cover it is chock full of excitement and historic photographs of these early vessels, and all his facts have been carefully researched for complete accuracy. Donahue is by trade a newspaper man—facts count and his works show it. The smoke and fire stories continue through several more days in his publication, including reports from Lake Michigan where smoke appeared to be the probable cause for many boats colliding, suffering damage and perhaps sinking.

Footnotes

[16] United States Life-Saving Service records, as compiled by Neal Bullington, Chief of Interpretation, United States Department of the Interior, National Park Service at Sleeping Bear Dunes National Lakeshore, Empire, Michigan.

[17] Work & Casualty Chart of the Great Lakes - 1894, U.S. Weather Bureau, as compiled by Neal Bullington, Chief of Interpretation, United States Department of the Interior, National Park Service at Sleeping Bear Dunes National Lakeshore, Empire, Michigan.

Section 1, Chapter 5

[18] Port Huron *Times Herald*, date unknown.

[19] "Many Suffered in Thumb Area Fire of 1871," The Saginaw *News*, date unknown, 1969.

[20] "The 1871 Fire," by Kate P. McGill. Part of a *Sesquicentennial Spotlight* published by the Sanilac County Historical Society at Port Sanilac, Michigan.

[21] *Bewabic Country,* by Herbert Larson. Carlton Press, New York, 1963.

[22] *History of the Great Fires in Chicago and the West*, by Rev. E.J. Goodspeed. 1871.

[23] Ibid.

Section 2, Chapter 1

[24] Excerpts from the Detroit *Evening News*, Sept., 1881.

Footnotes

[25] *Forest Fires and Forest Fire Control in Michigan,* by Mitchell and Robson, Michigan Dept. of Conservation / U.S. Dept. of Agriculture—Forest Service, 1950.

[26] "Meteorological Causes of the 1881 Fire in Michigan's Thumb Area," by Mark D. Schwartz, Department of Geography, San Francisco State University, San Francisco, California. A paper published in Volume #5, 1990 American Meteorological Journal.

[27] "The Heavens Rained Fire," by Doug Moreland. Detroit *Free Press,* Sept. 27, 1981.

[28] *Huron County Illustrated History.*

[29] Ibid.

Section 2, Chapter 2

[30] A clipping from an unknown newspaper, perhaps the Saginaw *News*, dated Sept. 9, 1963.

[31] *In the Beginning*, a family history of the Finkel family, contributed by Linda (Finkel) Siewert of Bad Axe.

[32] "1881—That's how Thumb residents recall great fire," Saginaw *News*, Saginaw, Mich., Mar. 4, 1951.

[33] *It Happened Here One Spring :A Centennial History of Port Crescent, Vanished Lumbering Village, 1868-1968,* by June Nelson.

[34] "The Fire of '71" by Kate P. McGill, printed as part of the *Sesquicentennial Spotlight* series, Sanilac County Historical Society.

Footnotes

[35] *The 1881 Fire*, by an unknown author. Submitted in 1987 by Lois Johnson of the Marlette Historical Society.

Section 2, Chapter 3

[36] Michigan Historic Marker #141, Huron County. Michigan Historical Commission.

[37] *The Flaming Forest,* published by the *Tuscola County Advertiser*, Caro, Michigan. Rudy Petzold, Publisher.

Section 2, Chapter 4

[38] A report taken from a July 7, 1957 edition of the Saginaw *News*, courtesy of editor Paul Chaffee.

[39] Article by John D. Tucker, in the Saginaw *News*, Sept. 16, 1958.

[40] The Saginaw *News*, Sept. 16, 1958.

[41] Ibid.

[42] "1881 Fire Still A Vivid Memory," by James L. Kerwin, *The Detroit News,* Sept. 22, 1981.

[43] The *Times Record* of Valley City, North Dakota.

[44] Taken from a 50-year anniversary article in the Huron County *Tribune*.

Footnotes

Section 2, Chapter 5

[45] *The Red Cross In Peace and War*, by Clara Barton. Published by the American Historical Press, 1899.

[46] "Crucible Of Fire Puts Red Cross To The Test," by Art 0'Shea, *The Detroit News*, May 21, 1981.

[47] The Sebewaing *Blade* & Unionville *Crescent* newspapers, 1961.

[48] "Red Cross Seeks Relief Effort Details," The Saginaw *News,* July 29, 1980.

[49] "Red Cross Using Thumb 1881 Fire Sketch," The Saginaw *News*, Sept. 23, 1961.

Section 3, Chapter 2

[50] *This Ontonagon Country,* by James K. Jamison. Published by R. Drier, Calumet, Mich., 1965.

Section 3, Chapter 3

[51] *The Detroit Evening News,* Aug. 27, 1896.

[52] "Ontonagon No More—City Completely Destroyed," *Chicago Record*, Aug. 26, 1896.

[53] "Hoodlum Element Rules," The Milwaukee *Journal*, Aug. 28, 1896.

Footnotes

[54] "Instant Aid Needed By Ontonagon Fire Sufferers," Detroit *Tribune*, Aug. 27, 1896.

[55] "Ontonagon Fire," the Houghton *Gazette,* date unknown.

[56] "Disastrous Ontonagon Fire Of '96 Recalled By Pioneer Woman," Ontonagon *Herald*, Sept. 21, 1956.

[57] "Woodbury Tells Of Ontonagon Fire," Ontonagon *Herald,* Aug. 26, 1964.

Section 3, Chapter 4

[58] The Matchwood Minutes," a regular column in *The Cloverland Press,* 1891.

[59] *Ewen Centennial Book - 1889 to 1989*, contributed by Mr. K.J. Moilanen of Ewen.

[60] L'Anse *Sentinel*, June 24, 1893.

[61] *Ewen Centennial Book - 1889 to 1989.*

[62] "Isle Royale Cottages Burn; Boats Keep Off," *The Detroit News*, Sept. 12, 1908.

[63] "61 Fires, Still Burning In U.P.; Rain Hoped For," Marquette *Mining Journal*, Oct. 24, 1947.

[64] "364 Forest Fires Burned 4,690 Acres In Peninsula: Estimated Damage $41,630," Marquette *Mining Journal,* Nov. 28, 1949.

[65] Marquette *Mining Journal*, date unknown.

[66] Marquette *Mining Journal*, date unknown.

Footnotes

[67] *Superior Heartland,* by C. Frederick Rydholm. A two-volume historical set self-published, 221 Lakewood Lane, Marquette, MI 49855, 1990.

[68] Ibid.

[69] Norway *Current,* May 11, 1889.

[70] Iron Mountain *Press*, May 24, 1906.

[71] *The Detroit News*, May 23, 1906.

[72] *Alger County: A Centennial History—1885 - 1895,* by The Alger Historical Society, Munising, Michigan.

[73] Ibid.

[74] The Detroit *News Tribune*, Oct. 18, 1908.

[75] Ibid.

[76] *The Detroit News*, Oct. 21, 1908.

[77] Ibid.

Section 3, Chapter 5

[78] *Forest Fires and Forest Fire Control in Michigan*, by Mitchell and Robson. Michigan Dept. of Conservation / U.S. Dept. of Agriculture—Forest Service, 1950.

[79] *The Detroit News*, May 19, 1906.

[80] Ibid.

Footnotes

[81] *From The Land Of The Great Lakes*, by Holger Rosenstand, page 102. Published by The Danish Interest Conference, The Lutheran Church in America, Des Moines, Iowa [Originally published in Danish at Copenhagen, Denmark, 1901].

[82] Article by editor Larry Easton in *The Soo*, Oct., 1991. This is a magazine published by the Soo Line Historical and Technical Society. A great deal of the material for Easton's article was gleaned from Rose Schultz and the files of the IXL Museum at Hermansville.

Section 4 Chapter 1

[83] *Eleventh Biennial Report of the State Game, Fish and Forestry Booklet*, 1909.

[84] *The Detroit News,* Oct. 16, 1908.

[85] Ibid.

[86] Ibid.

[87] Ibid.

[88] *The Detroit News*, Oct. 17, 1908.

[89] Ibid.

[90] *The Detroit News*, Oct. 19, 1908.

[91] Ibid.

[92] Ibid.

Footnotes

[93] *The Metz Fire of 1908*, by Herbert Nagel. Presque Isle County Historical Society.

[94] *The Detroit News*, Oct. 19, 1908.

[95] *The Detroit News*, date unknown.

Section 4 Chapter 2

[96] *The Detroit News*, Oct. 17, 1908.

[97] Ibid.

[98] Ibid.

[99] *The Detroit News*, Oct. 20, 1908.

[100] *The Detroit News*, Oct. 21, 1908.

[101] *The Detroit News*, Oct. 17, 1908.

[102] Ibid.

[103] *The Detroit News*, Oct. 19, 1908.

[104] Ibid.

[105] *The Detroit News*, Oct. 20, 1908.

[106] Ibid.

[107] *The Detroit News*, Oct. 21, 1908.

Section 4 Chapter 3

[108] *The Metz Fire of 1908*, by Herbert Nagel. Published by the Presque Isle County Historical Society.

[109] Ibid.

[110] Ibid.

[111] Ibid.

Section 5 Chapter 1

[112] Letter from Bishop Williams to his wife in Detroit, Oct. 18, 1908.

[113] Detroit *Free Press*, July 30, 1992.

[114] Bay City *Times*, July 14, 1911.

[115] *The Detroit News*, July 13, 1911.

[116] Ibid.

[117] Ibid.

[118] *The Detroit News*, July 12, 1911.

[119] Ibid.

[120] Ibid.

Section 5 Chapter 2

[121] *The Detroit News*, July 12, 1911.

[122] *The Detroit News*, July 14, 1911.

[123] Ibid.

[124] Ibid.

[125] Ibid.

[126] Ibid.

[127] Ibid.

[128] Bay City *Tribune*, July 14, 1911.

Section 5 Chapter 3

[129] *Along the Historic Riviere aux Sables*, by Neil Thornton. Chapter 17—"The Fire of 1911." Published by Printer's Devil Press, Box 85, Tawas City, Michigan 48764, 1987.

Bibliography

Books & Papers

Alger County: A Centennial History—1885 - 1895, by The Alger Historical Society, Munising, Michigan.

Along the Historic Riviere aux Sables, by Neil Thornton. Published by Printer's Devil Press, Box 85, Tawas City, Michigan 48764, 1987.

Bewabic Country, by Herbert Larson. Carlton Press, New York, 1963.

Birch Creek, First Farming Settlement, contributed by the Menominee Historical Society.

Ewen Centennial Book - 1889 to 1989, contributed by Mr. K.J. Moilanen of Ewen.

From The Land Of The Great Lakes, by Holger Rosenstand. Published by The Danish Interest Conference, The Lutheran Church in America, Des Moines, Iowa. [Originally published in Danish at Copenhagen, Denmark, 1901.

History of the Great Fires in Chicago and the West, by Rev. E.J. Goodspeed, 1871.

Huron County Illustrated History.

In the Beginning, a family history of the Finkel family, contributed by Linda (Finkel) Siewert of Bad Axe.

It Happened Here One Spring :A Centennial History of Port Crescent, Vanished Lumbering Village, 1868-1968, by June Nelson.

Menominee Revisited, written in the late 1800s by Josephine Ingalls Sawyer. Published by Mid-Peninsula Library Cooperative of Iron Mountain, MI, 1982.

Menominee County Book for Schools, by Ethel Schuyler, 1941.

Bibliography

Sesquicentennial Spotlight series, Sanilac County Historical Society.

Steaming Through Smoke and Fire, by James Donahue. Published by The Historical Society of Michigan, 1990.

Superior Heartland, by C. Frederick Rydholm. A two-volume historical set self-published, 221 Lakewood Lane, Marquette, MI 49855, 1990.

The Flaming Forest, published by the *Tuscola County Advertiser*, Caro, Michigan

The Metz Fire of 1908, by Herbert Nagel. Published by the Presque Isle County Historical Society.

The Holland Fire of October 8, 1871, by Donald L. vanReken. Self-published, 1982.

This Ontonagon Country, by James K. Jamison. Published by R. Drier, Calumet, Mich., 1965.

Periodicals

Bay City *Tribune*.

Bay City *Times*.

Chicago *Record.*

Cloverland Press.

De Grondwet, De Wachter, and *De Hollander*.

Detroit *Tribune*.

Detroit Evening News.

Bibliography

Detroit *Free Press.*

Detroit *News Tribune.*

Holland *Sentinel.*

Houghton *Gazette.*

Huron County *Tribune*.

Iron Mountain *Press.*

L'Anse *Sentinel*.

Manistee *Standard.*

Marquette *Mining Journal.*

Menominee *Herald-Leader*.

Milwaukee *Journal.*

Norway *Current.*

Ontonagon *Herald.*

Port Huron *Times Herald.*

Saginaw *News.*

Sebewaing *Blade* & Unionville *Crescent* .

The Soo, a magazine published by the Soo Line Historical and Technical Society.

Times Record of Valley City, North Dakota.

Bibliography

Government & Research Reports

The U.S. Commission of Agriculture Report on Forestry; 1872.

Climatic Conditions Preceding Historically Great Fires in the North Central Region, by Haines and Sando. Published 1969 by the North Central Forest Experiment Station, St. Paul, Minnesota.

Eleventh Biennial Report of the State Game, Fish and Forestry Booklet, 1909.

Forest Fires and Forest Fire Control in Michigan, by Mitchell and Robson. Michigan Dept. of Conservation / U.S. Dept. of Agriculture—Forest Service, 1950.

Meteorological Causes of the 1881 Fire in Michigan's Thumb Area, by Mark D. Schwartz, Department of Geography, San Francisco State University, San Francisco, California. A paper published in Volume #5, 1990 American Meteorological Journal.

United States Life-Saving Service records, United States Department of the Interior, National Park Service at Sleeping Bear Dunes National Lakeshore, Empire, Michigan.

Work & Casualty Chart of the Great Lakes - 1894, U.S. Weather Bureau.

Index

A

B

Index

C

Index

D

E

F

Index

G

H

Index

I

J

Index

K

L

Index

M

Index

Index

Q

Index

S

Index

T

U

V

W

Index

Y